GUIDE TO HUMAN RIGHTS RESEARCH

UNIVERSITY OF
W

Jack Tobin
Administrative Director
Human Rights Program, 1984-1992

with the assistance of

Jennifer Green
Administrative Director
Human Rights Program

A Publication of the
Harvard Law School
Human Rights Program

The Harvard Law School Human Rights Program, founded in 1984, fosters coursework, the participation of students in human rights activities, professional careers that include work to protect human rights, assistance to the worldwide human rights community, and research and scholarship. Through its student summer internships with nongovernmental organizations worldwide, its visiting fellows from all over the world who spend from two months to a year at the Law School, its visiting speakers and its applied research, the Program forges cooperative links with a range of human rights workers and organizations. It plans and directs international conferences on human rights themes. A brochure describing the Program's activities, including opportunities for visiting fellows (activists and scholars), is available on request.

Director: Professor Henry J. Steiner. *Projects Director:* Makau wa Mutua. *Administrative Director:* Jennifer M. Green. *Address:* Pound Hall 401; Harvard Law School; Cambridge, Massachusetts 02138; USA. *Tel:* (617) 495-9362. *Fax:* (617) 495-1110.

TABLE OF CONTENTS

Chapter Two. General Human Rights Research Tools and Sources

Chapter Three. Human Rights Materials on
Intergovernmental Organizations (IGOs) and Basic Treaties

Chapter Four. Selected Human Rights Topics, Fields and Themes

Chapter Five. Human Rights and United States Foreign Policy

Preface

The idea that a guide for human rights research be prepared within the Harvard Law School Human Rights Program grew out of the Program's productive association with Human Rights Internet. Jack Tobin, then administrative director of HRP, undertook this complex and challenging task, fitting it into the time remaining after his other work for HRP. His persistence and ambition led to a lengthy and inclusive draft in 1992 that was close to the final structure of this *Guide to Human Rights Research.* After Jack left HRP that year on a Fulbright Fellowship to Japan, Jennie Green, the present administrative director, brought the project to completion. I am very grateful to Jack for his spacious conception of what this *Guide* should be, and for his work and invention on an exacting mission full of perplexity and detail. I am as grateful to Jennie for bringing the project to publication.

Both Tobin and Green drew on the advice and criticism of librarians and scholars, who were generous with their time in commenting on one or another portion of the *Guide* and, in some cases, helping to write it. The acknowledgements below by Jack Tobin name such persons.

In its breadth as well as clarity, the *Guide* makes an important contribution to human rights work. It will introduce students to this growing field, as well as facilitate research by human rights scholars and activists. The Human Rights Program, which provided the staff time and the necessary funding for this project out of its general resources, is proud to have made this *Guide* possible.

Henry J. Steiner
Jeremiah Smith, Jr. Professor of Law
Director, Human Rights Program

x

Acknowledgements

Essential to the production of the *Guide to Human Rights Research* within the Human Rights Program (HRP) was the wealth of holdings of the Harvard Law and other Harvard University libraries. Equally important are the professional and non-professional staff of these libraries, who were helpful to my making use of the Harvard resources.

I am greatly indebted to Henry Steiner for his willingness to grapple with bibliographic matters, and for his numerous suggestions and comments on drafts.

Fred Chapman, director of the library of the Swiss Institute of Comparative Law and a former colleague at the Harvard Law Library, provided essential critical comments on the structure of the *Guide*. Laurie Wiseberg, Executive Director of Human Rights Internet was, as usual, a wise, generous, and constructive critic. David Weissbrodt, Briggs & Morgan Professor of Law at the University of Minnesota Law School, took time to read the manuscript and to offer many helpful suggestions. Jan Stepan, of the Swiss Institute of Comparative Law and a former mentor at Harvard, scanned an earlier draft with his usual keenness of eye and mind. Makau wa Mutua, Projects Director of HRP, provided a human rights lawyer's perspective as well as help with Africa-related materials, and essential collegial support.

Librarians Lyonette Louis-Jacques of the University of Minnesota Law Library, and Nina Cascio of the Charles B. Sears Law Library at the State University of New York at Buffalo, offered expert critique and additional citations. Harvard Law librarians who offered many helpful suggestions include Associate Librarian Robert Buckwalter, Bibliographer for International Law Bridget Reischer, Senior Reference Librarian Alan Diefenbach, and Reference Librarians Michael Jimenez and Naomi Ronen. David Paul, Documents Librarian of the Harvard College Library, provided advice and help in tracking down elusive materials. Reed Boland, editor of the *Annual Review of Population Law*, helped with sources on population and women's rights.

I am especially grateful to Nina Cascio and Jeanette Yackle for writing the section on online research. Nina also provided careful and thorough references throughout the *Guide* about what resources are available on computer networks.

Numerous outside readers gave comments and suggestions for additional references. Philip Alston was especially helpful in giving this project the benefit of his years of experience and research. Aziz Abu-Hamad and Dan Simon provided much helpful advice on resources on the Middle East; Deborah Anker gave expert assistance to the section on refugee law; Ken Anderson contributed to the sections on humanitarian law and international trade law; Abram Chayes commented on the environmental section; Rebecca Cooke and Celina Romany assisted with the women's rights section; Eric Heinze gave extensive comments on the section on the rights of sexual minorities; and Jim Ross assisted with sources from and about Asia and reviewed the text to give us the views of a human rights lawyer.

Jonathan Selbin provided research assistance and a fine editor's eye for detail. John Fountain, Maria Stavropoulou and Rebecca Sharpless also provided valued research assistance at critical times.

Wendilea Brown of the HRP staff brought her cool head and invaluable expertise to problems of logistics and computers. She provided essential assistance and great support. Ethan Thomas did his usual fine job of turning a mass of type into an attractive book. I am also grateful to Sandy Margolin and Ellen Miller for their patient and painstaking assistance with the *Guide's* production.

I know personally the persistent and painstaking effort that a project of this duration demands. I am extremely grateful to Jennie Green, my successor as administrative director of HRP, for the excellent work that she did in taking over the *Guide* a year ago, completing it and leading it to publication.

This *Guide* is dedicated to the memory of Herbert Anaya, murdered in 1987 in El Salvador by a right-wing death squad, and to the staff of the nongovernmental Human Rights Commission of El Salvador, who allowed me the privilege of sharing in their work and who taught me the meaning of commitment to human rights.

Jack Tobin

CHAPTER ONE.
INTRODUCTION AND OVERVIEW

I. Introduction

Chapter One gives the researcher a general orientation. It stresses the introductory and basic sources for research in human rights and provides the researcher with a general framework before he or she turns to the specific information in the later chapters. Those chapters repeat some of the references of Chapter One in the context of their more detailed coverage of specific topics.

The scope and shape of the *Guide* reflect the conviction that the field of human rights, as an arena of action and inquiry, must be addressed from a variety of disciplines. Human rights issues reach into many aspects of life — politics, international relations, economics, ethics, health, education, to name just a few — and can be effectively understood only by employing the scholarly disciplines which address these aspects. The human rights researcher must be able to work within disciplines other than law.

At the same time, the *Guide* maintains a focus on human rights legal issues and stresses the rights set forth in the principal postwar human rights documents. The *Guide* is strongly anchored in law both because of the continuing centrality of legal texts and modes of argument in human rights scholarship and advocacy, and because of the author's professional training and background.

The *Guide* presupposes an audience whose primary language of research is English, and who are in situations that permit access to the research materials and documentation described here. Although some works in languages other than English are mentioned, the *Guide* does not cover that vast and rich terrain. Because of problems of access, the English-language sources themselves are disproportionately from the United States, Europe, Canada, and Australia, with little representation of the English-speaking Caribbean, Africa, Asia, or other areas where English is widely used.

This work supplements existing guides to U.S. law, and to foreign, comparative and international legal research. It covers some English-language foreign and comparative legal materials. The *Guide* provides detailed treatment of U.S. government materials which relate to human rights; it does not do so for other countries.

Researchers seeking comprehensive information on non-U.S. legal systems, translations of codes and laws, casebooks, etc. should consult the general works on legal research suggested below. (See Section II. D.) Such sources are often essential to research which examines a particular country's observance of international human rights obligations. Domestic law must be closely examined to assess compliance, and the research tools and techniques for accessing such information may be different from those used in researching the international law of human rights.

This *Guide* gives extensive information about research tools such as bibliographies, research guides, manuals and indices, which lead the researcher to the needed documents, facts, or analysis. In most cases these are distinct from works which deal with substantive aspects of human rights. In other cases, however, the substantive works themselves — books, articles, encyclopedias — are research tools. Especially for unfamiliar matters, an introductory article or book is often the quickest way to identify key institutions and controversies, and the most promising sources of useful information.

With this in mind, but without attempting to provide a comprehensive list of the best-known or "best" books and articles on human rights, the *Guide* occasionally suggests frequently drawn-upon books, articles or other sources that provide good introductions or orientations to human rights as a whole, or to a particular topic. It includes a list in Chapter One of frequently-consulted substantive works which can provide initial orientation to a range of issues. The *Guide* is not, however, an exhaustive bibliography. Rather than list all of the possible sources for a given topic, it aims to provide the researcher with the most promising sources which will lead to a comprehensive research strategy.

The *Guide* also provides information about resources available on computer databases or "online." Section VI of this chapter gives an introduction to conducting such research. Throughout the *Guide*, the annotations note when a resource is available online. These notations are brief and assume some knowledge of the relevant computer network. Abbreviations and other terms of art used are explained in Section VI of this chapter.

II.   Bibliographic Access to Human Rights Information

Indices differ in their coverage of sources and selection policies. Some indices treat only periodicals, while others also include books, government documents, research reports, and other monographic literature. Some indices are selective, scanning only "relevant" articles or excluding pieces such as book reviews, editorial comments, and research notes. Highly relevant sources may not be covered in an otherwise quite useful index. For example, *Public Affairs Information Service* does not index either the frequently useful *New York Review of Books* or the *New Yorker*, which has articles on human rights from time to time. The *Review* and the *New Yorker* are indexed by the *Readers' Guide* and by *Magazine Index*.

In addition to the published sources discussed in this section, information on a topic may appear in unpublished form, such as conference reports or working papers and drafts. These sources are sometimes accessible through individuals who are active in the field as researchers, advocates or government officials, or through nongovernmental organizations.

Another category of materials, the proceedings of meetings of scholarly associations, is a good source of recent discussions of issues related to human rights. One useful source is the reports from the annual meetings of the *Proceedings of the American Society of*

International Law. Although sometimes published annually as serials, conference proceedings are often hard to locate through periodical indices. The following four reference tools provide various avenues of access to the scholarly conference literature: *Index to Social Sciences and Humanities Proceedings*; *Directory of Published Proceedings*; *Bibliographic Guide to Conference Publications*; and *Index of Conference Proceedings*.

A.   Serials

Serials, a bibliographic category comprising magazines, journals, newspapers, yearbooks and other periodic reports, are published by governmental, intergovernmental, and nongovernmental entities. They provide facts, analysis, bibliographies and other research tools which often have not yet appeared in monographs.

Serial literature — most familiar as articles in journals and magazines — varies in subject and in the level of scholarship. The sources range from theoretical journals to popular magazines and newspapers. Easy access to periodical articles, especially those in mass circulation or commercially important publications, is usually available through bibliographies or indexing services such as those discussed below.

Access to less well-known serials may require use of indices which specialize in publications of governments, international organizations or nongovernmental organizations, or other research tools.

Online: For a convenient, brief description of most current online indexing services, see the *Gale Directory of Databases*. There are two main issues and two updates per year. The directory briefly describes, indexes and updates more than 4,300 databases.

1.   Indices to Law or Law-Related Serials

Legal periodical indices provide access to law review articles, articles in legal newspapers, and articles in scholarly journals closely related to law. The most important indices, in order of importance, are:

Legal Resource Index (LRI). Los Altos, CA: Information Access Corporation, 1980-.

> The foremost index to U.S. and Commonwealth legal journals, indexing articles from more than 750 English-language law and law-related journals and newspapers. The LRI uses modified Library of Congress subject headings, and thus has "human rights" as a subject. A paper version of LRI, the *Current Law Index*, appears monthly, and provides essentially the same coverage of journals, but does not include legal newspapers. LRI extends back to 1980 and is updated monthly on microfilm.

> *Online*: LRI is available online in LEXIS (LGLIND file in LAWREV library) and WESTLAW (LRI database), and on CD-ROM. It is also available online in BRS (LAWS), DIALOG (file 150), and Knowledge Index (LEGAI).

Index to Legal Periodicals (ILP). **New York: H.W. Wilson Co., 1928-.**

Monthly. Although the LRI indexes many more items than ILP, both indices should be checked, since ILP indexes some things not covered by LRI. The ILP must be used for historical (i.e., pre-1980) searching.

Online: The *Index to Legal Periodicals* is online (1981 to date) on LEXIS (ILP file in LAWREV or LEXREF libraries) and WESTLAW (ILP database). It is also online in WILSONLINE (ILP), and BRS (WILP).

Legal Journals Index. **Hebden Bridge, West Yorkshire: Legal Information Resources Ltd., 1986-.**

This index, published under the auspices of the British and Irish Association of Law Librarians, indexes several hundred periodicals, such as *International Journal of Refugee Law, Interights Bulletin* and *Immigration and Nationality Law & Practice.* Several of these titles are not indexed in LRI or ILP.

Index to Foreign Legal Periodicals. **Chicago: American Association of Law Libraries, 1960-.**

Provides access to articles in non-English languages, non-U.S. legal journals, and collections of legal essays. It also indexes a considerable number of English-language law journals, in particular all the important U.S. law journals devoted to comparative, international and non-U.S. law.

Online: The *Index to Foreign Legal Periodicals* is available online through RLG's Citadel, from 1985 to present.

Annual Legal Bibliography (ALB). **Cambridge, MA: Harvard Law School Library, 1961-1981.**

This work is useful for law and law-related materials in a variety of languages for the years 1961-1981. Indexed by broad topic headings are all books and most articles received by the Harvard Law Library during this twenty-year period. The ALB indexed almost 2,000 periodicals in law and related fields from a large number of countries, including some 560 periodicals not covered by either the *Index to Legal Periodicals* or the *Index to Foreign Legal Periodicals.* It is thus the best and most comprehensive index of its sort for the period in question. There is no cumulative index for the paper version, so each annual volume must be checked.

The microfiche version is cumulative, however, making matters easier. See *The Harvard Legal Bibliography, 1961-1981.* Honolulu, HI: Harvard Law Library and Law Library Microform Consortium, 1985.

Public International Law: A Current Bibliography of Articles. **Berlin, NY: Springer-Verlag, 1975-.**

Published twice yearly, with headings in English and German, this index surveys about a thousand periodicals in a variety of languages in the fields of economics, history, law and political science, indexing only those articles that treat international law topics. Essays from collected works are also indexed. Each issue provides citations to some fifty or more articles concerning international human rights under the decimal heading 12.4. Other relevant headings are "Aliens and Refugees" (12.3) and "Self-Determination" (12.6).

The Harvard Monthly. **Cambridge, MA: Harvard College, 1885-.**

A bibliography of periodicals held in the Harvard University library system. It is also available at many other university libraries, which can facilitate inter-library loans.

2. Indices to Serials in Other Disciplines

International Political Science Abstracts. **Oxford: International Political Science Association, 1951-.**

Quarterly. Selective listing of articles from 600 English-language and foreign-language periodicals. Includes abstracts in English for English-language articles, author index and subject index with broad terms and names of countries.

Monthly Bibliography. **Geneva: United Nations Library, 1978-.**

Part I *(Books, Official Documents, and Serials)* is a separately bound volume which lists publications received by the U.N. library in Geneva. Part II *(Selected Articles)* lists articles from about 700 periodicals indexed at the U.N. library in Geneva and the Dag Hammarskjold (U.N.) Library in New York. Materials are classified by subject which simplifies locating materials on topics such as human rights (generally), or women, education, or health. Both parts contain author, title and subject indices.

PAIS International in Print. **New York: Public Affairs Information Service, 1991-.**

This print index has recently absorbed *PAIS Foreign Language Index*, and continues *PAIS Bulletin.*

PAIS Foreign Language Index. New York: Public Affairs Information Service, 1972-1990.

Covers 400 journals and 2,000 non-serial publications in French, German, Italian, Portuguese, and Spanish.

PAIS Bulletin. **New York: Public Affairs Information Service, 1915-1990.**

Published twice monthly with annual cumulations. Indexes over 800 English-language journals and 6,000 non-serial publications (i.e., monographs, government documents, pamphlets, directories, reports of public and private agencies and materials from the U.S. Congress) in business, sociology, government, public administration, public policy, political science, and international relations. Emphasis is on contemporary social, economic and political issues, and the making and evaluating of public policy.

The limitations of PAIS are that it does not cover some general interest magazines, nor does it index many academic journals which are not concerned with public policy matters.

Online: *PAIS International* includes the three publications immediately above, covering 1976 to date. Contains over 300,000 citations, with brief abstracts. PAIS International database is online in WESTLAW (PAIS database), DIALOG (file 49), BRS (PAIS), and DATA-STAR (PAIS). It is also available through RLG's Citadel, 1980 to the present.

Refugee Abstracts. **Geneva: Centre for Documentation on Refugees, U.N. High Commissioner for Refugees, 1982-.**

Quarterly. Indexes journal articles dealing with refugee issues. Essential source, containing the following sections: an annotated bibliography of scholarly books, articles, reports, and documents; an annotated list of practice-oriented manuals and documents; book reviews; the texts of resolutions and other documents of international organizations; and information on upcoming conferences, meetings and courses.

Social Sciences Citation Index. **Philadelphia: Institute for Scientific Information, 1973-.**

Indexes the principal journals of the social sciences and a few humanities journals. This index uses citation analysis, which indexes citations to literature found in the references or footnotes of articles, in addition to the articles themselves. The index can be used to locate the works in books, periodicals or elsewhere that have cited a particular author. This approach facilitates finding works that address a specific theory, concept or interpretation. Access is by author, title words, and corporate affiliation (university, department, research organization) of author.

Online: This is online as *Social Scisearch*, which also includes more than 2,000 journals in the natural, physical and biomedical sciences, in DIALOG (file 7) and as a DIALOG database in WESTLAW (SOCSCISRCH database). It is also available in BRS (SSCI) and DATA-STAR (SSCI).

Social Sciences Index. **New York: H.W. Wilson, 1974-.**

Includes about 300 of the most widely used journals in anthropology and ethnic studies, political science, economics and international studies, psychology and sociology. For most research that would include the use of this index, there will be other, more specialized indices to expand coverage to a wider selection of journals. Researchers may wish to consult some of the specialized indices listed below.

Online: *Social Sciences Index* is online from 1983 to date in WILSONLINE (SSI) and BRS (WSSI).

Human rights research can be expanded to other indices of traditional social science as well as humanities materials, such as *ABC Pol Sci, Abstracts in Anthropology, Abstracts on Criminology and Penology, British Humanities Index, Communications Abstracts, Historical Abstracts, Humanities Index, Population Index, Psychological Abstracts, Social Work Research and Abstracts* and *Sociological Abstracts*. Regional indices may also be helpful; examples include *Canadian Periodical Index, Current Bibliography on African Affairs, Guide to Indian Periodical Articles, Hispanic American Periodical Index*, or *Middle East Abstracts and Index*. The researcher might also need to consult indices in fields such as ethnic studies, journalism, and labor. In addition, *Philosopher's Index, Religion Index One, Catholic Periodicals* and other religious indices often list articles which provide ethical and moral perspectives on the international human rights debate. The *Philosopher's Index* is especially good for articles analyzing the concept of a "right" from theoretical perspectives.

A good source for periodical indices for various geographical regions (and for reference works in all areas of knowledge) is the reference classic, Sheehy, E., ed. *Guide to Reference Books*. 10th ed. Chicago and London: American Library Association, 1986. 1560 pp. (and Balay, R., ed. *Guide to Reference Books, Covering Materials from 1985-1990*. Supplement to the Tenth Edition. Chicago: American Library Association, 1992. 613 pp.) Also useful in this regard is Holler, F., ed. *Information Sources of Political Science*. 4th ed. Santa Barbara, CA and Oxford: ABC-Clio Information Services, 1985. 417 pp.

Online: The *Canadian Periodical Index* is available online in Info Globe from 1977 to date.

Online: *Historical Abstracts* is available online in DIALOG (file 39) and as a DIALOG database on WESTLAW (HIST-ABS), and in Knowledge Index (HIST2) from 1973 to date.

Online: The *Humanities Index* is online from 1984 to date in WILSONLINE (HUM), OCLC Epic, and OCLC FirstSearch.

Online: *Philosopher's Index* is online from 1940 to date in DIALOG (file 57) as a DIALOG database on WESTLAW (PHIL-IND), and in Knowledge Index (SOCS3).

Online: *Religion Index One* is one of several indices included in the database RELIGION INDEX from 1975 to date in DIALOG (file 190), in WESTLAW (RELIGION) as a DIALOG database, in WILSONLINE, in BRS (RELI), and in Knowledge Index (RELI2).

Online: *Sociological Abstracts* is online from 1963 to date in DIALOG (file 37), in WESTLAW (SOC-ABS database, 1973 to date) as a DIALOG database, in BRS (SOCA,SOCZ), in DATA-STAR (SOLA), in Knowledge Index (SOCS1), in OCLS FirstSearch, and in OCLC Epic.

3. Indices to General and Popular Serials

Magazine Index. **Foster City, CA: Information Access Corp., 1976-.**

Monthly, on microfilm. Indexes about 400 magazines.

Online: Magazine Index is online from 1959-1970 and 1973 to date in DIALOG (file 47) in WESTLAW (MAGINDEX) as a DIALOG database, in BRS (MAGS), in DATASTAR (MAGS) and in Knowledge Index (MAGA I). Also available on CDROM and INFOTRAK 2000.

Readers' Guide to Periodical Literature. **New York: Wilson, 1901-.**

Issued semi-monthly; cumulated annually. Covers about 175 general-interest periodicals.

Online: *Reader's Guide* is online from 1983 to date in WILSONLINE (RDG), BRS (WRGA), OCLC EPIC, and OCLC FirstSearch.

4. Indices to "Alternative" Serials

Alternative Press Index. **College Park, MD: Alternative Press Center, 1969-.**

Quarterly (irregular). Subject index to more than 200 liberal, radical and underground periodicals, most of them not indexed elsewhere. This is an especially important index for researchers interested in points of view outside the political mainstream.

The New Periodicals Index. **Boulder, CO: Mediaworks, Ltd., 1977-1983.**

Semiannual. Indexes all articles from a list of alternative and "new age" magazines, journals, newspapers and newsletters.

Whitaker, C.S., ed. *Alternative Publications: A Guide to Directories, Indexes, Bibliographies and Other Sources.* **Jefferson, NC: McFarland, 1990. 90 pp.**

Covers the underground press, and small presses. One of the few such guides available.

B. *Monographs*

Individually-authored books make up the bulk of this category, but it is broader, including collections of essays, dissertations and theses, and a variety of other non-serial publications, such as one-time reports and studies. Items in all of these subcategories may be authored by individuals, by intergovernmental or nongovernmental organizations, by governmental agencies, or other bodies.

1. Books and Collections of Articles: Catalogs and Indices

Some of the periodical indexing services discussed earlier — PAIS is one example — selectively index books. Books on human rights topics are also cited in the human rights bibliographies discussed below. The major access tool for monographs is usually the library catalog where the researcher is working. However, the publishing explosion of the past two decades has made it impossible for any single library to collect all important published materials. Thus, even for researchers at major research libraries, a surprising amount of important material may only be available at other libraries. Published catalogs of other libraries, or the *National Union Catalog*, available from the U.S. Library of Congress in Washington, DC and widely distributed, are essential in locating relevant material.

Some libraries produce periodic listings of their recently cataloged books which can help locate recently published works. However, such lists are usually not widely distributed. Many libraries treat significant reports produced by intergovernmental organizations such as the United Nations, or important governmental reports and studies, as books for cataloging purposes. This facilitates the researcher's task, since such items are separately cataloged, and thus accessible through the catalog by author, title, subject heading and sometimes by key word. Also important are the following online facilities.

> *Online*: The two major cataloging databases in the United States are RLIN and the OCLC. RLIN, the Research Libraries Information Network, is an online database reflecting the holdings of major U.S. academic (including law) libraries such as Berkeley, Columbia, Harvard, Michigan, and Yale, as well as important law libraries like the Los Angeles County Law Library. OCLC, the Online Computer Library Center, includes the acquisitions of many U.S. university libraries, law firm libraries and smaller law libraries. For access to these databases, consult your librarian.

> *Online*: A growing amount of electronic cataloging is being done through individual libraries, rather than through OCLC or RLIN, and important holdings of human rights materials may be located through these catalogs. Getting in touch with a reference librarian is the best way to determine whether a local electronic catalog would help with specific research.

> *Online*: An increasingly valuable resource is access to the electronic catalogs of other libraries through the INTERNET. Through INTERNET connections, library staff at most major research libraries can dial directly into the catalog of another library and search that library's catalog as if it were their own.

(a)   General Catalogs and Indices

Catalog of New Foreign and International Law Titles. Ann Arbor, MI: Ward and Associates, 1989-.

> Bimonthly. Lists by subject all law and law-related books recently acquired by major research law libraries in the United States. Subject indices published every two months can alert researchers to new works.

Harvard Law Library, ed. *Catalog of International Law and Relations, Part I, 1817-1963; Part II, 1964-1981*. Munich; New York: K.G. Saur, 1985.

> Microfiche. Especially useful tools for historical research in human rights are the published microfiche catalogs of the Harvard Law Library. The catalog provides entries by author, title and subject of all materials in the international and comparative law collection which were cataloged between 1817 and 1981.

Harvard Law Library, ed. "Foreign and Comparative Law, Subject Index, 1817-1981." Appendix D in *Guide to the Card Catalogs of Harvard Law School Libraries, 1817-1981*. Munich; New York: K.G. Saur, 1986.

> Microfiche. Contains entries arranged by subject for materials cataloged before August 1, 1981, which refer to countries outside the common law system. It also contains entries for works that compare three or more countries, and materials in the Ancient, Canon, Moslem and Roman law collections. Author and title entries for the materials appear in Parts I and II of the *Catalog of International Law and Relations* described above.

(b)   Indices Containing Material of Special Interest to United Nations Programs

Current Bibliographical Information. New York: United Nations, 1971-.

> This is the Dag Hammarskjold Library's monthly acquisitions list; it includes non-U.N. publications and selective articles from more than 700 periodicals. It also includes author and subject indices.

Monthly Bibliography. Geneva: United Nations, 1978-.

> Part I (*Books, Official Documents, and Serials*) is a separately bound volume which lists publications received by the U.N. library in Geneva. Items are classified to simplify locating materials on topics such as human rights (generally), women, education, or health. There are also author, title and subject indices.

2.   Dissertations and Theses

Dissertations and theses are underutilized research materials. As increasing numbers of students research human rights topics, this material becomes a more important resource. Unfortunately, relatively few dissertations or theses are represented in library catalogs.

Some libraries do catalog theses and dissertations produced by their own students: for example, the Harvard Law Library incorporates graduate dissertations written by degree candidates at the law school into the law library's collection as monographs. They are thus accessible by author, title, subject and key word searches through the library catalog, or through online bibliographic utilities such as RLIN or OCLC.

Theoretically, the best dissertations find their way into print and are subsequently cataloged as books. There are, however, many useful dissertations which for a variety of reasons are not published. Also, the time lag between the completion of a dissertation and its appearance in monograph format can be considerable. Researchers interested in accessing dissertations should consult the following resources.

Dissertation Abstracts International. **Ann Arbor, MI: University Microfilms International, 1938-.**

> Provides abstracts of doctoral dissertations produced in the United States and abroad. Access is by subject, author, or university. Coverage of scholarly production from the third world is, however, limited.
>
> *Online*: DAI is one of several indices comprising the online database *Dissertation Abstracts Online,* covering 1861 to date. It is available in DIALOG (file 35), in WESTLAW (DAO database) as a DIALOG database, in BRS (DISS), in OCLC EPIC, and in Knowledge Index (REFR5).

Masters Abstracts International. **Ann Arbor, MI: University Microfilms International, 1962-.**

> A small number of American colleges and universities cooperate in this quarterly, which provides abstracts.
>
> *Online*: *Dissertation Abstracts Online* (1962 to date, with abstracts 1988 to date) in DIALOG, BRS and OCLC EPIC.

C.   *Publications by the United States Government, Nongovernmental Organizations and Intergovernmental Organizations*

1.   Publications by the United States Government

These materials are discussed in detail in Chapter Five. This section merely highlights a few major sources as part of Chapter One's overview.

Many important U.S. government publications are serials and are indexed by the relevant periodical indices. Others are cataloged as monographs and are accessible through library catalogs. Virtually all U.S. government publications are accessible through the *Monthly Catalog of United States Publications*, the main current bibliography of publications issued by all branches of the U.S. government. Congressional publications are well-indexed by *CIS/Index*. The annual *Treaties in Force* provides citations to the texts of treaties to which the United States is a party. The Department of State *Dispatch*, the successor publication to the recently-terminated *Department of State Bulletin*, publishes official U.S. foreign policy statements, and the unofficial *International Legal Materials* (see pp. 14-15) contains a range of useful executive and legislative documents, judicial decisions, and drafts and final texts of treaties. The *Lawyer's Monthly Catalog* is also useful for U.S. government documents.

> *Online*: *Monthly Catalog of United States Publications* is available online from 1976 to date in DIALOG (file 66), in WESTLAW (GPO-CTLG database) as a DIALOG database, in BRS (GPOM), in OCLC EPIC, and OCLC FirstSearch.

> *Online*: *CIS/Index* is available online in DIALOG (file 101) and in WESTLAW (CIS database) as a dialog database from 1970 to present.

> *Online*: *International Legal Materials* is online in LEXIS from 1980 to date (in the ILM file) in the INTLAW, ITRADE, or LAWREV libraries.

For historical research, *Foreign Relations of the United States*, prepared by the Department of State, is a comprehensive collection of U.S. official documents on foreign relations. The 25-year publication time lag, however, limits its usefulness. The Department of State also publishes other documentary compilations, with less delay: *A Decade of American Foreign Policy: Basic Documents, 1941-1949*; *American Foreign Policy: Basic Documents, 1950-1955*; *American Foreign Policy: Current Documents*; and *American Foreign Policy: Basic Documents, 1968-1980*.

2.   Publications by Intergovernmental Organizations (IGOs)

Some important indices to the publications of intergovernmental organizations relevant to human rights are *UNDOC: Current Index* and the *Yearbook of the United Nations* (for U.N. materials); *International Labour Documentation* (for publications and documents of the International Labour Organisation); and *International Bibliography* (for the publications of a wide range of intergovernmental organizations, but which recently ceased publication). There are many more such tools, however, and the reader should consult Chapter Three for a detailed discussion of sources.

3.   Publications by Nongovernmental Organizations (NGOs)

Human rights nongovernmental organizations are vital to the international human rights movement. These organizations are usually defined as private organizations which do not seek formal state power and which use as their normative basis the rights enunciated in the major human rights treaties and other international instruments. These rights may include civil and political rights; economic, social and cultural rights; and the more recent rights to a clean environment, to development and peace. They may also include the rights of women, children, the disabled, indigenous peoples and sexual minorities.

A major defining feature of human rights NGOs is normative reference to international human rights standards. In fact, there are many other organizations — development NGOs are a good example — which could be included in the definition, since their activities address issues such as hunger, poverty, disease, housing, and employment that also figure in human rights instruments. Their publications are important for human rights research, since they sometimes document economic and social conditions and provide analyses which, while not using the rhetoric of rights, indicate the sources of problems.

NGOs vary in size and influence, and range from large and well-known international NGOs such as Amnesty International, to small, relatively unknown, and more vulnerable groups. Some of the larger groups now exercise significant influence in U.S. national policy debates about human rights worldwide. Typically, human rights NGOs monitor and publicize human rights conditions, conduct public education, and provide legal and humanitarian services to victims. Many of these organizations publish reports, newsletters and (less frequently) magazines which describe their work and the situation of human rights locally. Few of the major human rights NGOs devote resources to monitoring economic, social and cultural rights.

Bound reports of some of the most influential groups, such as Amnesty International, Human Rights Watch, the International Commission of Jurists, and the Lawyers Committee for Human Rights, are collected and cataloged by university, research, and law libraries. Reports of less prominent organizations are collected and cataloged much less frequently. Serial publications of "non-prominent" human rights NGOs receive similar treatment, making them much harder to locate and their contents less visible through periodical indices.

Because of this uneven coverage, the Human Rights Internet *Reporter* (see p. 69) is an important research tool for the activities and publications of human rights NGOs. The *Reporter* provides broad bibliographic coverage of the documents and publications of NGOs, with some coverage of significant academic works and intergovernmental organization documents. Internet has initiated a new publication, *Human Rights Tribune/ Tribune des Droits Humains* (see p. 55), which provides useful news and comment on the NGO movement. The bulk of the NGO documents in Human Rights Internet's extensive collection have been reproduced on microfiche by Inter Documentation Company (IDC) of the Netherlands. This collection, which is updated periodically and currently covers publications between 1980-1988, is an invaluable source of research material: *Human Rights Documents* [microform]. Leiden, The Netherlands: IDC, 1983-. (See p. 69.)

Non-current Amnesty International publications and selected documents are contained in a microfiche collection: *Amnesty International, 1962-1987,* Amnesty International, London. Netherlands: IDC Microform Publishers, 1989 (see p. 68). Current Amnesty International publications are available by subscription, or through one of the national or regional offices, addresses of which appear in AI's annual report and in many of its publications.

Publications by nongovernmental organizations are discussed in detail in Chapter Two, Section IV.

D.   Leading Works on Legal Research

Some leading works on legal research are Cohen, M., R. Berring and K. C. Olson. *How to Find the Law.* 9th ed. St. Paul, MN: West Publishing Co., 1989. 716 pp.; Jacobstein, J. M. and R. M. Mersky. *Fundamentals of Legal Research.* 5th ed. Westbury, NY: Foundation Press, 1990. 734 pp.; Price, M., H. Bitner and S. Bysiewicz. *Effective Legal Research.* 4th ed. Boston: Little Brown, 1979. 643 pp. In addition to U.S. legal research, these works provide basic information on foreign, international and comparative legal sources. With a focus on international law, the following publication is very useful: The George Washington Journal of International Law and Economics, eds. *Guide to International Legal Research,* 2d ed. Salem, NH: Butterworth Legal Publishers, 1993. 536 pp. This *Guide* was first published as a double issue of the *Journal* in vol. 20, nos.1-2 (1986) and then in book form in 1990. Two good sources for foreign law sources and issues are Germain, C. *Germain's Transnational Law Research: A Guide for Attorneys.* Ardsley-on-Hudson, NY: Transnational Juris Publications, Inc., 1991, and Reynolds, T. and A. Flores. *Foreign Law: Current Sources of Codes and Basic Legislation in Jurisdictions of the World.* Littleton, CO: F.B. Rothman, 1989-.

III.   Current Awareness

A.   Human Rights Developments

In addition to sources noted above such as the *Legal Resource Index* and *Current Law Index*, the following materials allow a researcher to keep abreast of some — not all — developments in the human rights field generally, and in its subfields. Listed below are some periodicals that systematically provide updates on developments such as the ratification of human rights treaties, significant action by human rights bodies, changes in international procedures, or relevant court decisions or new statutes. More detailed information on most of the following publications is provided in later sections of the *Guide* concentrating on particular topics or regions.

American Society of International Law. *International Legal Materials.* **Washington, DC: American Society of International Law, 1962-.**

> International Legal Materials (I.L.M.), published six times a year, is an important source of international law materials which frequently concern human rights. I.L.M. publishes the texts of draft or recently ratified treaties, decisions of international tribunals, and other international legal documents such as declarations and resolutions of international bodies. I.L.M. also reproduces sections from the Department of State's *Dispatch* which provide information on current U.S. actions on multilateral treaties. I.L.M. occasionally publishes the texts or excerpts of domestic court decisions which have major implications for international law. A concluding section briefly notes other significant international documents, such as reports of intergovernmental organizations.

Online: ILM is online from Jan. 1980 in LEXIS (in the ILM file) in the INTLAW, ITRADE, or LAWREV libraries.

The Economist. London: The Economist Newspaper Ltd., 1843-.

Essential for international and business news, and also has key economic information. Frequently has articles on different countries bearing on human rights.

HR Documentation DH. Geneva: International Service for Human Rights, 1989-.

Lists documents, compilations of voting results, and other information on U.N. human rights activities.

Human Rights Case Digest. London: British Institute of Human Rights, 1990-.

Bimonthly which gives summaries of European Court and Commission of Human Rights judgments and decisions, and Article 32 and 54 decisions of the Committee of Ministers.

Human Rights Internet Reporter. Ottawa: Human Rights Internet, 1976-.

Contains a bibliography of NGO literature; past issues also contain news, short articles, and comments about the human rights movement.

Human Rights Law Journal. Kehl am Rhein; Arlington, VA: N.P. Engel, 1980-.

Contains scholarly articles, updates and primary sources like committee reports, conferences, resolutions, declarations, and judicial opinions, frequently accompanied by commentary. Also provides status of ratifications.

Human Rights Monitor. Geneva: International Service for Human Rights, 1988-.

Covers human rights developments at the United Nations and specialized agencies, NGO activities, and occasional information on other international bodies.

Human Rights Quarterly. Baltimore: Johns Hopkins University Press, 1981-.

Scholarly articles from several disciplines, plus frequent articles covering activities at the annual sessions of the Commission on Human Rights and the Sub-Commission for the Prevention of Discrimination and the Protection of Minorities.

Human Rights Tribune. Ottawa: Human Rights Internet, 1992-.

Contains news of the human rights movement, and NGO and U.N. events.

The Review. **Geneva: International Commission of Jurists, 1969-.**

> Semi-annual articles review the sessions of the Commission on Human Rights and Sub-Commission; also includes brief articles on human rights conditions in various countries. Formed by the union of *Bulletin of the International Commission of Jurists* (1954-1968) and *Journal of the International Commission of Jurists* (1957-1968).

The Women's Watch. **Minneapolis, MN: International Women's Rights Action Watch, Humphrey Institute of Public Affairs, 1987-.**

> Quarterly newsletter on seminars, meetings, court decisions, legislative changes, and other developments in law and policy relating to the Convention on the Elimination of All Forms of Discrimination against Women.

B.   *Country Conditions*

For information about a specific country or region, the sources listed in Section A, above, will be relevant. Researchers should also consult the reports of human rights NGOs, government reports and U.S. congressional hearings, and the reports of intergovernmental organizations (such as U.N. bodies or the regional systems of human rights protection). Newspaper indices are also good sources of current information. Key indices include many that are available online, allowing simultaneous searches of a number of newspapers. Periodical indices which cover general or popular periodicals are also useful.

Annually published yearbooks such as the Europa publications, published in London by Europa Pub. Ltd., for different areas of the world (various dates) are useful for general background information about the economy, political system and recent history of countries. Also useful are the lengthy *Area Handbook* and *Country Studies* series published by the Library of Congress and American University in Washington. Finally, publications of the Joint Publications Research Service and the Foreign Broadcast Information Service can be consulted for recent translations of excerpts from non-U.S. publications and broadcasts. (See pp. 84-85 for more information on these resources.)

A good picture of the evolution of human rights conditions in a particular country or region over the past ten-to-twelve years is available in past issues of the *Human Rights Internet Reporter*, described above, and by using the microfiche collections of Amnesty International and Human Rights Internet. (See pp. 68-69.)

IV.   Principal Scholarly Journals on Human Rights

More information on scholarly journals is provided in Section III of Chapter Two.

Boletin, Comision Andina de Juristas. Lima: La Comision, 1982-.

Canadian Human Rights Yearbook. Toronto: Carswell, 1983-.

Columbia Human Rights Law Review. New York: Columbia University School of Law, 1972-.

> *Online*: Selected articles available in full text in WESTLAW (CLMHRLR database) from 1984 (Vol. 15) to date.

Europaische Grundrechte. Kehl am Rhein: Engel Verlag, 1974-.

Harvard Human Rights Journal. Cambridge, MA: Harvard Law School, 1988-.

Human Rights Law Journal. Kehl am Rhein: N.P. Engel, 1980-.

Human Rights Quarterly. Baltimore, MD: Johns Hopkins University Press, 1979-.

Israel Yearbook on Human Rights. Tel Aviv: Tel Aviv University Faculty of Law, 1971-.

Mennesker og Rettigheter. Oslo: Det Norske Menneskerettighetsprosjektet, 1983-.

Netherlands Quarterly of Human Rights. Utrecht: Studie-en Informatiecentrum Mensenrechten, 1983-.

New York Law School Journal of Human Rights. New York: New York Law School, 1983-.

> *Online*: Selected articles available in full text in WESTLAW (NYLSJHR database) from 1990 (Vol. 7) to date.

The Review. Geneva: International Commission of Jurists, 1969-.

Revista Chilena de Derechos Humanos. Santiago, Chile: Programa de Derechos Humanos, Academia de Humanismo Christiano, 1985-.

Revista Instituto Interamericano de Derechos Humanos. San Jose, Costa Rica: El Instituto, 1985-.

Revista Latinoamericana de Derechos Humanos. Lima: Red Latinoamericana de Abogados Catolicos, MILC, Pax-Romana, 1988-1989.

Revue Trimestrielle des Droits de l'Homme. Bruxelles: Editions Nemises, 1990-.

Revue des Droits de l'Homme. Paris: A. Pedone, 1968-.

Turkish Yearbook of Human Rights. Ankara: Institute of Public Administration for Turkey and the Middle East, Human Rights Research and Documentation Center, 1979-.

V.   List of Principal Works in Human Rights

Throughout the *Guide* occasional suggestions are made of books and articles that provide useful introductions to specific fields of human rights. This section is more comprehensive. It suggests a larger number of books about human rights that will aid the novice as well as researchers experienced in human rights work. The list does not purport to include *all* books that, from one or another perspective, are thought to be among the most searching or innovative writings in the field — though many of the books here noted fit that description. These frequently consulted books should be widely available.

A.   *General Treatises on International Law with Sections on Human Rights*

Akehurst, M. *A Modern Introduction to International Law.* 6th ed. London: HarperCollins Academic, 1987. pp. 76-81.

Brownlie, I. *Principles of Public International Law.* 4th ed. New York: Oxford University Press, 1990. pp. 553-601.

Chen, L. *An Introduction to Contemporary International Law: A Policy-Oriented Perspective.* New Haven, CT: Yale University Press, 1989. pp. 197-223.

Encyclopedia of Public International Law. Amsterdam; New York: North Holland Pub. Co., l981-. (See especially Vols. 5, 7 and 8.)

Henkin, L. "International Law: Politics, Values and Functions," 1989 *Recueil des Cours IV.* 19-416. (See especially chapters X, XI and XII.)

Janis, M. *An Introduction to International Law.* 2d ed. Boston: Little Brown and Co., 1993. pp. 241-272.

Jennings, R. and A. Watts. *Oppenheim's International Law.* 9th ed. Harlow, Essex, England: Longman Group UK Limited, 1992. (See especially Vol. 1.)

O'Connell, D.P. *International Law.* 2d ed. Vol. 2. London: Stevens and Sons, 1970. pp. 743-793, 956-959.

Schachter, O. *International Law in Theory and Practice.* Dordrecht; Boston; London: M. Nijhoff Publishers, 1991. pp. 330-361.

von Glahn, G. "Laws of War." In *Law Among Nations: An Introduction to Public International Law.* 6th rev. ed. 669-892. New York: Macmillan Pub. Co., 1992.

B.   General Treatises or Nutshells
        Specifically on Human Rights

Buergenthal, T. *International Human Rights in a Nutshell.* St. Paul, MN: West Pub. Co., 1988. 283 pp.

Sieghart, P. *The International Law of Human Rights.* Oxford: Clarendon Press, 1983. 569 pp.

C.   Casebooks

Berger, V. *Case Law of the European Court of Human Rights.* Dublin: Round Hall Press, 1989. 291 pp. (Vol. 1: 1960-1987; Vol. 2: 1988-1990.)

Buergenthal, T. et al. *Protecting Human Rights in the Americas: Selected Problems.* 3rd ed. Kehl; Arlington, VA: N.P. Engel, 1990. 561 pp.

Henkin, L., et al. *International Law: Cases and Materials.* 3d ed. St.Paul, MN: West Pub. Co., 1993. pp. 595-676.

Lillich, R. *International Human Rights: Problems of Law, Policy, and Practice.* 2d ed. Boston: Little, Brown Company, 1991. 1062 pp.

Newman, F., and D. Weissbrodt. *International Human Rights: Law, Policy and Process.* Cincinnati: Anderson Pub. Co., 1990. 812 pp.

Sohn, L., and T. Buergenthal. *International Protection of Human Rights.* Indianapolis: Bobbs-Merill, 1973. 1402 pp.

Steiner, H. and D. Vagts. *Transnational Legal Problems.* 3d ed. Mineola, NY: Foundation Press, 1986. pp. 405-479, 653-695.

D.   General Texts on Human Rights

In order to give the researcher an overview of the type and range of texts in the human rights field, a brief list of frequently consulted works follows. This is a partial listing; researchers interested in the annotations to these references or in further works in a specific field should consult the relevant section(s) below.

Alston, P., ed. *The United Nations and Human Rights: A Critical Appraisal.* Oxford: Clarendon Press; New York: Oxford University Press, 1992. 765 pp.

Alston, P. and K. Tomasevski, eds. *The Right to Food.* Boston: M. Nijhoff; Utrecht: Stichting Studie- en Informatiecentrum Mensenrechten, 1984. 229 pp.

An-Na'im, A., ed. *Human Rights in Cross-Cultural Perspectives: A Quest for Consensus.* Philadelphia: University of Pennsylvania Press, 1992. 479 pp.

An-Na'im, A. *Toward an Islamic Reformation: Civil Liberties, Human Rights, and International Law.* Syracuse, NY: Syracuse University Press, 1990. 253 pp.

An-Na'im, A. and F. Deng, eds. *Human Rights in Africa: Cross-Cultural Perspectives.* Washington, DC: The Brookings Institution, 1990. 399 pp.

Bassiouni, M., ed. *International Criminal Law.* 3 vols. Dobbs Ferry, NY: Transnational Publishers, 1986. (Vol. 1: Crimes; Vol. 2: Procedure; Vol. 3: Enforcement.)

Brownlie, I. *Treaties and Indigenous Peoples.* Oxford: Clarendon Press; New York: Oxford University Press, 1992. 105 pp.

Cassese, A. *Human Rights in a Changing World.* Philadelphia: Temple University Press, 1990. 245 pp.

Cassese, A., ed. *The International Fight Against Torture.* Baden-Baden: Nomos Verlagsgesellschaft, 1991. 186 pp.

Cassese, A. *International Law in a Divided World.* Oxford: Clarendon Press; New York: Oxford University Press, 1986. 429 pp.

Cassese, A., et al. *Human Rights and The European Community.* 3 vols. Baden-Baden: Nomos Verlagsgesellschaft, 1991.

Centre for Human Rights. *United Nations Action in the Field of Human Rights.* New York: United Nations, 1988. 359 pp.

Claude, R.P., and B.H. Weston, eds. *Human Rights in the World Community.* 2d ed. Philadelphia: University of Pennsylvania Press, 1992. 463 pp.

Crawford, J. *The Rights of Peoples.* Oxford: Clarendon Press; New York: Oxford University Press, 1992. 236 pp.

Delissen, A. et al., eds. *Humanitarian Law of Armed Conflict: Challenges Ahead. Essays in Honor of Frits Kalshoven.* Boston; Dordrecht: M. Nijhoff, 1991. 668 pp.

Diemer, A. et al. *Philosophical Foundations of Human Rights.* Paris: United Nations Educational, Scientific and Cultural Organization, 1986. 340 pp.

Dijk, P. van and G.J.H. van Hoof. *Theory and Practice of the European Convention on Human Rights.* 2d ed. Deventer; Boston: Kluwer Law and Taxation Publishers, 1990. 657 pp.

Donnelly, J. *The Concept of Human Rights.* New York: St. Martin's Press, 1985. 120 pp.

Donnelly, J. *International Human Rights.* Boulder, CO: Westview Press, 1993. 206 pp.

Donnelly, J. *Universal Human Rights in Theory and Practice.* Ithaca, NY: Cornell University Press, 1989. 295 pp.

Fawcett, J. *Application of the European Convention on Human Rights.* Oxford: Clarendon Press; New York: Oxford University Press, 1987. 444 pp.

Forsythe, D. *Human Rights and World Politics.* 2d rev. ed. Lincoln, NE: University of Nebraska Press, 1989. 316 pp.

Goodwin-Gill, G. *The Refugee in International Law.* Oxford: Clarendon Press; New York: Oxford University Press, 1983. 318 pp.

Gormley, W. P. *Human Rights and Environment: The Need for International Cooperation.* Leyden: Sijthoff, 1976. 255 pp.

Grahl-Madsen, A. *The Status of Refugees in International Law.* 2 vols. Leyden: Sijthoff, 1966-1972.

Hannum, H. *Autonomy, Sovereignty and Self-Determination: The Accommodation of Conflicting Rights.* Philadelphia: University of Pennsylvania Press, 1990. 503 pp.

Hannum, H., ed. *Guide to International Human Rights Practice.* 2d ed. Philadelphia: University of Pennsylvania Press, 1992. 308 pp.

Harris, D. *The European Social Charter.* Charlottesville, VA: University Press of Virginia, 1984. 345 pp.

Hathaway, J. *The Law of Refugee Status.* Toronto: Butterworths; Austin, TX: Butterworth Legal Publishers, 1991. 252 pp.

Henkin, L. *The Age of Rights.* New York: Columbia University Press, 1990. 220 pp.

Henkin, L., ed. *The International Bill of Rights: The Covenant on Civil and Political Rights.* New York: Columbia University Press, 1981. 523 pp.

Hevener, N. *International Law and the Status of Women.* Boulder, CO: Westview Press, 1983. 249 pp.

Horowitz, D. *Ethnic Groups in Conflict.* Berkeley: University of California Press, 1985. 697 pp.

Howard, R. *Human Rights in Commonwealth Africa.* Totowa, NJ: Rowman & Littlefield Publishers, 1986. 250 pp.

International Dimensions of Humanitarian Law. Geneva: Henry Dunant Institute; Dordrecht; Boston: M. Nijhoff Publishers, 1988. 328 pp.

Jabine, T. and R. Claude, eds. *Human Rights and Statistics: Getting the Record Straight.* Philadelphia: University of Pennsylvania Press, 1992. 458 pp.

Laqueur, W. and B. Rubin, eds. *The Human Rights Reader.* 2d ed. New York: New American Library, 1989. 516 pp.

Lauterpacht, H. *An International Bill of the Rights of Man.* New York: Columbia University Press, 1945. 230 pp.

Lawson, E., ed. *Encyclopedia of Human Rights.* New York: Taylor & Francis, 1991. 1907 pp.

Mayer, A. *Islam and Human Rights: Tradition and Politics.* Boulder, CO: Westview Press, 1991. 258 pp.

McDougall, M., H. Lasswell and L. Chen. *Human Rights and World Public Order.* New Haven, CT: Yale University Press, 1980. 1016 pp.

McGoldrick, D. *Human Rights Committee.* Oxford: Clarendon Press; New York: Oxford University Press, 1991. 576 pp.

Meron, T. *Human Rights and Humanitarian Norms as Customary Law.* Oxford: Clarendon Press; New York: Oxford University Press, 1989. 263 pp.

Meron, T. *Human Rights in Internal Strife: Their International Protection.* Cambridge, U.K.: Grotius, 1987. 172 pp.

Meron, T., ed. *Human Rights in International Law: Legal and Policy Issues.* Oxford: Clarendon Press, 1984. 2 vols. 566 pp.

Meron, T. *Human Rights Law-Making in the United Nations.* New York: Oxford University Press, 1986. 351 pp.

Merrills, J. *The Development of International Law by the European Court of Human Rights.* New York: Manchester University Press, 1988. 235 pp.

Nardin, T., and D. Mapel, eds. *Traditions of International Ethics.* Cambridge; New York: Cambridge University Press, 1992. 326 pp.

Plender, R. *International Migration Law.* rev. 2d ed. Dordrecht; Boston: M. Nijhoff Publishers, 1988. 587 pp.

Rhoodie, E. *Discrimination Against Women: A Global Survey of the Economic, Educational, Social and Political Status of Women.* Jefferson, NC: McFarland, 1989. 618 pp.

Robertson, A., and J. Merrills. *Human Rights in the World.* 3rd ed. New York: Manchester University Press, 1989. 314 pp.

Rodley, N. *The Treatment of Prisoners Under International Law.* Paris: United Nations Educational, Scientific and Cultural Organization; Oxford: Clarendon Press; New York: Oxford University Press, 1987. 374 pp.

Schwarzenberger, G. *International Law.* Vol. 2, *The Law of Armed Conflict.* London: Stevens and Sons, 1968.

Shue, H. *Basic Rights.* Princeton, NJ: Princeton University Press, 1980. 231 pp.

Sieghart, P. *The Lawful Rights of Mankind: An Introduction to the International Code of Human Rights.* Oxford; New York: Oxford University Press, 1985. 252 pp.

Steiner, H. *Diverse Partners: Non-Governmental Organizations in the Human Rights Movement.* Cambridge, MA: Harvard Law School Human Rights Program and Human Rights Internet, 1991. 90 pp.

Steiner, H., ed. *Ethnic Conflict and the U.N. Human Rights System.* Cambridge, MA: Harvard Law School Human Rights Program, forthcoming, 1994.

Thornberry, P. *International Law and the Rights of Minorities.* Oxford: Clarendon Press; New York: Oxford University Press, 1991. 451 pp.

Tolley, H. *The U.N. Commission on Human Rights.* Boulder, CO: Westview Press, 1987. 300 pp.

Van Dyke, V. *Human Rights, Ethnicity and Discrimination.* Westport, CT: Greenwood Press, 1985. 259 pp.

Vasak, K. and P. Alston, eds. *The International Dimensions of Human Rights.* 2 vols. Westport, CT: Greenwood Press; Paris: United Nations Educational, Scientific and Cultural Organization, 1982.

Vincent, R. J. *Human Rights and International Relations.* New York: Cambridge University Press, 1986. 186 pp.

VI.   Online Research: Using Computer Databases[1]

What is a database? In the context used here, it is any collection of information which is in machine readable form and can be searched by computer. The type of information that is contained in databases includes: *bibliographic* (containing short references to documents or other materials); *full text* (containing the entire text of documents); *referral* (similar to directories, containing references to names, addresses, descriptions of people, organizations, companies, etc.); and *numeric* (containing numbers or statistics).

Why would one use a database? It is often much faster to search an index or other information in a database than in its equivalent print format. Databases also offer more flexibility: it is usually possible to combine two or more search terms simultaneously, to generate information that meets the specific needs of the searcher. It is also possible to search many sources simultaneously. In a full text database, one often has the option to search every word of all of the documents the database contains, making it possible to find even a single occurrence of a relevant word in any document in the database.

Full text databases provide immediate access to entire documents that may not be easily or conveniently available in print format. It is also possible to search many more indices or materials than the usual library would have access to if it had to buy the printed version of each document. Often the online or database version of an index is more up-to-date than its print equivalent. Also, some materials, like news wire services, do not exist as a searchable source in print format.

For all the usefulness and benefits of online databases, there are some shortcomings. First, there is no one database that can provide access to all relevant human rights information for all time periods. Instead, there are hundreds of different databases, some containing human rights information on a focused topic, and others covering human rights in addition to other topics. One reason for this is that information services, including databases, in many different disciplines are relevant for human rights research. Another reason is that there are many different producers of human rights or human rights-related databases, including nongovernmental organizations (NGOs), intergovernmental organizations (IGOs), governments, educational institutions, and commercial companies or vendors. The scope of materials covered by a single database will always be limited, and it is important for the researcher to learn what kind of materials, subjects, and time periods are covered in a given database. (See Section E, below, for several directories to databases.)

A second drawback of online databases is that the techniques and search strategies for different databases are not uniform, so searching skills cannot necessarily be applied across different databases. Third, expense is often a concern. Subscription rates for some databases are very high; communications costs can also be high if it is necessary to have

---

[1] Nina Cascio, international law librarian, Charles B. Sears Law Library, State University of New York at Buffalo, and Jeanette Yackle, head of reference, International, Foreign and Comparative Law, Harvard Law Library, authored this section.

the computer dial up a database on a long distance phone line. Finally, some information is simply not available in database format, or, if equipment fails or electricity is unavailable or unreliable, an online database search may not be possible.

While researchers can often perform database searches independently, sometimes it is necessary to rely upon a librarian or information specialist to perform a search.

A.   *Gaining Access to Databases*

How can one gain access to databases? The simplest method is to visit a university, college, or public library and speak to a librarian. Many libraries have computerized online catalogs allowing one to search the library's collection. Many academic libraries with online catalogs have also made available various commercially produced online indices, such as the *Social Sciences Index*, *Public Affairs Information Service*, and the *Legal Resource Index*. Libraries also often provide these and other databases in CD-ROM format, where the data is stored on a compact disk instead of accessed through phone lines.

Many libraries have access to either the Online Computer Library Center (OCLC) or Research Libraries Information Network (RLIN), which allow one to search the holdings of many libraries and research institutions in North America and abroad. Through the Internet, an international communications network, it is possible to access information which includes the online catalogs of university libraries throughout the world. It is also common for libraries to have subscriptions to online databases, such as DIALOG, BRS, Dow Jones, and others, which a librarian will search for a patron, sometimes for a fee to cover the cost of accessing the database. If a particular library does not provide access to a desired database, librarians can often provide a referral to another library. It is possible for individuals to subscribe to commercial online databases, but often the cost is prohibitive.

There are many specialized databases that have been created by IGOs such as the United Nations, by NGOs, and by educational and research institutions. Many of these are not available through commercial online services, but some of these organizations and institutions can provide searches for outside users. Identifying these databases will be discussed in the sections on IGO- and NGO-produced databases that follow.

B.   *Legal Databases*

Throughout this *Guide*, there are many references to sources that are available on LEXIS and WESTLAW, the two major legal research databases in the United States. They provide access to case, statutory, and administrative law for the United States on both the federal and state levels, and include secondary sources (law review articles, periodical indices, encyclopedias, looseleaf services, news sources). Foreign law sources (British, Chinese, Commonwealth, European Community, French, Polish, and more) and international law sources (e.g., decisions of the International Court of Justice) are available on one or both systems.

NEXIS is the full-text news service that is available with LEXIS. It has the full text of news stories from many newspapers, wire services, newsletters, magazines, and television and radio broadcast transcripts. DIALOG, a major database vendor, has recently contracted with West Publishing Company to make many of its databases (bibliographic indices, directories, and full text materials) searchable through WESTLAW. To determine the databases that are available in LEXIS/NEXIS, consult the LEXIS/NEXIS *Library Contents and Alphabetical List*, updated at least once a year; to ascertain the databases that are available in WESTLAW and on DIALOG through WESTLAW, consult the WESTLAW *Database List*, which is periodically updated. The scope and availability of databases available through LEXIS/NEXIS and WESTLAW change, so it is necessary to consult these updated guides or check the lists online for the most current information.

Most academic law libraries or law schools in the United States have entered into "educational contracts" with Mead Data Central for LEXIS/NEXIS, and West Publishing Company for WESTLAW, to provide "unlimited access" to enrolled law students and law faculty for conducting research related to the law school curriculum. Both LEXIS/NEXIS and WESTLAW are relatively expensive to search outside the educational setting.

Despite the increasing appearance of foreign legal sources in LEXIS/NEXIS and WESTLAW, there is far from good coverage of most jurisdictions of the world. There are many other online legal research systems around the world that could prove useful for various aspects of human rights research. For example, QL (Quicklaw) from Canada provides access to Canadian federal and provincial law, in addition to specific files containing summaries of Canadian Charter of Rights cases (CRC database), bibliographic descriptions of human rights periodical articles (HRB database), and Canadian news (CNW and CPN databases). There are legal databases from Australia, Austria, Belgium, Denmark, Finland, France, Germany, Israel, Italy, Japan, Luxembourg, the Netherlands, New Zealand, Norway, the Philippines, Portugal, South Africa, Spain, Sweden, Switzerland, the United Kingdom, and other countries. However, access to such foreign databases from the United States may be difficult or impossible.

The book, *International Access to Legislative Information: A Preliminary Investigation*, edited by W. S. Chiang and K. Price (Sarasota, FL: UNIFO, 1992), includes papers from a workshop set up to explore new ways to provide efficient access to legislation from all over the world. Appendix 1 (pp. 52-61) includes a proposal for an International Legal Information Network (ILIN) which would include creation of a cooperative online index to current national legislation and international treaties with an electronic document delivery capability.

C.   *Databases Produced by Nongovernmental Organizations (NGOs)*

Human Rights NGOs worldwide have been collecting, organizing, and making available information gathered in the course of their work. The information often consists of news clippings, journal articles, reports, or books. Sometimes it includes data gathered by the NGO itself from victims of or witnesses to human rights abuses. NGOs may also collect legal decisions, laws and regulations, and statements of government policies. Some NGOs have created manual systems (such as card files) to organize their information, and many have created computer databases.

In recent years, effort has been made to encourage human rights NGOs to develop organized information systems according to a standard format. A major actor in this effort has been HURIDOCS (Human Rights Information and Documentation System). HURIDOCS encourages the use of a standard format to record individual pieces of information so that all users of the information system can effectively and efficiently locate relevant items and transfer information efficiently. HURIDOCS also encourages the use of a common thesaurus from which subject terms can be taken to facilitate the retrieval of information within an organization and between organizations. Various thesauri are described elsewhere in this *Guide*. To contact HURIDOCS, write Torggate 27, 0183 Oslo 1, Norway.

There are some human rights NGOs that gather publications of other NGOs to make them available to researchers. The leading such NGO is Human Rights Internet (HRI), located at the Human Rights Research and Education Centre at the University of Ottawa, 57 Louis Pasteur, Ottawa, Ontario, K1N 6N5 Canada. HRI promotes human rights education, stimulates research, and encourages information-sharing and other communication among those committed to human rights.

Human Rights Internet has created a database containing the full texts of directories of human rights organizations and a bibliographic database containing citations to and abstracts of human rights publications. The information in these databases is used to create some of HRI's publications, among them the *Human Rights Internet Reporter*, the *Human Rights Tribune*, and various directories of human rights organizations. (These publications are described in Chapter Two, Section IV.) These databases can be searched on-site, or requests can be made by phone, fax or mail. There may be fees charged for searches and photocopying.

Databases created by human rights NGOs are not generally available as commercial online databases. Policies regarding access to NGO in-house databases vary depending on the goals and purpose of each NGO as well as the availability of resources. If access to a specific NGO database is provided to outside users, the search is generally performed by a member of the organization. Direct inquiry is usually the best way to discover whether a particular NGO has an in-house database, and what its access policy is for external users. Some NGO directories, as well as UNESCO's *World Directory of Human Rights Teaching and Research Institutions* (Oxford and New York: Berg, 1988), indicate whether specific NGOs maintain a database or utilize computerized methods of data processing. Information in printed directories may be out-of-date, however, so contacting the organization is the best way to obtain accurate information.

To identify NGOs working in a specific human rights area, use the UNESCO directory, the HRI directories, and others listed elsewhere in this *Guide*.

D.   *Databases Produced by Intergovernmental Organizations (IGOs)*

IGOs have long been collecting information to support their work. Many of the databases provide access to legislation while others contain bibliographic references to books, periodical articles, reports, documents, statistics, and other data important to the work of the IGO. A growing number of these databases are available commercially, though many are still available only for the internal use of the particular IGO.

1.   U.N. Databases

In 1983, a resolution of the U.N. Economic and Social Council mandated the creation of **ACCIS (Advisory Committee for the Co-ordination of Information Systems),** whose purposes were to make U.N. information sources more accessible to member states and to streamline the U.N. information infrastructure. ACCIS created a database called **DUNDIS** which keeps track of U.N. information systems and databases, and produces specialized guides to U.N. information systems and databases.

Several databases created by U.N. agencies are presently available through commercial vendors. Others are available only to U.N. system organizations, and some are accessible by users external to the United Nations at various specified search sites. Although the ACCIS guides are created primarily for those working within the U.N. system, they are very useful for external users. Through the following guides it is possible to ascertain whether outside users can gain access to specific databases and whether commercial vendors exist.

Directory of United Nations Databases and Information Services. **4th ed. Compiled by Advisory Committee for the Co-ordination of Information Systems (ACCIS). New York: United Nations, 1990. 484 pp.**

> Serves as a guide to 872 computerized databases and information systems/services created or operated by or in association with U.N. organizations and agencies. Part I alphabetically lists each of the U.N. organizations and specialized agencies and includes a description of their functions and machinery, and a list of their information services and databases.
>
> Part II (yellow pages) alphabetically lists services under broad subject categories. Each entry includes the name of the information service, the U.N. organization with which it is affiliated, the year the information service started, the holdings, subject scope, geographic coverage of the information service, printed products produced, a list of databases maintained, and other information.
>
> Part III (blue pages) is an alphabetical list of databases arranged by broad subject areas. In each entry descriptive information is provided, including database name and acro-

nym, U.N. affiliated organization, managing service, date established, status, subject and geographic scope, time period covered, frequency of updating, language of data, indexing and classification tools, availability, printed products, software, operating system, distribution media, online hosts, a contact person, and more.

The last Part contains a name/acronym index and three subject indices (in English, French and Spanish). The information in this directory is maintained in the DUNDIS database.

ACCIS has also produced several guides on U.N. information sources on specific topics. All of the guides provide information on databases and their availability to external users. Among the guides available include those listed below.

ACCIS Guide to United Nations Information Sources on International Trade and Development Finance. New York: United Nations, 1990.

ACCIS Guide to United Nations Information Sources on the Environment. New York: United Nations, 1988.

ACCIS Guide to United Nations Information Sources on Food and Agriculture. Rome: Food and Agriculture Organization of the United Nations, 1987.

ACCIS Guide to United Nations Information Sources on Health. New York: United Nations, 1992.

Directory of United Nations System Databases on Non-Governmental Organizations. New York: United Nations, 1988.

To keep up to date with newly created databases in the U.N. system and other developments, consult the following newsletter.

ACCIS Newsletter. **Geneva: ACCIS, 1983-.**

Bimonthly. The aim of this newsletter is to provide up-to-date information on publications and developments in information systems and technology within the U.N. system. To subscribe, write to the Editor, ACCIS Newsletter, ACCIS Secretariat, Palais des Nations, 1211 Geneva 10, Switzerland.

Among the many databases produced by the United Nations and its agencies that could prove useful for different aspects of human rights research are the following few examples. It may be necessary to contact the organization to arrange to have a search performed. Many of these databases contain the data used to create printed publications put out by the organization.

BIBLIOFILE produced by United Nations International Children's Emergency Fund (UNICEF). 1983-.

This bibliographic database covers information worldwide on child care child development, economic development, education, health, nutrition, social development, social welfare, water and women.

ECO-Line produced by the World Health Organization (WHO) and the Pan American Health Organization. 1984-.

This database, currently being developed, covers environmental legislation, pesticides, pollution, toxic substances, and toxicology.

Health Legislation Database produced by the World Health Organization (WHO). 1919-.

This database provides access to legislation on health and the environment worldwide and on the specific subjects of AIDS, health, nutrition, occupational hygiene, pharmaceuticals, and tobacco.

LABORDOC produced by the International Labour Organisation (ILO). 1965-.

This is a bibliographic database, with worldwide coverage of economic policy, employment, labor legislation, labor policy, labor relations, management, project evaluation, rural development, social development, social security, technological change, and working conditions.

LABORLEX-ILOLEX produced by the International Labor Organisation (ILO). Starting dates vary.

This trilingual (English, French, Spanish) database contains the ILO conventions, ILO Recommendations, the Triennial Report of the Committee on Freedom of Association (1985-present), Comments of the Committee of Experts on the Application of Conventions and Recommendations (1987-present), the Annual Report of the Conference Committee on the Application of Standards (1987-present), the Reports of Committees and Commissions established under articles 24 and 26 of the ILO constitution to investigate representations and complaints, ratification lists by convention and by country, and the ILO constitution. This database is also available on CD-ROM, distributed by Kluwer Academic Publishers.

LABORLEX-NATLEX produced by the International Labour Organisation (ILO). 1968-.

This database contains worldwide coverage of labour and social security legislation; it is frequently updated.

REFLIT (Refugee Literature Database) produced by the U.N. High Commissioner for Refugees (UNHCR), Centre for Documentation on Refugees (CDR). 1979-.

> This is a bibliographic database providing access to over 8,000 items in English, French, Spanish and German.

2.   European IGOs

Both the European Communities and the Council of Europe have created databases, some of which are available to the public.

The **Commission of the European Communities (EC)** sponsors many different groups of databases. Some of the legal databases in particular could prove to be useful for human rights research. **CELEX** is a database which provides access to the *Official Journal of the European Communities* (the C and L series). Specifically, CELEX contains primary legislation (treaties establishing the EC and amendments), secondary legislation, supplementary legislation, preparatory documents, case law (from the European Court of Justice), and Parliamentary questions. CELEX is available on LEXIS (ECLAW file in the INTLAW or Europe libraries) and WESTLAW (CELEX database). It is also available on CD-ROM.

SCAD is a bibliographic database providing access to EC publications, the main acts of EC legislation, selected periodical articles on EC topics, and opinions or statements by workers or employers organizations on Commission policy and work. SCAD is also available on CD-ROM.

The **European Community Host Organization (ECHO)** includes over 20 multilingual European databases. **DIANEGUIDE**, one of the ECHO databases, is a directory of European databases. **EURISTOTE** is a guide to theses and studies that have been carried out since the 1950s on all aspects of EC policy, and includes a list of academics studying European integration.

For more information on EC databases, the researcher should consult *EC 1992 and Beyond: Access to Information*, Washington, DC: The Division, 1992. (See especially, "Online to Europe" by Colin Hensley (pp. 39-53), a revised version of a December 1989 article from *Database* magazine).

The **Council of Europe** also has created important databases. They provide online access to European Court of Human Rights and European Commission of Human Rights materials. These databases are not currently publicly available, but may be in the future. For more information about access, contact the Human Rights Information Centre, Council of Europe, B.P. 431R6, 67006 Strasbourg CEDEX, France.

The Council of Europe has also published a feasibility study on the creation of a database on human rights research, described below.

Lassen, N. *Feasibility Study on the Creation of an Accessible Computerized Database on Human Rights Research Projects and Programmes in Europe; and, Survey of Human Rights Research in Europe.* **Strasbourg: Council of Europe Directorate of Human Rights (Human Rights Documentation Centre), 1990. 220 pp.**

> This study was prepared for the Commission of the European Communities by the Danish Center of Human Rights and the Netherlands Institute of Human Rights. Introductory material describes the rationale for creation of the database, its general framework, and recommendations on how to proceed. The bulk of this publication consists of the contents of the model database created, resulting in a descriptive survey of human rights research in Europe. Individual researchers, university institutes and nongovernmental organizations were consulted for this survey. According to the study, up-to-date printouts from this database will be available upon request. Includes indices by subject (index-term), title, and country.

E.   *Directories for Commercially Available Databases*

How can one find out what commercially available databases exist, and how can one identify those databases dealing with particular subjects? One useful method is to consult directories of online databases. One such directory is listed below.

Gale Directory of Databases. **Detroit: Gale Research, 1993-.**

> This directory was formed by the merger of Gale's *Computer-Readable Databases*, Cuadra/Gale's *Directory of Online Databases*, and Cuadra/Gale's *Directory of Portable Databases*. Vol. 1 (*Online Databases*) briefly describes approximately 5,200 online databases available publicly from the producers or via online services. It also includes lists of database producers and databases available through specific online services, a geographic index and a subject index. Vol. 2 (*CD-ROM, Diskette, Magnetic Tape, Handheld, and Batch Access Database Products*) briefly describes 2,900 database products available in "portable" form and through batch processing. This directory is available online through Data-Star, ORBIT, Questel, and DIALOG.

There are also a number of directories that indicate whether a particular publication is available in computerized format. Such publications include the two listed below.

Nobari, N. ed. *Books and Periodicals Online.* **New York: Library Alliance, 1987-.**

> The sixth edition (1993) incorporates the three editions of *Directory of Periodicals Online—Indexed, Abstracted & Full-Text* (*News, Law & Business; Science & Technology*; and *Medical & Humanities*), which the editor has acquired from InfoGlobe in Toronto, Canada. For each publication listed, it is possible to determine which databases contain the publication in full-text format, or only provide indexing by citation and/or abstract. The time periods covered and whether the publication is selectively or comprehensively represented in the databases listed are included. Over 43,000 publications appearing in 1,800 databases from around the world are accessible through this directory. Also included are a directory of publishers, a directory of producers and vendors, a list of titles by databases, and a list of titles available on CD-ROM.

Orenstein, R. M., ed. *Fulltext Sources Online.* **Needham, MA: BiblioData, 1988-.**

> Semiannual. This directory lists over 4,000 journals, magazines, newspapers, newsletters, newswires, and TV and radio transcripts available online in full text. It includes dates of coverage, frequency of updating, lag times, and degree of coverage. The database vendors represented include BRS, Data-Star, Data Times, DIALOG, Dow Jones, FT Profile, Info Globe, Infomart, Mead Data, NewsNet, QL, Reuters, STN, WESTLAW, Burrelle's and Genios. Includes geographic and subject indices.

Keep in mind that database availability through specific vendors or services is constantly changing, so that even some of the references to database availability found throughout this *Guide* may prove to be inaccurate in short order. It is best to consult up-to-date sources or a librarian for information about the current availability of a given database.

F. *The Internet*

The Internet is a loose collection of thousands of computer networks available to millions of researchers in institutions all over the world. This section will provide a brief introduction to the relevant networks for those conducting human rights research. The guides discussed below should be consulted to help users familiarize themselves with how this computer network functions. Internet updates should be consulted regularly because resources are constantly changing: materials are continuously added, deleted or moved between parts of the network. A computer-support person can be key to guide one through the necessary paths to gain access — the different steps vary, depending on the computer used and location.

1. Introductory Aids

Kehoe, B.P. *Zen and the Art of the Internet: A Beginner's Guide.* **2d ed. Englewood Cliffs, NJ: Prentice Hall, 1993.**

> The first edition is available as an anonymous FTP (ftp.cs.widener.edu); anonymous;; cd pub/zen. The second edition is not yet available on the computer network.

Krol, E. *The Whole Internet User's Guide & Catalog.* **Sebastopol, CA: O'Reilly & Associates, 1992.**

> Widely available. Lists various resources available on the Internet and gives a detailed explanation of how to search for resources. Gives excellent detailed instructions on how to solve various problems as they occur.

LaQuey, T. with J. C. Ryer. *The Internet Companion: A Beginner's Guide to Global Networking.* **Reading, MA: Addison-Wesley Publishing Corporation, 1993.**

> This is the best book which gives a general introduction. It explains terms and basics at the complete novice level and has a useful appendix for further information. Beginners may want to read this book and then consult the Krol book for more complex problems.

A description of recent materials available through the Internet provides a good introduction and might whet the appetite of a researcher for further exploration of this new tool.

2.   Joining an Internet "List"

To pursue a specific research topic, one could sign up for a list available on the computer network (called a "listserv"). Such a list would allow for the exchange of information among researchers with a common interest. If one had a query about a research topic it would be possible to send the question by electronic mail (or directly from one computer to another) to the people on this list for assistance.

One of the best resources on the INTERNET is the Int-Law listserv, which is used mainly by law librarians who specialize in international and foreign law. This is a good listserv to monitor to see the type of topics which are discussed. Also, if a researcher is having trouble finding an important source, this might be the first place to send out a query; librarians are a generous and knowledgeable group of people. Researchers can subscribe to this listserv at Int-Law@UMMINN1.BITNET.

3.   Specific Systems which Might be Helpful

The **"Cornell Law" menu-based system (or "gopher")** is a specialized service devoted to law which includes several subcategories of interest. Two worth highlighting are the Library Resources (online catalogs) and Foreign and International Law: Primary Documents and Commentary.

> **Library Resources** explains how to connect to and search online library catalogs. For example, without leaving the computer it is possible to search the online catalog of hundreds of colleges and universities. The relevant bibliographic records can be downloaded into an individual's electronic mail files and even transferred into word processing files. (This could greatly simplify tasks such as writing bibliographies.)

> The **Foreign and International Law** section on the Cornell menu has one particularly useful resource. Cornell has included the Fletcher School of Law and Diplomacy collection of machine-readable multilateral treaties, several of which are important human rights documents. Additional treaties are continuously added. This section allows searches by "key word" for related treaty articles. To access, simply use the address jade.tufts.edu. Other searches in the Cornell Law gopher would lead to the Maastricht Treaty, United Nations Committee on Economic Development documents, the tables of contents of international law journals or the United States Central Intelligence Agency *World Fact Book*. To access, simply use the address fatty.law.cornell.edu.port 70.

For researchers interested in the rights of indigenous peoples, an excellent paper by Steven C. Perkins entitled "Researching Indigenous Peoples Rights Under International Law" is available full-text through the Washington and Lee Law Library file transfer protocol, or "FTP site." This article includes an excellent directory of organizations which are active in supporting indigenous peoples rights and how to contact them, in addition to a good current bibliography. The Washington and Lee Law Library site is accessed via telnet liberty.us.wlu.edu; login lawlib if one wants to know what other sources are available. To simply obtain a copy of the Perkins paper you would access it via ftp liberty.us.wlu.edu; login anonymous; cd pub/lawlib.

Commercial databases, which charge telecommunication fees, can also be accessed though Internet. *EcoNet/PeaceNet* is a U.S.-based international communication system dedicated to serving organizations and individuals working for human rights, peaceful dispute resolution, disarmament, environmental protection and other social justice issues.

This computer network has made international access more affordable by establishing relationships with similar networks in Australia, Brazil, Canada, England, Nicaragua, Russia and Sweden so a user can be in constant communication with a wide range of internationally active organizations and individuals. Electronic gateways allow EcoNet users to send telex and fax messages nearly anywhere in the world and electronic mail to users on many other electronic systems. This is an excellent resource for communication for financially-strapped human rights groups. EcoNet/Peacenet is a service of the Institute for Global Communications, 18 de Boom Street, San Francisco, CA 94107.

CHAPTER TWO.
GENERAL HUMAN RIGHTS RESEARCH TOOLS AND SOURCES

I. Human Rights Research Guides, Bibliographies, and Encyclopedias and Restatements

A. General Human Rights Research Guides

Andrews, J.A. and W.D. Hines. *Keyguide to Information Sources on the International Protection of Human Rights*. New York: Facts on File Publications, 1987. 169 pp.

> The best general research manual available. Part I gives general background on the international instruments and institutions, and includes a general review of the literature. Part II provides access to information sources, with useful brief annotations, and covers the important English-language secondary literature. Part III is a good annotated list of selected intergovernmental and nongovernmental human rights organizations.

Garling, M. *Human Rights Research Guide: Library Holdings in London on Human Rights, Censorship and Freedom of Expression*. London: Writers and Scholars Educational Trust, 1978. 77 pp.

> Contains brief descriptions of libraries and documentation collections in London which have significant holdings of materials on censorship, broadly defined.

Holler, F. *Information Sources of Political Science*. 4th ed. Santa Barbara, CA: ABC-Clio Information Services, 1985. 417 pp.

> Not a human rights guide, but a comprehensive guide to reference sources of political information.

Reynolds, T. "Highest Aspirations or Barbarous Acts...The Explosion in Human Rights Documentation: A Bibliographic Survey." *Law Library Journal* 71 (1978): 1-48.

> Although now dated, this pioneering article is still useful, especially for its discussion of the documentation of relevant intergovernmental organizations.

Vincent-Daviss, D. "Bibliographic Essay." In *Guide to International Human Rights Practice*. 2d ed., edited by H. Hannum, 249-266. Philadelphia: University of Pennsylvania Press, 1992.

> A brief, but directed, list of suggestions for finding books, articles and documents. Emphasizes reference materials, international and regional documentation systems, and advice on how to obtain the most up-to-date information. Includes an explanation of U.N. document symbols. Specific topic sections include practice-oriented materials, teaching materials and resources, the International Labour Organisation, refugees, and physical security and the administration of justice.

Whalen, L. *Human Rights: A Reference Handbook.* **Santa Barbara, CA; Oxford: ABC-Clio, 1989. 218 pp.**

> Does not add a great deal to the existing guides and bibliographies, but useful for a general orientation to the field.

Wiseberg, L., ed. *A Guide to Establishing a Human Rights Documentation Centre: Report of a UNESCO-UNU International Training Seminar on the Handling of Documentation & Information on Human Rights: 22-24 November 1988.* **Ottawa: Human Rights Internet, 1990. 80 pp.**

> Wiseberg's chapter, "Suggestions for Building a Core Collection of Human Rights Documentation" (pp. 52-78), lists and annotates reference works, scholarly studies, NGO material, and documents of intergovernmental organizations. Wiseberg's listing points out the core items which are essential for any documentation center, and provides citations to supplementary materials.

B.   *Regional Research Guides*

Louis-Jacques, L., and S. Nevin. *Human Rights in the Soviet Union and Eastern Europe: A Research Guide and Bibliography.* **s.l.: s.n., 1989. 61 pp.**

> Already dated, but still a first-rate guide to the issues in the region and the primary and secondary literature of this rapidly changing field. Research guide discusses how to find sources of information on human rights in Ukraine, the Baltic states (Estonia, Latvia, and Lithuania), Albania, Bulgaria, Czechoslovakia, Hungary, Poland, Romania, and the former East Germany, Soviet Union, and Yugoslavia. Good treatment of relevant Library of Congress classification, periodical indices and indexing terms, online sources, and background sources. Good discussion of the Helsinki Final Act and its literature. Final section critically appraises the literature available in English on human rights in the selected countries. Bibliography excludes much material on Soviet Jewry and on other religious, ethnic and racial minorities in Eastern Europe and the former Soviet Union.

Perkins, S. "Latin American Human Rights Research 1980-1989: A Guide to Sources and a Bibliography." *Denver Journal of International Law & Policy* **19 (Fall 1990): 163-267.**

> A detailed guide and bibliography focused on legal materials. Good treatment of the human rights documents of the Organization of American States and the United Nations. Part I (Introduction) is a useful brief guide to Latin American legal materials generally. Part V lists publications and articles on human rights in Latin America since 1980, arranged by region, by country and by topic.

Third World Resources. **Oakland, CA: Third World Resources. 1985-.**

> A quarterly review of resources from and about the third world. Not a human rights guide per se, but much of the information it provides is highly relevant to human rights research. Provides annotated lists of books, periodicals, pamphlets and articles, and

audiovisuals on human rights and social justice themes in the third world. Includes "Resource Guides" which focus on specific regions.

Vincent-Daviss, D. "The Occupied Territories and International Law: A Research Guide" (Symposium on Human Rights and Israeli Rule in the Territories). *New York University Journal of International Law & Politics* **21 (Spring 1989): 575-665.**

Brings together and annotates a great deal of English-language material relevant to the study of human rights in the Israeli-occupied territories. Primary material includes Israeli official reports, U.S. hearings and reports, and U.N. documents. Secondary material includes sources on the background of the Arab-Israeli conflict, and materials on general international human rights, refugee law, self-determination, and terrorism.

C.   *Human Rights Bibliographies*

1.   Principal General Human Rights Bibliographies

Several bibliographies which should be consulted at the outset of almost any human rights research follow.

Center for the Study of Human Rights, Columbia University. *Human Rights: A Topical Bibliography.* **Boulder, CO: Westview Press, 1983. 299 pp.**

Still the best scholarly bibliography covering the field generally, emphasizing law, the social sciences and philosophy. Includes English-language books and articles which are likely to be available in most research libraries. Arranged by subject. Contains few references to NGO publications.

Friedman, J. and M. Sherman, comps. and eds. *Human Rights: An International and Comparative Law Bibliography.* **Westport, CT: Greenwood Press, 1985. 868 pp.**

An extensive (4,000-plus entries) bibliography with a focus on international and comparative legal aspects of human rights. Contains references to books, articles, and documents of international organizations in a variety of languages.

Greenfield, R., I. Jhappan, and L. Wiseberg. "A Bibliography of Human Rights Bibliographies." In *Teaching Human Rights,* **98-134. Washington, DC: Human Rights Internet, 1981.**

A well-annotated list of international human rights and related bibliographies which have been separately published. Also includes a selection of bibliographies appearing in treatises on international human rights. English-language sources predominate. Also includes collections of documents. Although dated, still an extremely useful source. Bibliographies are organized in the following categories: international human rights bibliographies; topic-specific bibliographies; country-specific bibliographies; and audio-visual bibliographies.

Louis-Jacques, L. and D. Weissbrodt. "Bibliography for Research on International Human Rights Law." *Hamline Law Review* 13 (Summer 1990): 673-717.

An excellent, concise bibliography focused on legal materials.

2.   Other General Human Rights Bibliographies

Agi, M. *5,000 Titres sur les Libertes: Une Selection d'Ouvrages Disponibles en Langue Francais*. Paris: Librarie des Libertes, 1984. 270 pp.

Organized in three sections: index to themes, words and key words; unannotated list of books; human rights thesaurus. Entries from literature, art, history, natural sciences, and philosophy. In French.

Alston, P. "Select Bibliography." In *The United Nations and Human Rights: A Critical Appraisal*, 677-748. Oxford: Clarendon Press, 1992.

Very helpful list of sources. Includes U.N. documents and books and articles, divided into sections on the different U.N. human rights bodies, the International Labour Organisation, human rights coordination, and general issues. Not annotated.

Amnesty International. *Human Rights Education: Bibliography*. London: AI International Secretariat, May 1992. 63 pp.

Annotated. Includes publications on formal and informal education (for educators and for use at the primary and secondary levels) and on the training of professionals (including security forces, medical personnel and public officials). Primary languages are English, French, Spanish, Dutch and German.

Friedman, J., and L. Wiseberg, eds. "Bibliography." In *Teaching Human Rights*, 78-97. Washington, DC: Human Rights Internet, 1981.

Somewhat dated, unannotated alphabetical list of articles, monographs and documents compiled from the readings listed in the human rights syllabi presented earlier in the same volume.

Goehlert, R. *Human Rights Policy: A Selected Bibliography*. Monticello, IL: Vance Bibliographies, 1984. 8 pp.

Unannotated, alphabetical listing of articles (from about 1974 to 1981).

Goldblatt, M. and P. Ward. *Recent Titles in Law For the Subject Specialist*. Ann Arbor, MI: Ward and Associates, 1984-.

Quarterly. Selection and reference tool which presents recent acquisitions of law libraries in 23 subject areas. Contributors include some 60 academic, bar, and law firm libraries, the Library of Congress and (when available) some 300 Federal administrative agency libraries. Covers all material except journal articles (i.e., new books, government documents, new serial titles and title changes, audiovisual materials, and computer databases and programs.) The most relevant volume to human rights researchers is *Constitional Law, Human Rights and Citizenship.* Other relevant titles include *Military and Security Law.*

Human Rights Research and Education Bulletin/Droits de la Personne. **Ottawa: Human Rights Research and Education Centre, University of Ottawa. 1985-.**

A quarterly in English and French which describes the activities of the Centre and contains brief articles. The *Bulletin* often includes select bibliographies.

O'Connor, B., comp. and ed. *International Human Rights, A Bibliography, 1970-1975.* **Rev. ed. Notre Dame, IN: Center for Civil and Human Rights, University of Notre Dame Law School, 1980. 172 pp.**

Contains about 2,400 English-language entries, including books, periodical articles, and documents. Subject/geographic index.

Shimane, R. and R. Rich, comps. *International Human Rights: A Selected Bibliography.* **Asa V. Call Law Library, Bibliography, No. 91. Los Angeles: University of Southern California Law Center, 1979. 81 pp.**

Unannotated list of books and articles treating human rights in general, human rights and the United Nations, the European human rights convention, the American convention, and humanitarian intervention. Entries are arranged under nine broad headings.

Stanek, E. *A Bibliography of Selected Human Rights Bibliographies, Documentary Compilations, Periodicals, Reports, and Reference Books Essential for the Study of International and Comparative Law of Human Rights.* **Monticello, IL: Vance Bibliographies, 1987. 12 pp.**

Unannotated alphabetical list of materials on civil and human rights; many items deal with Canada and the Canadian Charter of Rights and Freedoms. Has a section listing human rights periodicals, yearbooks and other serials with information on the international, national and comparative human rights law.

Stanek, E. *Human Rights: A Selected Bibliography of Monographs, Essays, Serials, and Basic Compilations of Documents, and Bibliographies Pertinent to International Protection of Human Rights.* **Monticello, IL: Vance Bibliographies, 1987. 31 pp.**

Unannotated alphabetical list of materials on civil rights, human rights, and foreign affairs.

Vasak, K., ed. "Selected Bibliography on International Human Rights Law." In *The International Dimensions of Human Rights*. Revised and edited for the English edition by Philip Alston, 688-738. Westport, CT: Greenwood Press, 1982.

> Multilingual entries arranged alphabetically. Includes compilations of documents, publications of international and regional organizations, analytical works on general human rights questions, as well as those discussing international and regional organizations. Unannotated.

3.   Specialized and Regional Human Rights Bibliographies and Indices

Benamati, D. and D. Voisinet. "Selected Readings on International Courts and the Protection of Human Rights." *Connecticut Journal of International Law* 2 (Spring 1987): 391-396.

> A very basic, unannotated list of some English-language analytical works and sources of information on the European Court of Human Rights, the Inter-American Court of Human Rights, and emerging regional organizations. Omits most materials published prior to 1980, and U.N. sources.

"Bibliography." In *Human Rights and Development in Africa*, edited by C. Welch and R. Meltzer, 301-316. Albany: State University of New York Press, 1984.

> Unannotated bibliography with a section on research guides and bibliographic sources, followed by a list of references to books and articles arranged by broad subject or regional categories.

"Bibliography of Asian Studies." In *Journal of Asian Studies*. Ann Arbor, MI: Association for Asian Studies, 1956-.

> Annual. Extensive classified list of English-language books, periodical articles, pamphlets, and other publications on all phases of life and culture in Asia.

Caccia, I., comp. *Charter Bibliography: An Indexed Bibliography on the Canadian Charter of Rights and Freedoms*. Saskatoon, Saskatchewan: Canadian Human Rights Reporter, 1985. 62 pp.

> Lists collected essays, books and articles. Subject index according to sections of the Charter.

Cascio, N. "Human Rights in South and Southeast Asia: A Selective Bibliography." In *Asian Perspectives on Human Rights*, edited by C. Welch and V. Leary, 235-298. Boulder, CO: Westview Press, 1990.

> Annotated bibliography with the following headings: international law in third world context; international human rights law in Asian focus; human rights and religious

traditions; law; the national dimension of human rights; women and human rights; minorities and indigenous populations; human rights and development; ethnic conflict and human rights; case studies and human rights missions; bibliographies and directories; continuing bibliographies. Includes English-language material published since 1976 addressing human rights in South Asia, including Bangladesh, India, Nepal, Pakistan and Sri Lanka, and in Southeast Asia, including Indonesia, Malaysia, the Philippines, and Thailand.

Delorme, R. *Latin America: Social Science Information Sources, 1967-1979.* **Santa Barbara, CA: ABC-Clio, 1981. 262 pp.**

Provides information on 5,600 books and periodical articles published between 1967 and 1979 on all areas of Latin America. Most citations are to English-language materials.

Delorme, R. *Latin America, 1979-1983: A Social Science Bibliography.* **Santa Barbara, CA: ABC-Clio, 1984. 225 pp.**

Provides 3,728 citations to works in English, Spanish and Portuguese published from 1979 through September 1983.

Delorme, R., comp. *Latin America, 1983-1987: A Social Science Bibliography.* **New York: Greenwood Press, 1988. 391 pp.**

Updates the previous two bibliographies.

Hamalengwa, M. et al., comps. *The International Law of Human Rights in Africa: Basic Documents and Annotated Bibliography.* **Dordrecht; Boston: M. Nijhoff, 1988. 427 pp.**

Provides the texts of African and global instruments. Bibliography of some 300 English-language entries is unannotated, despite the title.

Hispanic American Periodicals Index (HAPI). **Los Angeles: UCLA Latin American Center Publications, 1970-.**

Annual subject and author index to articles of interest to Latin Americanists. Appears in some 200 journals published in South and Central America, the United States, Europe and the Caribbean. Covers leading journals in all major disciplines of the social sciences and humanities.

Online: HAPI is available online on RLG's Citadel from 1970 to present.

Latin American Center, Hispanic Law Division. *Index to Latin American Legislation (World Law Index Pt. 1).* **2 vols. Boston: J.K. Hall, 1961. 1474 pp.**

Online: This database contains over 40,000 abstracts describing national laws, decrees, decree-laws, and regulations of the Spanish-speaking nations of Latin America, as well as Brazil, Haiti, the Philippines, Portugal, Spain and the Portuguese-speaking African countries. The database continues the printed publication *Index to Latin American Legislation 1950-1960* plus its supplements. It is updated quarterly with coverage from 1976 to present, and is available online through RLG's Citadel.

Kavass, I. *Gorbachev's Law: A Bibliographic Survey of English Writings on Soviet Legal Developments, 1987-1990.* **Buffalo: W. S. Hein, 1991. 379 pp.**

Lists and describes books, articles, papers and other publications in English about law and related subjects in the Soviet Union. Author bibliography lists items by authors' names. Annotations are informative, and treatment of collections of articles seems especially good. Entries are also listed by subject. Contains several useful brief introductory sections: "New Research Aids on the Soviet Union," "Recent Collections of Soviet Documents in English," and "New Periodicals about the Soviet Union."

Kavass, I. *Soviet Law in English: Research Guide and Bibliography 1970-1987.* **Buffalo: W. S. Hein, 1988. 653 pp.**

An annotated bibliography of about 1,600 books and articles arranged alphabetically by author. Entries are also arranged by subject, including sections on human rights, dissidents, the individual and the law, psychiatric abuse, and religion. First chapter is an historical introduction to the field of Soviet legal research.

Legal Aspects of Apartheid: A Selective Bibliography of Books and Articles and United Nations Documentation in English, 1950-1983. **New York: Dag Hammerskjold Library, ST/LIB/SER. B/34, 1984. 49 pp.**

Unannotated listing of (1) books and articles and (2) U.N. documentation. Entries in these two sections are arranged alphabetically by author or title.

Library of Congress, comp. and ed. *Human Rights in Latin America 1964-1980. A Selective Annotated Bibliography.* **Washington, DC: U.S. Government Printing Office, 1983. 257 pp.**

Covers books, significant pamphlets and journals. Brief annotations in English.

Lulat, Y. G.-M. *U.S. Relations with South Africa: An Annotated Bibliography.* **Vol. 2,** *Periodical Literature and Guide to Sources of Current Information.* **Boulder, CO: Westview Press, 1991. 468 pp.**

Partially annotated bibliography of books, journal articles, government documents, NGO materials, substantive magazine and newspaper articles published since the late 19th century.

The Mideast File. **Oxford; Medford, NY: Learned Information, 1982-1988.**

Quarterly updated index to political, economic, historical, military and other information published about the Middle East in books, periodicals, official gazettes, and other media. Most of the cited material is in English, 20% in Arabic, and 15% in other European languages.

Nowak, M. "Selected Bibliography." *Human Rights Law Journal* 7 (1986): 399-402.

> Contains about 40 entries, most dealing with the African Charter on Human and Peoples' Rights.

Nyquist, C. "Research Problems and Library Resources on Human Rights in Africa." In *Human Rights and Development in Africa*, edited by C. Welch and R. Meltzer, 287-300. Albany, NY: State University of New York Press, 1984.

> Discussion of the main tools, sources and obstacles to research.

Otto, I. and M. Schmidt-Dumont. *The Arab-Israeli Conflict Since the Outbreak of the Intifadah: A Selected Bibliography.* Hamburg: Deutches Ubersee-Institut, Ubersee-Dokumentation, Referat Vorderer Orient, 1990. 98 pp.

> In English and German. Includes books and articles, organized by subject, in several languages. Contains about 430 entries covering the period from December 1987.

Perry, G. *The Palestine Question: An Annotated Bibliography.* Belmont, MA: Association of Arab-American University Graduates, 1990. 138 pp.

> Selected, annotated bibliography aimed at the non-expert, not the specialized researcher. Limited to English-language titles, and largely to books. Emphasis on titles published during the 1980s.

"Selected Bibliography." *University of Chicago Law Review* 58 (Spring 1991): 859-869.

> Unannotated listing on legal and constitutional developments in Eastern Europe.

Silverburg, S. *The Palestinian Arab-Israeli Conflict: An International Legal Bibliography.* Monticello, IL: Vance Bibliographies, 1982. 27 pp.

> Unannotated. Includes official or public documents, books, periodical literature, newspaper articles and unpublished materials.

The following three items listed below, by D. Vincent-Daviss, are aimed at U.S. law students, and are well-annotated bibliographies of human rights literature and guides to related human rights materials in English.

Vincent-Daviss, D. "Human Rights Law: A Research Guide to the Literature—Part I: International Law and the United Nations." *New York University Journal of International Law & Politics* 14 (Fall 1981): 209-319.

> A good introduction to international law research, to general human rights research, and to research on the U.N. Charter, the Universal Declaration of Human Rights, and U.N. human rights bodies.

Vincent-Daviss, D. "Human Rights Law: A Research Guide to the Literature—Part II: International Protection of Refugees, and Humanitarian Law." *New York University Journal of International Law & Politics* 14 (Winter 1982): 487-573.

> Good introduction to English-language materials on the history, development and present workings of relevant international law and organizations. Annotations are complemented by brief background sketches of laws and institutions.

Vincent-Daviss, D. "Human Rights Law: A Research Guide to the Literature—Part III: The International Labour Organisation and Human Rights." *New York University Journal of International Law & Politics* 15 (Fall 1982): 211-287.

> An excellent introduction. Annotations to ILO-produced materials and to the literature analyzing the ILO's contribution are complemented by introductory essays on the history and development of the ILO, its instruments, and its mechanisms of supervision and implementation.

Whisman, L. "Selected Bibliography: Articles and Cases on International Human Rights Law in Domestic Courts." *International Lawyer* 18 (Winter 1984): 83-88.

> Covers years 1980-1984.

D.   Encyclopedias and Restatements

Encyclopedia of Public International Law. 12 vols. Amsterdam; New York: North Holland Pub. Co., 1981.

> The Encyclopedia contains short articles surveying developments in the field generally or on a specific topic, and brief bibliographies which are often quite good. Vol. 8 (Human Rights and the Individual in International Law-International Economic Relations) contains short, introductory articles on a large number of topics relating to human rights, followed by brief bibliographies. Vol. 5 (International Organizations in General—Universal Organizations and Cooperation) and Vol. 7 (History of International Law—Foundations and Principles of International Law - Sources of International Law - Law of Treaties) are also useful.

Lawson, E. *Encyclopedia of Human Rights.* New York: Taylor & Francis Inc., 1991. 1907 pp.

> An alphabetically arranged series of entries consisting largely of excerpts from U.N. documents. Contains a subject index. Does not appear to be very useful, except for some appendices such as a selected bibliography of materials from Human Rights Internet's database (covering years 1985-89, arranged by country and by subject), and the reproduction of a comprehensive list of U.N. studies and reports on human rights issues (U.N. Doc. E/CN.4/Sub.2/1990/2).

Restatement of the Law Third, the Foreign Relations Law of the United States. **2 vols. St. Paul, MN: American Law Institute Pub., 1987-.**

Summary of foreign relations law by the American Law Institute, an association of judges, legal academics and lawyers "who are selected on the basis of professional standing." Though not an official U.S. document, the Restatement is considered to be an authoritative explanation of existing law and is often cited by courts, scholars, and lawyers. Secs. 701-703, 711-713, in Vol. II are especially relevant. See also Supplement 1988 and regularly-issued annual supplements.

Online: The full text of the *Restatement* is online in WESTLAW in the REST-FOREL database.

II. Human Rights Treatises, Nutshells, and Collections of Articles

Following is an annotated list of treatises, nutshells and collections of articles, which expands the list provided in Chapter One. Researchers interested in some of the basic human rights casebooks should see that list in Chapter One.

Buergenthal, T. *International Human Rights in a Nutshell.* **St. Paul, MN: West Publishing Co., 1988. 283 pp.**

A good brief overview. Very useful as a quick reference.

Hannum, H., ed. *Guide to International Human Rights Practice.* **2d ed. Philadelphia: University of Pennsylvania Press, 1992. 308 pp.**

An excellent introduction to the field. (See p. 82 for a full annotation.)

Janis, M. and R. Kay. *European Human Rights Law.* **Hartford, CT: University of Connecticut Law School Foundation Press, 1990. 405 pp.**

A textbook, with large excerpts from sources, which gives an introduction to European human rights law. Text presentations alternate with notes and questions for students. The first three chapters treat institutions and procedures; the last treat four areas of substantive adjudication by the European Court of Human Rights: torture and cruel, inhuman or degrading treatment, respect for private and family life, freedom of expression, and the right to a fair and public hearing.

Meron, T., ed. *Human Rights in International Law: Legal and Policy Issues.* **2 vols. Oxford: Clarendon Press, 1984.**

Intended as a textbook covering principal human rights areas, and as a reference book. Each of its 13 articles concludes with teaching suggestions, a syllabus, a minisyllabus, a bibliography, and a minibibliography. A good basic introduction to the field and some of its major components.

Sieghart, P. *The International Law of Human Rights.* **Oxford: Clarendon Press, 1983. 569 pp.**

A good source for locating texts of articles in a number of human rights instruments which deal with the same right. Part I provides an historical introduction. Parts II and III set out the texts of the substantive articles of eight major international human rights instruments, ordered according to subject matter. Texts are followed by cross-references, comment, a brief history of the right concerned, references to interpretations and applications of the right by competent independent institutions, and a summary of the contents of any relevant subsidiary instruments. Part IV reproduces procedural articles, and describes the functions of the major human rights supervisory and enforcement bodies.

III.   Human Rights Journals and Newsletters

A.   *Scholarly Journals*

Africa Today. **Denver: Africa Today Associates, 1954-.**

Quarterly. Scholarly articles on human rights, politics, economics. Each issue contains "Africa Rights Monitor," a section on human rights in the region.

The African Studies Review. **Waltham, MA: African Studies Association, 1970-.**

Scholarly articles. Published three times per year.

All-European Human Rights Yearbook. **Kehl am Rhein; Arlington, VA: N.P. Engel, 1991-.**

A new annual publication which focuses on implementation and strengthening of human rights standards and practice throughout Europe. It is intended that scholarly works from proceedings of international conferences, articles examining domestic and international human rights developments in Europe, and significant case law will be published in this series. The first volume provides the proceedings of a conference on the role of the Council of Europe, the CSCE and the European Communities in an all-European system of human rights protection.

Anuario de Derechos Humanos. **Madrid: Universidad Complutense, Facultad de Derecho, Instituto de Derechos Humanos, 1982-.**

Annual, in Spanish, containing scholarly articles and book reviews.

Arab Law Quarterly. **London: Graham and Totman, 1985-.**

Published on behalf of the Society of Arab Comparative and International Law, which aims to provide a forum for discussion of Arab law, especially in the context of the relationship between Arab and non-Arab countries in the commercial field. Many articles focus on questions such as humanitarian intervention, constitutional law, the

Islamic inheritance system, registration of foreigners, and the legal systems of different Arab countries. The journal also publishes various legal documents such as orders and revisions in legal codes.

Boletin. **Lima: Comision Andina de Juristas, 1980-.**

In Spanish. Quarterly containing scholarly articles, documents, book reviews, and an activities and events section.

Canadian Human Rights Yearbook/Annuaire Canadienne des Droits de la Personne. **Toronto: Carswell, 1983-.**

In English and French. Published annually by the University of Ottawa Human Rights Research and Education Centre. Contains articles, case notes and essays on law and other themes, and a bibliography on the Canadian Charter of Rights and Freedoms.

Codesria Bulletin. **Dakar, Senegal: Council for the Development of Economic and Social Research in Africa, 1973-.**

Information on the rights of social scientists in Africa, and on social science and politics of the region. Scholarly and policy-oriented articles. Published quarterly.

Columbia Human Rights Law Review. **New York: Columbia University School of Law, 1972-.**

Semi-annual. Scholarly articles on civil rights and human rights, book reviews and student notes. Often predominately United States-focused.

Online: Selected articles available in full text online from 1984 (Vol. 15) to date in WESTLAW (CLMHRLR database).

Democratic Jurisprudence. **Association of Democratic Scholars. Seoul, Korea, 1990-.**

Quarterly, in Korean. Each issue contains approximately ten 30-page articles by young scholars working on their PhDs or by those who have recently obtained their doctorates. Focus is on analyses comparing issues in Korea with those in Germany, the United States and Japan.

Digest of Middle East Studies. **Milwaukee, WI: University of Wisconsin-Milwaukee, 1991-.**

Quarterly. Survey and review of materials published on the Middle East. Provides index.

Europaische Grundrechte. **Kehl am Rhein: Engel Verlag, 1974-.**

Semimonthly, formerly *Grundrechte*. In German. Each issue contains one scholarly article. Provides summaries and occasional full texts of decisions of the European Court of Human Rights, the Court of Justice of the European Communities, and courts of member states of the Council of Europe. Current proceedings section gives summaries of complaints declared admissible by the European Commission of Human Rights.

Harvard Human Rights Journal. **Cambridge, MA: Harvard Law School, 1988-.**

Annual. Scholarly articles, student notes reviewing current issues in human rights, book reviews, and notes on human rights internships. Formerly *Harvard Human Rights Yearbook.*

Human Rights and Justice. **Seoul, Korea: Korean Bar Association, 1983-.**

Monthly. Korean-language publication which contains scholarly articles with focus on practical legal human rights problems in Korea. Each edition contains about 10 articles and is approximately 100 pages in length.

Human Rights Law Journal. **Kehl am Rhein; Arlington, VA: N.P. Engel, 1980-.**

Monthly, merged with *Human Rights Review* in 1980. Essential reading for updates on the European human rights scene. Provides extracts of European Court and Commission of Human Rights decisions and reports, pending proceedings, CSCE documentation and scholarly articles. Vol. 10, the "Ten Years' Cumulative Index" (1980-1989), usefully brings together a large number of references to human rights instruments, national court decisions relevant to human rights (such as the Argentine Supreme Court and Court of Appeals judgments convicting former military commanders), resolutions and reports of international organizations, decisions and judgments of international tribunals, provisions of selected national constitutional and other laws. Provides an annual list of the current ratification status of the international human rights instruments.

Human Rights Quarterly. **Baltimore, MD: Johns Hopkins University Press, 1979-.**

Formerly *Universal Human Rights.* Essential reading. Contains scholarly articles from a variety of disciplines (focuses are law, sociology and the social sciences), book reviews, and occasional shorter notes. Presents comparative and international research on public policy within the scope of the Universal Declaration of Human Rights. Sponsored by the Urban Morgan Institute for Human Rights, College of Law, University of Cincinnati.

Human Rights Review. **See** *Human Rights Law Journal.*

Human Rights Yearbook. **Moscow: General Editorial Board for Foreign Publications, Nauka Publishers, 1983-.**

Published irregularly. The first three issues covered materials for 1981, 1982-83 and 1984. Fourth issue, published in 1987, covered 1985. Intended to offer the foreign reader authentic information on Soviet legislation and mechanisms of protection in the area of human rights. Texts of enactments are given, as well as articles commenting on the new legislation.

Israel Yearbook on Human Rights. **Tel Aviv: Faculty of Law, Tel Aviv University, 1971-.**

Contains scholarly articles, comments, and book reviews, often on Israeli or other Middle East human rights questions. Contains Israeli judicial decisions relating to human rights.

Journal of Human Rights Law and Practice. **Lagos, Nigeria: Civil Liberties Organisation, Nigeria, 1991-.**

Three issues per year. Scholarly articles, book reviews, case reviews, and conference reports.

Journal of Palestine Studies. **Berkeley: University of California Press, 1971-.**

Quarterly focused on the Arab-Israeli conflict. Includes special reports on developments in human rights and peace talks; reviews of current titles in English, Arabic and Hebrew; and documents and source material. Also provides chronology of major social, economic, political and military events over the quarter, and includes a bibliography of periodical literature.

Law and Society. **Seoul, Korea: Research Group for Law and Society, 1989-.**

Quarterly. Korean language journal issued by young professors and scholars working at universities in Korea. Scholarly and theoretical perspectives on efforts to reform the legal system. Each journal consists of about ten 30-page articles.

Lokayan Bulletin. **Delhi: Lokayan, 1983-.**

Bimonthly. Contains theoretical articles on human rights, democracy, and related questions. Focus is on India.

Mas alla del Derecho/Beyond Law. **Bogota: Instituto Latinoamericano de Servicios Legales Alternativas, 1991-.**

Three times a year. In English. Theoretical and policy-oriented articles on social change, human rights and legal services in Latin America and the Caribbean.

New York Law School Journal of Human Rights. **New York: New York Law School, 1983-.**

Semiannual. Student-edited journal containing scholarly articles, notes and book reviews on international human rights and U.S. civil rights topics. Continues *New York Law School Human Rights Annual.*

Online: Selected articles in full text online from 1990 (Vol. 7) to date in WESTLAW (NYLSJICL database).

The Palestine Yearbook of International Law. **Nicosia, Cyprus: Al-Shaybani Society of International Law, 1984-.**

Annual containing scholarly articles, reports of judicial decisions, texts of legislation, special reports, book reviews, and bibliography. Focus is on human rights-related matters.

Revista Chilena de Derechos Humanos. **Santiago, Chile: Academia de Humanismo Cristiano, 1985-.**

Published three times a year, in Spanish. Scholarly and policy articles.

Revista IIDH. **San Jose, Costa Rica: Instituto Interamericano de Derechos Humanos, 1985-.**

In Spanish, semi-annual. In addition to scholarly articles on human rights in Latin America, contains summaries of the activities of the Inter-American Court of Human Rights and the Inter-American Commission on Human Rights; texts of opinions, decisions and orders of the Court; reports of the Commission; resolutions of the Organization of American States General Assembly; and summaries of human rights activities in the U.N.

Revista Latinoamericana de Derechos Humanos. **2 vols. Lima: Red Latinoamericana de Abogados Catolicos, 1988-1989.**

In Spanish. Contains scholarly articles, book reviews, and documents. Roman Catholic, liberation theology perspective.

Revue Trimestrielle des Droits de l'Homme. **Bruxelles: Editions Nemesis, 1990-.**

Quarterly, in French. Focus is on decisions of the European Court of Human Rights. Some attention to decisions of the courts of Western European nations; occasional articles on U.S. and Canadian decisions.

Rivista Internazionale dei Diritti dell'Uomo. **Milan: Universita Cattolica del Sacro Cuore, 1988-.**

In Italian, three issues yearly. Scholarly articles, notes and decisions of the European Court and Commission of Human Rights, Resolutions of the European Council of Ministers, and summaries of Italian court decisions on human rights. Focus of the journal is on the European human rights system.

South African Human Rights and Labour Law Yearbook. **Cape Town: Oxford University Press, 1990-.**

Twenty-seven chapters review human rights and labor law issues since January 1989. Representative human rights chapter titles include: capital punishment, censorship under the emergency, conscription, constitutional reform, detentions, education, forced removals, legal representation and the courts, and policing. Labor law titles include: collective bargaining, changes in Transkei labor relations, redundancy and retrenchment, strikes and lock-outs, and unfair discrimination in employment.

South African Journal on Human Rights. **Braamfontein, SA: Revan Press, 1985-.**

Published three times per year. Scholarly articles, cases and comments, and book reviews. "Human Rights Index" describes human rights-related events in South Africa.

The Thatched Patio. **Colombo, Sri Lanka: International Centre for Ethnic Studies, 1988-.**

Bimonthly. Focuses on ethnic conflict and related questions. Articles cover issues across the world; emphasis is on South Asia.

Turkish Yearbook on Human Rights. **Ankara: Institute of Public Administration for Turkey and the Middle East, Human Rights Research and Documentation Center, 1979-.**

Double-volume issue published every other year. Scholarly articles in French and English on human and civil rights in Turkey.

B.   *Activist Newsletters and Publications on Current Developments*

A few of the publications, primarily those available in English, are listed below. Some are published by human rights groups and others are general news publications. The researcher should also consult other general publications on the region, which may include articles on the human rights situtation. The researcher may also wish to consult publications in the languages of the country or region, by local human rights organizations and others.

1.   General

ACLU International Civil Liberties Report. **Los Angeles, CA: American Civil Liberties Union International Human Rights Task Force, 1992-.**

Semiannual newsletter of this newly created task force. Articles include topics such as reports on ACLU work for U.S. ratification of international treaties, recent developments in international human rights litigation in U.S. courts, the use of international human rights law in civil rights cases.

Academic Freedom. **Geneva: World University Service, 1990-.**

Irregular. Newsletter reporting on academic freedom issues.

Amnesty International Newsletter. **London: Amnesty International Publ., 1971-.**

Monthly. Articles on human rights violations around the world and the organization's efforts to address them. Includes "urgent actions" so readers can take action. Continues *AIR, Amnesty International Review.*

Bulletin of Human Rights. **Geneva: United Nations, 1978-.**

Quarterly. Information on human rights-related activities at the United Nations. A selected list of Commission on Human Rights documents is included in each issue.

Bulletin of the Lawyers Committee for Human Rights. **New York: LCHR, 1980-.**

Quarterly. Contains brief articles on the activities of the Lawyers Committee for Human Rights.

CCR News. **New York: Center for Constitutional Rights, 1992-.**

Semiannual. Provides updates on CCR cases in U.S. courts and the international human rights system, brief articles on specific human rights issues (e.g., rape as torture, human rights for indigenous peoples), news about organization's activities, and list of CCR publications. Organization also produces annual report, *Center for Constitutional Rights Docket [year].*

CIJL Bulletin. **Geneva: Centre for the Independence of Judges and Lawyers, 1979-.**

Semiannual. Brief articles on human rights violations against lawyers and judges.

Freedom Review. **New York: Freedom House, 1991-.**

Six times per year. Continues *Freedom at Issue,* published between 1970-1990.

Human Rights. **Chicago: American Bar Association's Section of Individual Rights and Responsibilities, 1970-.**

Four times per year. Publication of the American Bar Association's Section of Individual Rights and Responsibilities. Contains non-scholarly articles on human rights and civil rights topics. Gives summaries of selected lower and appellate court rulings on human and civil rights, and upcoming Supreme Court cases dealing with human and civil rights. Has occasional articles on international human rights.

Online: Selected articles available in full text online from 1987 (Vol. 14) to date in WESTLAW (HUMRT database).

Human Rights Research and Education Bulletin/Droits de la Personne Bulletin d'Information sur la Recherche et l'Enseignement. **Ottawa: Human Rights Centre, University of Ottawa, 1985-.**

Quarterly bilingual (English-French) publication of the Human Rights Centre, University of Ottawa. Contains news of the Centre and useful bibliographies.

Human Rights Tribune/Tribune des Droits Humains. **Ottawa: Human Rights Internet, 1992-.**

Quarterly. Focus is on issues and situations being debated in the human rights community. Discusses current debates about and within the movement. The "Departments" section contains a calendar of human rights events, plus short pieces on national and international law, country conditions, activities in international organizations, and NGO news. The *Tribune* is intended to provide, on a more frequent basis, the news and comments previously supplied by the *Human Rights Internet Reporter*. The *Reporter* will continue to be published, as a bibliography of (mostly) human rights NGO publications.

Human Rights Watch Quarterly Newsletter. **New York: Human Rights Watch, 1983-.**

Twelve-page membership newsletter. Issues focus on specific themes (e.g. human rights abuses in Latin America, freedom of expression, or women's rights) and provide country-by-country updates on the organization's work.

HURIDOCS News. **Oslo: Human Rights Information and Documentation System, 1985-.**

Twice annually. Provides information on current developments in the human rights documentation network, including standard formats for the exchange of information, software, training sessions on the handling of human rights documentation, etc.

International Newsletter on Treatment and Rehabilitation of Torture Victims. **Copenhagen: Rehabilitation and Research Centre for Torture Victims, 1988-.**

Quarterly. Intended to promote the mutual exchange of experience and research among professionals and centers working with torture victims, mostly concerning the psychological and physical sequelae of torture. Issues contain a feature article, presentations of relevant work, and a selected list of documents received at the Rehabilitation and Research Centre for Torture Victims documentation center. Forthcoming conferences and seminars are also indicated.

International Review of Contemporary Law. **Brussels: International Association of Democratic Lawyers, 1954-.**

Semiannual. Focuses on peace and disarmament, support for popular struggles against fascism and colonialism, and the provision of information on law in the socialist countries. Publication suspended 1971-1976.

Interights Bulletin. **London: International Centre for the Legal Protection of Human Rights, 1985-.**

Information on legal matters with a focus on Europe. "International Law Reports" section provides a subject arrangement of brief abstracts of noteworthy decisions of tribunals applying international human rights law. (Most cases in this section are from the European Court of Human Rights and the European Commission of Human Rights.)

The Law Group Docket. **Washington, DC: International Human Rights Law Group, 1982-.**

Twice a year. Articles include updates on efforts of the Law Group to further respect for human rights in the U.N., Inter-American system, and U.S. courts, as well as analyses of the Group's efforts to work with lawyers to build the rule of law.

PHR Record. **Boston, MA: Physicians for Human Rights, 1987-.**

Quarterly. Provides updates on organization's activities, particular efforts of physicians on human rights issues, and information about human rights and health.

The Review. **Geneva: International Commission of Jurists, 1969-.**

Semiannual. Contains brief articles on human rights conditions in individual countries, longer articles on human rights topics, including reviews of sessions of U.N. human rights bodies.

2.   Africa

Africa News. **Durham, NC: Africa News Service, Inc. 1980-.**

Weekly. Current awareness.

Africa Report. **New York: African-American Institute, 1960-.**

Bimonthly. General journalistic articles on politics and economics; occasional articles on human rights.

African Human Rights Newsletter. **Banjul, The Gambia: African Centre for Democracy and Human Rights Studies, 1991-.**

In French and English. Quarterly providing current news on human rights in Africa, including African human rights NGOs and the African Commission on Human and Peoples' Rights, and on Africa-related matters at the United Nations and other international bodies.

Constitutional Rights Journal. **Lagos, Nigeria: Constitutional Rights Project, 1991-.**

Quarterly news reporting on human rights, with focus on Nigeria.

Facts and Reports: Press Cuttings on Angola, Mozambique, Guinea Bissau, Portugal and Southern Africa. **Amsterdam: Angola Committee, 1970-.**

Biweekly. Reproduces newspaper articles and texts of radio broadcasts, primarily from southern African sources. This is a good source of relatively recent information. Items are arranged by country; each issue contains an index to the previous issue, providing access by topic and country.

Jeune Afrique. **Paris: Les Editions J.A., 1980-.**

Weekly, in French. Current awareness, with emphasis on Francophone Africa.

Nairobi Law Monthly. **Nairobi: Kaibi, 1987-.**

Monthly. Articles on legal education, law, and rights awareness. The major human rights journal of Kenya.

New African. **London: IC Magazines, Ltd, 1978-.**

Monthly. Current awareness.

SAIRR News. **Johannesburg: South African Institute of Race Relations, 1984-.**

Quarterly newsletter. Contains information on the activities of members of the organization and on current developments in South Africa. Continues *Race Relations News*, 1938-1984.

Social and Economic Update. **Johannesburg: South African Institute of Race Relations. 1987-.**

Provides information and statistics on business and employment, education, energy, health and welfare, housing, land, transport, and water in South Africa.

West Africa. **London: West Africa Publishing Co., 1917-.**

Current awareness.

West Africa Annual. **Lagos: John West Publications, 1962-.**

Annual. Statistical information on the region.

3.   Asia

Aliran Monthly. **Pulau Pinang, Malaysia: Aliran Kesedaran Negaran, 1984-.**

The leading human rights publication in Malaysia. Articles on civil, political, economic, and cultural rights.

Alternative. Manila: Legal Resources Development Program of PROCESS Foundation, 1986-.

Policy-oriented articles on politics, development and human rights.

AMPO. Tokyo: Pacific-Asia Resources Center, 1969-.

Quarterly. Analyses of Japanese politics and society.

Asia Yearbook. Hong Kong: Far Eastern Economic Review, 1973-.

Annual. Contains statistical information on the region; individual country entries provides descriptions of political and economic developments over the past year.

B.U.R.M.A. Bangkok, Thailand: Burma Rights Movement for Action, 1991-.

Monthly newsletter published by Burmese exile community living in Thailand. Includes brief updates and articles on the civil war, human rights violations, the economy, refugees, politics and international actions on these issues.

Bulletin of Concerned Asian Scholars. Cambridge, MA: Bulletin of Concerned Asian Scholars, 1969-.

Quarterly. Political analyses of a broad range of topics in Asia.

Buraku Liberation News. Osaka: Buraku Liberation Research Institute, 1981-.

Published six times a year. Focuses on Buraku discrimination issues.

Burma Affairs. London: Burma Affairs Monitor, 1991-.

Bimonthly. News bulletin and forum for overseas Burmese and "friends of Burma." Burma Affairs Monitor is a group which monitors issues concerning Burma and which is "working towards the formation of a free, stable and democratic Burma."

CAHR Newsletter. Taipei: Chinese Association for Human Rights, 1987-.

Brief semi-annual newsletter describing human rights developments and activities of organization within Taiwan, and CAHR's international activities.

China Rights Forum. New York: Human Rights in China, 1990-.

Quarterly. Journal by Chinese human rights activists in the United States. Brief articles give updates on specific abuses and perspectives on theoretical issues. Each issue includes English and Chinese sections. Continues *Human Rights Tribune.*

ECDFC Monitor. Quezon City, Philippines: Ecumenical Commission for Displaced Families and Communities, 1986-.

    Quarterly. Brief articles providing updates on Filipinos displaced due to military/rebel clashes and operations and government infrastructure projects. Also discusses local and international efforts to address problems of the internally displaced in the Philippines.

Far Eastern Economic Review. Hong Kong: Far Eastern Economic Review, Ltd., 1946-.

    Weekly. In-depth news articles and analyses on political, economic and social developments in Asia.

From The Lawyers Collective. Bombay: R. Hazari for the Lawyers Collective, 1986-.

    Monthly. Articles on public interest law and policy in India.

Hotline: Justice and Peace Newsletter. Dhaka, Bangladesh: Commission for Justice and Peace.

    Bimonthly. Brief updates on human rights abuses in Bangladesh.

HRCP Newsletter. Lahore, Pakistan: Human Rights Commission of Pakistan, 1990-.

    Quarterly. Brief articles on specific human rights violations, patterns of abuses against certain groups, HRCP meetings and relevant international developments.

IMADR Bulletin. Tokyo: International Movement against All Forms of Discrimination and Racism, 1986-.

    Bimonthly. Contains brief articles on human rights in the Asian region and elsewhere, as well as information on IMADR activities and human rights events in Japan. IMADR works at the international level on Buraku and related issues, and is close to the Buraku Liberation League and the Buraku Liberation Research Institute.

Indochina Digest. Washington, DC: Indochina Project, 1987-.

    Weekly. Brief updates compiled by the Vietnam Veterans of America Foundation on developments in Vietnam and in U.S. policy towards Vietnam, Cambodia, and Laos. Articles based on wire service stories, published news accounts and staff reporting.

Indochina Interchange. New York: US-Indochina Reconciliation Project of The Fund for Reconciliation and Development, Inc., 1990-.

    Bimonthly. Brief updates about aid to and exchanges between the U.S. and Cambodia, Laos and Vietnam.

Indonesian Human Rights Forum. Jakarta, Indonesia: Indonesian Legal Aid Foundation (YLBHI), 1991-.

> Quarterly publication with discussions on human rights issues in Indonesia. Contributions by activists and scholars. Also contains brief news items.

Inform. Colombo, Sri Lanka: Sri Lanka Information Monitor.

> Monthly. Detailed, well-documented summaries of specific human rights situations. Also provides chronology summarizing highlights in human rights, and other political and economic developments.

INSEC Bulletin. Kathmandu, Nepal: Informal Sector Service Centre, 1991-.

> Bimonthly. Provides updates on human rights situations in South Asia, updates on INSEC activities, and other articles and editorials.

Japan Civil Liberties Union. *Universal Principle.* Tokyo: JCLU.

> Published twice a year. Newsletter containing current information on human rights issues in Japan, especially those in which the JCLU is participating.

Justice and Peace Review. Quezon City, Philippines: Ecumenical Movement for Justice and Peace, 1986-.

> Quarterly. Articles and interviews on human rights developments in the Philippines. Issues each have specific theme.

Konsumer. Penang, Malaysia: Consumers' Association of Penang, 1979-.

> Newspaper of the Consumers' Association of Penang, published every two weeks. Often contains material relevant to human rights in Malaysia.

Korea Update. New York: Korea Church Coalition for Peace, Justice and Reunification, 1991-.

> Quarterly newsletter. Articles provide information and analysis of political, economic and social conditions in Korea, and U.S. foreign policy towards Korea.

LAWASIA Human Rights Bulletin. Sydney, Australia: LAWASIA, 1982-.

> Published twice yearly until 1987; since then annually. Contains short factual accounts of human rights conditions in the Asia-Pacific region, drawn from various publications.

News Tibet. Dharamsala, India: Office of Tibet, 1964-.

Three times per year. Publication of the Dalai Lama and the Tibetan government-in-exile. Articles on various aspects of Tibetan life, including Buddhism, culture, politics, medicine, arts history and activities of Tibetans in exile.

Philippine Human Rights Monitor. Manila, Philippines: Ateneo Law School Human Rights Center, 1988-.

Monthly magazine published by human rights center at Jesuit university in the Philippines.

Philippine Human Rights Update. Quezon City, Philippines: Task Force Detainees of the Philippines, 1972-.

Monthly magazine published by the oldest and largest human rights monitoring organization in the Philippines. Covers wide range of civil, political, economic, social and cultural human rights violations. Issues periodically include detailed statistics on human rights violations.

Phnom Penh Post. Phnom Penh, Cambodia: Phnom Penh Post Publishing, Ltd., 1992-.

Biweekly newspaper on developments within Cambodia.

Slogan. Lahore, Pakistan: Tayyeb Iqbal Printers/Hina Jilani, 1989-.

Provides analytical articles, reports of human rights meetings, news clippings about significant human rights abuses, and reports of human rights investigations in Pakistan.

Tapol. London: Tapol, The British Campaign for the Release of Indonesian Political Prisoners, 1973-.

Published 5-6 times per year. Covers current human rights conditions, political trials, and foreign aid in Indonesia. Occasional coverage of developments in Malaysia and West Papua.

UCL Newsletter. Bangkok, Thailand: Union for Civil Liberty, 1984-.

Includes annual summary of civil liberties violations and articles on civil, political, and economic human rights violations. Focus is on Thailand; a few articles focus on Burma.

Women's Equality. New Delhi, India: All India Democratic Women's Association (AIDWA), 1989-.

Quarterly. Provides updates on AIDWA policies, analyses of legal developments, and reports of investigations into human rights abuses. Focuses on abuses against women in India.

Women's Link. **New Delhi, India: Programme for Women, Indian Social Institute, 1992-.**

> Bimonthly. Articles provide brief analyses of specific human rights abuses against women in India. Includes wide range of civil, political, economic, social and cultural abuses.

4.   Eastern Europe and the Former Soviet Union

Balkan War Report. **London: Institute for War and Peace Reporting, 1991-.**

> 10-12 issues per year; focused on the crisis in the former Yugoslavia. Incorporates *Yugofax.* Established by the Institute for War and Peace Reporting, a conflict-monitoring organization, and the Helsinki Citizens' Assembly, a network of politicians, academics and activists "working for the democratic integration of Europe."

Current Digest of the Soviet Press. **Columbus, OH: American Association for the Advancement of Slavic Studies, 1949-1992.**

> Selected translations from a large number of Soviet newspapers and periodicals.

> *Online.* Available on NEXIS from 1983-1992.

East European Reporter. **London: East European Reporter, 1985-.**

> An excellent source of information on current political debates in the region. Vol. 5, no. 1 (January/February 1992) is the first issue published from the new Hungarian headquarters of the journal. In the past, it was a good source of detailed analyses of political, social and cultural developments in Poland, Czechoslovakia, Hungary, the former East Germany, and the former Yugoslavia. Recent issues also cover Albania, Romania, the Baltic states, and Bulgaria. By drawing exclusively on material available in the region itself, the *Reporter* gave a platform to the independent opposition groups and initiatives. It continues this policy of attempting to allow Central and Eastern Europe to speak for itself. Its major shortcomings are a lack of attention to the non-Stalinist left, and to the voices of workers suffering the effects of the restoration of capitalism in the region.

Eastern Europe on File. **New York: Facts on File, Inc., 1991-.**

> Summaries of newspaper articles and other items from wire services, newspapers and radio broadcasts in the region.

Express Chronicle. **Moscow: A. Podrabinek, 1987-.**

> English-language translations of reports, documents and commentary from the Moscow Russian-language weekly "Ekspress-Khronika." Examples of the types of articles: Issue 1 of 1991 reported on the use of the state of emergency, problems of rehabilitating repressed individuals and nations, the situation in Azerbaijan and Karabakh, post-Communist "bolshevism" in Georgia, the KGB, and psychiatric abuse.

Glasnost News and Review. **New York: Center for Democracy in the USSR, 1990-.**

Bimonthly news journal, supported by the National Endowment for Democracy, providing news on human rights and politics during the end of the Gorbachev era. Free market perspective. Continues *Information Bulletin Glasnost*, 1987-1990.

Palach Press Bulletin. **London: The Press, 1976-1987.**

English translations of Charter 77 and other Czechoslovak documents of importance.

Radio Free Europe Research. **New York: Radio Free Europe, 1976-.**

Weekly, providing current situation reports on individual countries and background reports on topics such as arms control talks, dissent and the churches. Annual subject and author index.

Religion in Communist Lands. **Chistlehurst, U.K.: Centre for the Study of Religion and Communism, 1973-1991.**

Quarterly. Continued by *Religion, State and Society* , 1991-.

Summary of Available Documents. **London: Palach Press Ltd., 1976-1986.**

Irregular. English translations of Charter 77 documents and other Eastern European dissident literature.

Survey. **London: Congress for Cultural Freedom, 1956-.**

Irregular. Contains policy-oriented articles on Soviet politics and economics. Continued from 1957-1961 by *Soviet Survey.* In 1961, the title changed back to *Survey.*

Uncensored Czechoslovakia. **London: The Press, 1989-.**

Semimonthly. Full texts in English of all Charter 77 documents and VONS (Committee for the Defense of the Unjustly Prosecuted) statements, and news items and summaries of the content of other Czechoslovak independent periodicals. Continues *Palach Press Infoch Summary*, 1988-89.

Voice: Peace and Human Rights Bulletin. **Belgrade, Yugoslavia: Center for Antiwar Action, 1991-.**

Quarterly newsletter on developments in the former Yugoslavia, and the efforts of the Center for Antiwar Action.

5.   Latin America

Andean Newsletter. **Lima: Andean Commission of Jurists, 1986-.**

Monthly. Published in English and Spanish editions. Brief updates on human rights-related matters in the Andean countries. Until 1989, contained the useful *Drug Trafficking Update.* In 1989, the *Update* became a separate publication.

Drug Trafficking Update. **Lima: Andean Commission of Jurists, 1989-.**

Published in English and Spanish. Brief updates on human rights implications of the drug trade itself, as well as human rights violations committed in the course of the "war on drugs."

Haiti Insight. **Miami, FL: National Coalition for Haitian Refugees, 1990-.**

Monthly current awareness.

Latinamerica Press. **Lima: Noticias Aliadas, 1969-.**

Weekly Latin American news, with a liberation theology and human rights focus.

Latin American Weekly Report. **London: Latin American Newsletters Ltd., 1986-.**

Weekly Latin American news, including business and trade developments.

El Otro Derecho. **Bogota: Instituto Latinoamericano de Servicios Legales Alternativos, 1988-.**

In Spanish. Theoretical and practically-oriented articles examining law, legal services, human rights from a left-of-center, "alternative law" perspective which seeks to use and transform law in the interests of the oppressed.

Portavoz. **Bogota: Inter-American Legal Services Association. 1977-.**

Bimonthly newsletter, in Spanish. Information on human rights, legal services, and the "alternative law" movement in Latin America. Includes information on documents and publications in the field.

Update Latin America. **Washington, DC: Washington Office on Latin America, 1977-1991.**

Bimonthly news on issues which include human rights, congressional and executive actions, and military aid.

WOLA Briefing Series: Issues in International Drug Policy. **Washington, DC: Washington Office on Latin America, 1990-.**

Produced by the Washington Office on Latin America, a series of issue briefs some of which, such as *Peru Under Scrutiny: Human Rights and U.S. Drug Policy,* deal with human rights matters. The Washington Office on Latin America also produces *WOLA Policy Briefs,* published as mimeo/photocopied documents, parts of which are incorporated in subsequent full-length reports.

6.   Middle East

Al-Mohamoon al-Arab. **Cairo, Egypt: Arab Lawyers Union.**

Monthly newsletter (equivalents also published in Arabic and French). The ALU, established in 1944, is a confederation of national bar associations in most Arab countries.

Arab Organization for Human Rights. *Newsletter.* **Cairo, Egypt: The Organization, 1992-.**

Provides information on human rights developments in the region and the activities of the organization. Since 1983, the organization also has released an annual report in Arabic and English; it issues occasional human rights reports in English.

Arabia Monitor. **Washington, DC: International Committee for Human Rights in the Gulf and Arab Peninsula, 1993-.**

Monthly. Each issue is about ten pages long and contains 1-2 articles on specific human rights abuses, about 2 pages of news items and an urgent action appeal.

B'Tselem Update. **Jerusalem: B'Tselem, 1989-.**

Newsletter of Israeli organization which documents human rights violations in the Israeli-occupied territories and brings the violations to the attention of the general public and policy and opinion makers. The organization also issues reports on human rights conditions.

Egyptian Organization for Human Rights. [Titles vary.] Cairo: The Organization.

Occasional reports on the human rights situation in Egypt.

Human Rights Focus. **West Bank: Al-Haq, Law in the Service of Man.**

Newsletter of Al-Haq, one of the leading Palestinian human rights organizations in the Israeli-occupied territories and the West Bank affiliate of the International Commission of Jurists. In addition to its newsletter, Al-Haq produces an annual report and publications on specific human rights abuses in the occupied territories.

Kuwaiti Association for the Defense of War Victims. *Annual Report.* **Kuwait City, Kuwait: The Association, 1992-.**

> Annual. Describes activities of the organization during the year and human rights developments in the country.

Litigation Docket. **Jerusalem: Association for Civil Rights in Israel (ACRI).**

> Annual Report. Description of the cases begun or completed by ACRI in the year covered by the report.

Middle East International. **London: Middle East International, 1968-.**

> Articles, news analyses, book reviews and editorials. Includes brief updates on situations in countries throughout the region as well as longer analytical articles. 25 issues per year.

Middle East Report. **New York: Middle East Research & Information Project, 1988-.**

> Continues *MERIP Middle East Report*, 1986-1988. Current policy-oriented articles on politics. Nine issues per year.

Mideast Mirror. **London: Mideast Mirror, 1987-.**

> Daily translations of selected articles from Arabic, Hebrew, Persian, and other newspapers in the region. Available by mail or fax. Key for researchers who use English only.

Washington Report on Middle East Affairs. **Washington, DC: American Educational Trust, 1982-.**

> Monthly. Published by retired U.S. foreign service officers, ambassadors, and members of Congress. Contains analyses of developments in the region, actions by the U.S. Congress, political opinion pieces, chronologies, and clippings from other news sources. "Supports Middle East solutions which it judges to be consistent with the Charter of the United Nations and traditional American support for human rights, self-determination, and fair play."

IV.   Human Rights Nongovernmental Organizations (NGOs): Documentation and Directories

Since assessments of human rights conditions often entail criticizing the actions or inaction of a particular state, reports and documents of NGOs often provide the most reliable information on human rights conditions. Although no report is without bias, those by governments almost always reflect their interest in minimizing the quantity of violations or in denying government responsibility. Reports by intergovernmental organizations, although sometimes more objective, also tend to reflect the priorities and foreign policy considerations of states, and are often affected by political pressures from states.

Researchers using NGO materials should keep in mind that all NGOs are not equal. Some do highly professional work, others less so. The most trustworthy are usually those which make their fact-gathering methodology explicit. Some receive funding from governmental sources, and this should be taken into account. Recent years have seen governments creating governmental human rights bodies, which sometimes issue their own reports. Questions surrounding the independence of such governmental entities are addressed in *Report of the International Workshop on National Institutions for the Promotion and Protection of Human Rights,* Paris, 7-9 October, 1991, U.N. doc. E/CN.4/ 1992/43, 16 December 1991.

The accessibility of human rights NGO documentation has improved somewhat in recent years, but it is still often difficult or impossible to obtain materials from smaller groups, especially those operating in situations of heavy repression. For more information, see the discussion of NGO documentation in Chapter One, pp. 12-14.

Introductory accounts of the nature and activities of human rights NGOs can be found in the following publications.

> Shestack, J. "Sisyphus Endures: The International Human Rights NGO." *New York Law School Law Review* 24 (1978): 89-123.

> Steiner, H. *Diverse Partners. Non-Governmental Organizations in the Human Rights Movement.* Cambridge, MA: Harvard Law School Human Rights Program and Human Rights Internet, 1991. 90 pp.

> Weissbrodt, D. "The Contribution of International Nongovernmental Organizations to the Protection of Human Rights." In *Human Rights in International Law: Legal and Policy Issues,* edited by T. Meron, 403-438. Oxford: Clarendon Press, 1984.

> Wiseberg, L. and H. Scoble, "Monitoring Human Rights Violations: The Role of NGOs." In *Human Rights and American Foreign Policy,* edited by D. Kommers and G. Loescher, 179-210. Notre Dame, IN: University of Notre Dame Press, 1979.

A.   *Human Rights Organizations Regularly Publishing Reports*

Following are the addresses of nongovernmental human rights organizations which regularly produce the most widely consulted reports in English on countries or topics. Researchers should contact these organizations directly if publications are not available from libraries or a local nongovernmental organization.

> Amnesty International, International Secretariat, 1 Easton Street, London WC1X 8DJ, United Kingdom.

> Article 19, 90 Borough High Street, London, United Kingdom.

British Parliamentary Human Rights Group, House of Lords or House of Commons, Westminster Palace, London, SW1A OAA, United Kingdom.

Human Rights Watch, 485 Fifth Avenue, New York, NY 10017. Over 100 reports annually on human rights violations worldwide. Publications often appear in the name of one of HRW's regional divisions: Africa Watch, Americas Watch, Asia Watch, Helsinki Watch, and Middle East Watch. HRW also has four thematic, cross-regional projects: the Prison Project, Women's Rights Project, Arms Project, and the Fund for Free Expression.

International Commission of Jurists, 26 chemin de Joinville, CH-1216 Cointrin, Geneva, Switzerland.

International Human Rights Law Group, 1601 Connecticut Avenue N.W. Suite 700, Washington, DC 20009.

International League for Human Rights, 432 Park Avenue South, room 1103, New York, NY 10016.

Lawyers Committee for Human Rights, 330 Seventh Avenue, New York, NY 10017.

Minnesota Advocates for Human Rights (formerly the Minnesota Lawyers International Human Rights Committee), 400 Second Avenue South Suite 1050, Minneapolis, MN 55401.

Minority Rights Group, 379 Brixton Road, London, SW9 7DE, United Kingdom.

Physicians for Human Rights, 100 Boylston Street, Boston, MA 02116.

Washington Office on Latin America, 110 Maryland Avenue N.E., Washington, DC 20002.

B.   NGO Publications: Collections and Indices

Amnesty International, London. *Amnesty International, 1962-1987.* **Leiden, The Netherlands: InterDocumentation Co. Microform Publishers, 1989. 163 pp.**

Microfiche, with printed user instructions. Guide to the microform collection. Five volumes: A1 (country dossiers, 1975-1979 and 1980, in a geographic arrangement), A2 (country dossiers, 1981-85), A3 (country dossiers 1986-1987), B1 (Amnesty International publications, 1962-1980) and B2 (publications, 1981-1986). Also contains a cumulative inventory.

Human Rights Documents [microform]. Leiden, The Netherlands: InterDocumentation Co. Microform Publishers, 1983-.

The bulk of the NGO documents in Human Rights Internet's collection have been reproduced on microfiche. This collection covers publications between 1980-1988. The collection is kept up to date by supplements.

There is a cumulative guide to the microform collection, Wiseberg, L. *Human Rights Documents: Guide to the Microform Collection.* Parts I and II. Zug, Switzerland: InterDocumentation Co. (IDC), 1988. 419 pp. Incorporates material from 1987-88. The listing is not annotated, but is a comprehensive table of contents of the publications contained in the collection.

Human Rights Internet Reporter. Washington, DC: Human Rights Internet, 1976-.

Human Rights Internet is a documentation center and information clearinghouse which contains what is probably the best collection of NGO documentation in the world. It publishes the *Human Rights Internet Reporter,* which continues to provide the best coverage and the most detailed indexing of human rights NGO documents. The *Reporter*'s emphasis is on the materials produced by nongovernmental organizations and only secondarily on academic publications.

The *Reporter* abstracts hundreds of publications each issue, with emphasis on materials produced by human rights NGOs. Scholarly material is also abstracted, but less comprehensively. Since Volume 11 (December 1985), the *Reporter* has been maintained in a computer database for free-text searching. Several sections contain short articles on current human rights topics, information on developments in international law, in the human rights NGO community, and information on human rights conferences and awards.

The bibliography section provides abstracts of NGO documents, accessible through three indices: geographic (by country and region); organizational (by NGO name), and subject (by detailed subject categories). With the appearance of the *Human Rights Tribune,* the *Reporter* will continue to be published, but will consist solely of a bibliography section.

Vernau, J., comp. *An Index to "Index on Censorship."* London; New York: Hans Zell Publishers, 1989. 420 pp.

Indexes items from issue No. 1 (1972) to No. 100 (1988). Provides convenient access to major articles by country, and to all the names which have appeared in *Index.*

Verstappen, B., comp. and ed. *Human Rights Reports. An Annotated Bibliography of Fact-Finding Missions.* London: H. Zell, 1987. 393 pp.

An annotated listing of fact-finding reports published by NGOs and IGOs between 1970 and 1986. Entries are arranged by country, within geographic regions. Country, publisher and keyword indices are provided. Entries contain bibliographic information on the report, and a brief description of the purpose and results of the mission. Published for the Netherlands Institute of Human Rights.

C.   *Annual Reports*

Included here are substantial English-language reports on human rights conditions which appear annually, or with certain regularity. With the exception of the annual report by the U.S. State Department, all reports are by human rights NGOs. Although the reports listed here are those which are most debated and analyzed by the professional and academic human rights sector, and thus dominate the field, it should be kept in mind that they represent only a small, if powerful, part of the worldwide human rights movement.

Excluded here are the large number of reports and periodicals by NGOs from all over the world which deal with individual countries or regions and which, although often providing valuable, detailed information about human rights violations, are often published irregularly, and are difficult to obtain. Also not included are the many reports published by human rights NGOs on an irregular basis, which treat human rights conditions in single countries. For information on how to access these useful materials, see the section above on indices to NGO publications.

Researchers should bear in mind that none of the major U.S.-based human rights organizations systematically monitors economic, social and cultural rights. Information necessary to assess such rights can be found in the section on economic, social and cultural rights, or in the section dealing with the rights of indigenous peoples. Reports can reflect different political perspectives; because of this, researchers may wish to consult a variety of sources.

Amnesty International. *Amnesty International Report [year].* **London: Amnesty International Publications, 1976-.**

> Published under the title *Annual Report* between 1961-1975. Each report covers the year preceding publication. Brief country-by-country reports on human rights violations under AI's mandate: the release of prisoners of conscience, fair and prompt trials for all prisoners, and opposition to the death penalty, extrajudicial execution, "disappearance," torture, and cruel, inhuman or degrading treatment. Introduction provides an overview of human rights and a description of AI's work. Several appendices provide additional information.

Article 19. *Information, Freedom and Censorship: The Article 19 World Report 1988.* **Burnt Mill; Harlow; Essex, U.K.: Longman, 1988.**

> Covers events up to January 1, 1988. Concise country-by-country reports on 77 countries which attempt "to reflect the diverse global challenges raised by the violation of freedom of expression and information." Countries are not rated or classified. "Themes and issues" section classifies and provides annotations about impediments to the free exchange of ideas and information, describing the justifications put forward for censor-

ship, methods of censorship, targets of censorship, and the defenses of freedom of expression and information. See D'Souza, below, for coverage of 1988-1991.

Centre for the Independence of Judges and Lawyers of the International Commission of Jurists. *Attacks on Justice: The Harassment and Persecution of Judges and Lawyers.* **Geneva: Centre for the Independence of Judges and Lawyers of the International Commission of Jurists, 1989-.**

Annual summary of cases of summary execution, detention, "disappearances," physical attacks, threats of violence and professional sanctions against judges and lawyers who were persecuted while carrying out their professional duties.

D'Souza, F., ed. *Information, Freedom and Censorship: The Article 19 World Report 1991.* **London: Library Association Pub., 1991. 471 pp.**

Covers events during 1988-1991. See above description of 1988 Article 19 report.

Gastil, R. *Freedom in the World.* **New York: Freedom House, 1978-.**

Annual survey of the countries of the world on "Political Rights & Civil Liberties," including the United States. Attempts to rank countries in three categories: "free," "partly free," or "not free." Country reports are broadly descriptive, rather than linked explicitly to international human rights standards, in the manner of other human rights NGOs. Rankings are according to criteria of "political rights and civil liberties." The former include the right to vote and the existence of "fair and competitive elections." The latter include "freedoms of expression, religion and association...protecting the individual from political violence and from harms inflicted by courts and security forces." Entities defined as free "have free economic activity and tend to strive for equality of opportunity."

Freedom House's methodology and funding have provoked some controversy. See "Freedom House, Portrait of a Pass-Through," in *National Endowment for Democracy (NED): A Foreign Policy Branch Gone Awry.* s.l.: Council for Hemispheric Affairs/Inter-Hemispheric Education Resource Center, March, 1990. pp. 67-69.

Human Rights in Developing Countries. **Vol. 5. Oslo: Norwegian University Press, 1985-1989; Kehl: N.P. Engel, 1989. 464 pp.**

The fifth in a series of annual volumes, it provides information on the human rights situation in 14 countries receiving development aid from Canada, the Netherlands, and the Nordic countries. Equal weight is given to civil and political rights and economic, social and cultural rights. Each country report begins with a thumbnail sketch of the economy and development aid, and a set of social indicators. Countries described are Bangladesh, Botswana, China, Costa Rica, Guatemala, Indonesia, Kenya, Nicaragua, Pakistan, Peru, Philippines, Sri Lanka, Sudan, and Tanzania. Volume also includes three analytical articles on human rights and development.

Human Rights Watch. *The Bush Administration's Record on Human Rights in 1989.* **New York: Human Rights Watch, January 1990.**

> Good critique of U.S. human rights policy in selected countries. This report has not been continued; the annual analysis of U.S. foreign policy has been incorporated in the *Human Rights Watch World Report*, described below.

Human Rights Watch. *Human Rights Watch World Report [year].* **New York: Human Rights Watch, 1991-.**

> An essential annual report analyzing the U.S. administration's human rights policy in a number of countries monitored by Human Rights Watch, describing human rights developments in the countries under scrutiny and reviewing the activities of Human Rights Watch.

Human Rights Watch and Lawyers Committee for Human Rights. *The Reagan Administration's Record on Human Rights.* **New York: Human Rights Watch and Lawyers Committee for Human Rights, 1980-1989.**

> Annual issues, spanning the eight years of the Reagan administration, were published, the final volume appearing in January 1989. Good critique of U.S. human rights policy in selected countries. Sections entitled "U.S. Human Rights Laws," "Treaties," and "Refugee, Asylum and Immigration Policy" provide succinct treatments of current U.S. legislation dealing with human rights and an assessment of U.S. performance.

Humana, C., ed. *World Human Rights Guide.* **3d ed. New York: Oxford University Press, 1992. 393 pp.**

> These reports assemble information for over 100 countries on 40 selected rights, all but three of which are civil and political rights. By a process of scoring performance on a scale of one to four and weighting certain rights more than others, Humana assigned scores to countries, ranging from 98% for Finland and Norway, to 13% for Ethiopia. Humana's work, widely criticized for the selection and arbitrary weighting of rights, has resurfaced in the Human Freedom Index of the U.N. Development Program (UNDP), first published in the 1991 *Human Development Report*.

International Confederation of Free Trade Unions. *Annual Survey of Violations of Trade Union Rights [year].* **Brussels: ICFTU Press, 1984-.**

> Brief summaries arranged by geographic region. Appendices include a survey of complaints submitted by the ICFTU, National Affiliates and International Trade Secretariats to the International Labour Organisation's Committee on Freedom of Association; and a list of ICFTU actions in defense of trade union rights.

Lawyers Committee for Human Rights and Human Rights Watch. *Critique of the Department of State's Country Reports on Human Rights Practices for [year].* **New York: Americas Watch, 1978-.**

> Published annually since 1978 (between 1980 and 1990 in conjunction with Human Rights Watch; since 1991 by the Lawyers Committee for Human Rights). Covers a portion of the countries dealt with in the U.S. Department of State *Country Reports.* Introductions to several issues provide a good discussion of the techniques used by the U.S. State Department to shade the presentation of violations.

U.S. Department of State. *Country Reports on Human Rights Practices for [year].* **Washington: U.S. Government Printing Office, 1979-.**

> Published each February, the report is mandated by the Foreign Assistance Act. The report describes human rights conditions in most countries of the world, not including the United States. Two cautions are in order when using this report. First, the definition of human rights employed, with the exception of certain worker rights, excludes most economic, social and cultural rights. (Since 1990, Congress has required the State Department to include women's rights in its international human rights reporting and the material has been included in the annual reports.) Second, in human rights reports by a government, objectivity may suffer. As points of comparison, the reports of human rights NGOs should be consulted.

Weschler, J. *The Persecution of Human Rights Monitors: A Worldwide Survey.* **New York: Human Rights Watch, 1987-1990.**

> Reports on various forms of persecution against human rights monitors in a variety of countries. First edition published in 1987; second in 1988; final report in 1990. Information on persecution of monitors was then incorporated in the Human Rights Watch *World Report.*

D. *Election Monitoring*

Given the transitions from military to civilian governments in several countries during the mid-1980s and the emphasis placed by the U. S. government on formal mechanisms of democracy as a primary index of human rights observance, human rights NGOs, and subsequently American and European governmental agencies, began sending missions to observe the conduct of elections. (In a few cases, U.N. agencies have supervised the conduct of elections.) These missions resulted in a series of NGO reports. There was a spirited debate over the methodology and significance of such work, and over the extent of U.S. involvement. The International Human Rights Law Group (IHRLG) published several reports as part of its election-observing project.

For an especially useful introduction to IHRLG's approach to election monitoring, see Garber, L. *Guidelines for International Election Observing.* Washington, DC: International Human Rights Law Group, 1984. 101 pp. Other groups which regularly monitor elections include the Carter Center and the National Democratic Institute. What follows is a selection from the literature produced by the IHRLG and other organizations.

Arnold, M. *Zimbabwe: Report on the 1985 General Elections: Based on a Mission of the Election Observer Project of the International Human Rights Law Group.* Washington, DC: The Group, 1986. 142 pp.

Booth, J., et al. *The 1985 Guatemalan Elections: Will the Military Relinquish Power? Report of the Delegation.* Washington, DC: International Human Rights Law Group and the Washington Office on Latin America, 1985. 79 pp.

Carliner, D., et al. *Political Transition and the Rule of Law in Guatemala: Report of the Follow-up Delegation of the International Human Rights Law Group and the Washington Office on Latin America.* Washington, DC: International Human Rights Law Group and the Washington Office on Latin America, 1988. 46 pp.

Fauriol, G., and F. Loser. *Guatemalan Election Study Report.* Washington, DC: Center for Strategic and International Studies, 1986. 65 pp.

Garber, L. and E. Bjornlund, eds. *New Democratic Frontier: A Country by Country Report on Elections in Central and Eastern Europe.* Washington, DC: National Democratic Institute for International Affairs, 1992. 247 pp.

Hooper, M. *Election 1984, Duvalier Style: A Report on Human Rights in Haiti Based on a Mission of Inquiry.* New York: Americas Watch and Lawyers Committee for International Human Rights, 1984. 17 pp.

International Human Rights Law Group and the Washington Office on Latin America. *From Shadow into Sunlight: A Report on the 1984 Uruguayan Electoral Process.* Washington, DC: International Human Rights Law Group, 1985. 46 pp.

International Human Rights Law Group and Washington Office on Latin America. *A Political Opening in Nicaragua: Report on the Nicaraguan Elections of November 4, 1984.* Washington, DC: International Human Rights Law Group and Washington Office on Latin America, 1984. 60 pp.

E.   *Directories of Human Rights and Related Nongovernmental Organizations*

1.   Human Rights Organization Directories

Asian Regional Resource Center for Human Rights Education (ARRC). *A Directory of Asian Organizations Related to Human Rights Education Work.* **Bangkok, Thailand: ARRC, 1993. 34 pp.**

A listing of regional, national and local nongovernmental organizations which are engaged in human rights education work or which have the capacity to do so. Includes those NGOs involved in social development work that have human rights education programs or those that are interested in developing such programs.

Carver, R., and P. Hunt. *National Human Rights Institutions in Africa.* [Occasional Paper No. 1.] Banjul, The Gambia: African Centre for Democracy and Human Rights Studies, September 1991. 45 pp.

> Provides a short historical review of national human rights institutions in Africa, primarily the 17 official organs established between 1966-1990. The second part looks at mandates, modes of election and competence, and investigations by these human rights bodies. The third part analyzes institutions in Tanzania, Togo, Uganda, Zaire and the Gambia. An appendix provides a directory of national human rights institutions in Africa.

Directorio de Organismos de Derechos Humanos en Centroamerica. San Jose, Costa Rica: CODEHUCA, 1987. 90 pp.

> In Spanish. Information on human rights organizations in Central America.

Fenton, T. and M. Heffron, comps. and eds. *Africa: A Directory of Resources.* Maryknoll, NY: Orbis Books, 1987. 144 pp.

> Annotated entries describing organizations, books, periodicals, pamphlets, articles, and audiovisuals. Peace and social justice perspective.

Fenton, T. and M. Heffron, comps. and eds. *Asia and Pacific: A Directory of Resources.* Maryknoll, NY: Orbis Books, 1986. 137 pp.

> Annotated entries describing organizations, books, periodicals, pamphlets and articles, and audiovisuals. Peace and social justice perspective.

Fenton, T. and M. Heffron, comps. and eds. *Human Rights. A Directory of Resources.* Maryknoll, NY: Orbis Books, 1989. 156 pp.

> Annotated entries describing organizations, books, periodicals, pamphlets and articles, and audiovisuals. Emphasis is on materials useful for the teacher or activist. Peace and social justice perspective. This directory updates and expands the resources in the chapter on human rights in *Third World Resource Directory Indexes*, Orbis, 1984.

Fenton, T. and M. Heffron, comps. and eds. *Latin America and Caribbean: A Directory of Resources.* Maryknoll, NY: Orbis Books; London: Zed Books, 1986. 142 pp.

> Peace and social justice perspective. Annotated entries describe organizations, books, periodicals, pamphlets, articles, and audiovisuals.

Fenton, T. and M. Heffron, comps. and eds. *Middle East: A Directory of Resources.* Maryknoll, NY: Orbis Books, 1988. 144 pp.

> Annotated entries describing organizations, books, periodicals, pamphlets and articles, and audiovisuals. Peace and social justice perspective.

Fruhling, H. et al. *Organizaciones de Derechos Humanos de America del Sur.* **San Jose, Costa Rica: Instituto Interamericano de Derechos Humanos, 1989. 285 pp.**

In Spanish. Provides basic information on the structure, origins, mandates, activities and publications of 76 human rights NGOs in Argentina, Bolivia, Brazil, Colombia, Chile, Ecuador, Paraguay, Peru and Venezuela.

Ginger, A., J. Frankel, M. Kidane, eds. *Human Rights Organizations and Periodicals Directory.* **6th ed. Berkeley, CA: Meiklejohn Civil Liberties Institute, 1990. 194 pp.**

Looseleaf focused on U.S. organizations and sources. Organizations are arranged alphabetically. There are also subject and periodical indices, a federal agencies guide, and a geographical guide. Over 700 entries.

Le Guide des Droits de l'Homme: Afrique-Monde Arabe. **Paris: Editions Sans Frontiere, 1985. 158 pp.**

In French. Provides brief information on human rights groups in sub-Saharan Africa and the Arab world.

Human Rights Internet. *Asia: Human Rights Directory.* **Ottawa, Ontario: Human Rights Internet, forthcoming.**

A new updated edition on nongovernmental organizations in Asia is expected to be published in 1993. See also the Internet directory for Africa, Latin America and Asia, described below, p. 77.

Jinken dantai meibo (Directory of Human Rights Organizations). **Osaka: Buraku Kaiho Kenkyujo, 1991. 120 pp.**

In Japanese. Alphabetical listing with brief information, including activities, publications, addresses and phone numbers of Japanese organizations. Contains index by area of activity.

Parliamentary Human Rights Bodies: World Directory, 1990. **Reports and Documents, no. 17. Geneva: Inter-Parliamentary Union, 1990. 140 pp.**

Includes information on formal or informal human rights bodies in national parliaments; provides information on human rights bodies in international parliamentary assemblies and institutions; and lists national and international parliamentary assemblies and institutions in which no such human rights bodies exist.

Social and Human Science Documentation Centre and the Division of Human Rights and Peace. *World Directory of Human Rights Teaching and Research Institutions/ Repertoire mondial des institutions de recherche et de formation sur les droits de l'homme/Repertorio mundial de instituciones de investigacion y de formacion en materia de derechos humanos.* Deddington, Oxford, U.K.; New York; Berg; Paris: United Nations Educational, Scientific and Cultural Organization, 1988. 216 pp.

Includes indices.

Wiseberg, L., ed. *Human Rights Internet Directory: Eastern Europe & the USSR.* Cambridge, MA: Human Rights Internet, 1987. 304 pp.

Already somewhat dated, but provides a comprehensive picture of human rights organizations in the early period of *perestroika*. Introductory articles to country sections and accompanying bibliographies are useful.

Wiseberg, L., G. Lopez, and S. Meselson, eds. *Human Rights Directory: Latin America and the Caribbean.* Human Rights Internet Reporter, vol. 13, nos. 2 & 3. Cambridge, MA: Human Rights Internet and Programa de Derechos Humanos de la Academia de Humanismo Cristiano (Chile), 1990. 528 pp.

Bilingual (in Spanish and English). Comprehensive coverage of Latin American and Caribbean organizations, as well as outside organizations focused on the region or on one of its countries. Type of information is the same as that provided in Human Rights Internet, *Africa: Human Rights Directory and Bibliography*, listed below.

Wiseberg, L., and L. Reiner, eds. *Africa: Human Rights Directory and Bibliography.* Human Rights Internet Reporter, vol. 12, no. 4. Cambridge, MA: Human Rights Internet, 1989. 308 pp.

A directory of organizations, combined with a bibliography. Provides information on African organizations concerned with human rights or social justice and on outside organizations focused on Africa. Addresses, chief staff members, publications and descriptions of the development, nature and activities of NGOs and some IGOs are given. Information on groups is arranged according to whether the group's focus is Africa-wide, subregional or on individual countries. A bibliography of about 1,000 books, reports, documents, and articles follows the same arrangement. The bibliography excludes most material on human rights in South Africa.

Wiseberg, L., and H. Scoble, eds. *Human Rights Directory: Latin America, Africa, Asia.* Washington, DC: Human Rights Internet, 1981. 243 pp.

Latin American and African sections are superseded by newer directories devoted to these regions (listed above). Asia information is dated, but still occasionally useful. A new Asia directory is forthcoming.

Wiseberg, L. and H. Sirett, eds. *Human Rights Directory: Western Europe.* **Washington, DC: Human Rights Internet, 1982. 335 pp.**

> Although somewhat dated, still useful for its information about many organizations in the region.

Wiseberg, L., and H. Sirett, eds. *North American Human Rights Directory.* **Washington, DC: Human Rights Internet, 1984. 264 pp.**

> Still useful for descriptions provided of many organizations based in the United States and Canada, but addresses, phone and staff information are often out of date.

World Without War Council. *Raising the Curtain: A Guide to Independent Organizations and Contacts in Eastern Europe.* **2d ed. Seattle: World Without War Council, 1990. 77 pp.**

> Suggestive rather than comprehensive listing of independent or unofficial groups in Eastern Europe. Where possible, names, contacts and addresses are given, in addition to descriptions of organizations' activities.

2.   Human Rights-Related Organization Directories

Dembinski, L., ed. *International Geneva Yearbook: Organization and Activities of International Institutions in Geneva.* **Dordrecht; Boston; London: M. Nijhoff Pub., 1988-.**

> Part One consists of policy-oriented articles on international organizations. Part Two contains useful brief descriptions of United Nations bodies, with a summary of the year's activities, and a list of publications. Also included are (1) the specialized agencies and other bodies within the U.N. system, (2) several other intergovernmental organizations, (3) organizations with special status (such as the International Committee of the Red Cross, Inter-Parliamentary Union, Independent Commission on Humanitarian Issues, etc.), and (4) nongovernmental organizations. This latter list is especially useful for anyone seeking information on NGOs with offices in Geneva which do human rights-related work.

Fenton, T. and M. Heffron, comps. and eds. *Transnational Corporations and Labor: A Directory of Resources.* **Maryknoll, NY: Orbis Books, 1989. 166 pp.**

> Peace and social justice focus. Annotated lists of organizations, books, periodicals, pamphlets and articles, and audiovisuals. Organization, individual, title, geographic, and subject indices.

Hernandez, H. and E. Sanchez, eds. *Cross-Border Links.* **Albuquerque, NM: Inter-Hemispheric Education Resource Center, 1992. 257 pp.**

> English/Spanish annotated listing of all educational, social justice, labor, scholarly and business groups with a special interest in relations between Mexico, Canada and the

United States. Lists each organization's name, description of activity, key contact, address, phone and publications.

Inter-American Foundation. *A Guide to NGO Directories.* **Rosslyn, VA: Inter-American Foundation, 1990. 18 pp.**

Cites 32 directories of Latin American and Caribbean NGOs.

Japanese NGO Center for International Cooperation (JANIC). *Directory of Non-Governmental Organizations in Japan 1992: NGOs Active in International Cooperation.* **Tokyo: JANIC, 1992. 156 pp.**

The third edition (previous directories were published in 1988 and 1990) includes 173 Japanese organizations involved in a wide variety of cooperative, non-profit activities in developing countries around the world. NGOs are listed in four categories: (1) international cooperation; (2) support for foreign laborers and refugees living in Japan; (3) information dissemination and policy advocacy in Japan; (4) facilitation of networking among Japanese NGOs. Addresses, telephone and fax numbers, names of staff, and brief information on objectives, activities, finances, and membership are provided. Indexes NGOs by field, by geographic region, and alphabetically.

Knowles, L. *A Guide to World Hunger Organizations.* **Ellenwood, GA: Seeds/Alternatives, 1984. 104 pp.**

Describes the work of 19 organizations, including churches, which work against world hunger.

Research Centers Directory. **Detroit: Gale Research Co., May 1965-.**

Published annually, updated between editions by the quarterly *New Research Centers.* Detroit: Gale Research Co., 1965-.

Describes over 8,000 nonprofit research organizations in universities, foundations and other settings. Covers the full spectrum of research activities. Extensive coverage given to business, economics, and public policy. Entries provide the centers' founding dates, methods of governance and funding, purposes, and types of research. Also provides information on annual research budgets, and special capabilities.

U.N. Non-Governmental Liaison Service. *Who's Who on Debt and Structural Adjustment, A Directory of NGOs Involved in Research, Information and Advocacy.* **Geneva: NGLS, UNCTAD/NGLS/19, 1990. 227 pp.**

Lists about 160 organizations, from all regions of the world. Entries provide addresses and telephone numbers; frequently the name of a contact person; lists of activities (with examples); and descriptions of main target groups, objectives, institutions studied, publications and future plans. Organized by country. Four indices: by thematic area, geographic area of interest, institutions studied, and activities.

Zimmerman, D., N. Avrin and O. Della Cava, comps. *A Directory of International Migration Study Centers, Research Programs, and Library Resources.* **New York: Center for Migration Studies of New York, Inc., 1987. 299 pp.**

Provides information on the structure, staff, size and location of centers/programs concerned with international migration, as well as their current projects, research activities, publications and library resources. Western Europe and North American countries comprise two-thirds of the entries, which are organized geographically. Title and geographical indices.

V.   Human Rights Thesauri

Aitchison, J. *International Thesaurus of Refugee Terminology.* **Dordrecht; Boston: M. Nijhoff, 1989. 476 pp.**

A detailed thesaurus of refugee-related terms.

Caccia, I., comp. *Human Rights Thesaurus.* **Ottawa, Ontario: Human Rights Internet and Human Rights Research and Education Centre, University of Ottawa, 1993. 275 pp.**

In English and French. Contains about 2,000 terms, with scope notes and references to the relevant international instruments. Published in a limited edition in cooperation with the African Centre for Democracy and Human Rights Studies (Banjul) and the Arab Institute for Human Rights (Tunis) for testing by human rights groups.

Paenson, I. *Manual of the Terminology of the Law of Armed Conflicts and of International Humanitarian Organizations.* **London; Boston: M. Nijhoff, 1989. 844 pp.**

Quadrilingual (English-French-Spanish-Russian) manual and dictionary.

Stormorken, B. and L. Zwaak. *Human Rights Terminology in International Law: A Thesaurus.* **Strasbourg: Human Rights Documentation Centre; Dordrecht; Boston: M. Nijhoff Publishers, 1987. 234 pp.**

This thesaurus is intended to be used with human rights case law of national and international bodies. It is focused on rights defined in the major human rights international and regional instruments; it does not focus on violations.

VI.   Practice Manuals

Amnesty International. *A Guide to the African Charter on Human and Peoples' Rights.* **London: Amnesty International, 1991. 68 pp.**

A booklet for non-experts which explains one's rights under the African Charter, the role of the African Commission in promoting and protecting such rights, and how to make complaints about violations to the African Commission.

Amnesty International. *Protecting Human Rights. International Procedures and How to Use Them.* **London: Amnesty International, 1987-1989.**

> Provides practical information on procedures and organizations. The following have been issued: 1A. *The Human Rights Committee* (April 1987, IOR 03/01/87); 1B. *The Human Rights Committee: Examination of Individual Complaints under the Optional Protocol.* (April 1987, IOR 03/02/87); 1C. *"General Comments" of the Human Rights Committee* (April 1987 IOR 03/03/87); 2. *The Organization of African Unity and Human Rights* (May 1987, IOR 03/04/87); 3. *Summary of Selected International Procedures and Bodies Dealing with Human Rights Matters* (August 1989, IOR 30/01/89). Papers are available from Amnesty International offices. Each is approximately 10 pages of text and includes appendices such as texts of the relevant international instrument, charts of signatures and ratifications, and sample forms.

Byre, A.D. and B. Y. Byfield. *International Human Rights Law in the Commonwealth Caribbean.* **Dordrecht; Boston; London: M. Nijhoff Publishers, 1991. 398 pp.**

> Collection of papers from a workshop held in Jamaica in 1987, organized by Interights and the Organization of Commonwealth Bar Associations. The book is arranged thematically, each chapter devoted to papers and discussions on a particular human rights issue. Issues covered are the use of available remedies, liberty and security of the person, the right to a fair trial, access to court, the right to life and human dignity, freedom of expression, equality before the law, freedom of association, and the role of governments in NGOs.

de Chazournes, L. B., et al. *Practical Guide to the International Procedures Relative to Complaint and Appeals Against Acts of Torture, Disappearances, and Other Inhuman or Degrading Treatment.* **Geneva: World Organization Against Torture/S.O.S. Torture, 1988. 92 pp.**

> Provides practical information on how to use international bodies in denouncing acts of torture or other violations of human rights. Includes information on the Organization of American States, International Labour Organisation, U.N. Educational, Scientific and Cultural Organization, Organization of African Unity, International Committee of the Red Cross, U.N. High Commissioner for Refugees, and Council of Europe bodies, as well as other U.N. bodies which have jurisdiction over human rights matters.

Dijk, P. van and G.J.H. van Hoof. *Theory and Practice of the European Convention on Human Rights.* **2d ed. Deventer; Boston: Kluwer Law and Taxation Publishers, 1990. 657 pp.**

> Meant to be used as a textbook and as a guide for practicing lawyers. Provides a general survey of the history, structure and functioning of the Convention, then discusses the Convention's supervisory procedures and extensively analyzes the rights and freedoms of the Convention. Analysis is based primarily on the case law of the European Court of Human Rights and the European Commission of Human Rights.

Hannum, H., ed. *Guide to International Human Rights Practice.* **2d ed. Philadelphia: University of Pennsylvania Press, 1992. 308 pp.**

An excellent practical introduction to supervisory and implementation procedures and institutions. Part I provides an overview of international human rights law, strategies and procedures. Part II covers "communications" — procedures for making human rights complaints within the U.N. system. Part III describes the three regional systems for the protection of human rights. Part IV deals with other techniques and fora for protecting rights. Appendices provide a bibliographic essay by D. Vincent-Daviss, a checklist to help select the most appropriate forum, a model communication, addresses of intergovernmental organizations, ratification status of selected human rights instruments, and citations for major international human rights instruments.

Hannum, H. *Materials on International Human Rights and U.S. Criminal Law and Procedure.* **Washington, DC: Procedural Aspects of International Law Institute, 1989. 152 pp.**

See p. 195 for annotation.

How to Address a Communication to the African Commission on Human and Peoples' Rights. **Geneva: International Commission of Jurists, 1992. 32 pp.**

Booklet which is a practical guide for individuals, groups, and NGOs wishing to address communications to the African Commission or to obtain observer status. Annexes contain a communication form and checklist.

Indian Rights, Human Rights: Handbook for Indians on International Human Rights Complaint Procedures. **Washington, DC: Indian Law Resource Center, 1984. 129 pp.**

See p. 159 for annotation.

Isaacs, S. et al. *Assessing the Status of Women: A Guide to Reporting Using the Convention on the Elimination of All Forms of Discrimination Against Women.* **New York: International Women's Rights Action Watch, 1988. 44 pp.**

See p. 177 for annotation.

Schabas, W. *International Human Rights Law and the Canadian Charter: A Manual for the Practitioner.* **Toronto: Carswell, 1991. 357 pp.**

Designed to make international human rights law more accessible to the Canadian practitioner. The book has four main chapters: (1) a review of the theoretical basis for the use of international law; (2) a description of the various international instruments and tribunals; (3) a review of the use made by Canadian courts of international human rights law in the construction of the Charter; (4) an overview of international human rights case law, grouped by subject. Appendices contain reported Canadian cases referring to international human rights law; a table of international instruments cited by Canadian courts; and a table of international jurisprudence cited by Canadian courts.

Tardu, M.E. *Human Rights: The International Petition System.* **3 vols. Dobbs Ferry, NY: Oceana Publications, 1979-.**

Looseleaf. Somewhat dated, since last supplemented in 1985.

U.N. Centre for Human Rights. *Communications Procedures.* **Fact Sheet, no. 7. Geneva: Centre for Human Rights, 1989. 18 pp.**

Brochure with brief descriptions of procedures for reporting human rights violations to the United Nations, addresses of relevant U.N. human rights bodies, and a model communication.

U.N. Institute for Training and Research. *Manual on Human Rights Reporting Under Six Major International Human Rights Instruments.* **New York: U.N., 1991. 203 pp.**

A collection of articles on the system of periodic reporting established under six major human rights instruments, emphasizing practical aspects of the processes.

Weissbrodt, D. and P. Parker, comp. *Orientation Manual: The U.N. Commission on Human Rights, Its Sub-Commission, and Related Procedures.* **s.l.: Minnesota Advocates for Human Rights and the International Service for Human Rights, 1993. 100 pp.**

First published in 1988, this updated manual is designed for use by first-time participants and observers at the proceedings of the Commission on Human Rights, the Sub-Commission for Prevention of Discrimination and Protection of Minorities, and related bodies, which meet at the European headquarters of the United Nations in Geneva, Switzerland. It provides a brief overview of the major U.N. human rights organizations, discusses the rules and procedures of the Commission and the Sub-Commission, and is full of essential nuts-and-bolts information, ranging from instructions on getting to the NGO and government credentials office, to the location of free copy machines.

Appendices and Supplementary Materials contain a range of useful information, such as a bibliography, lists of members of the Commission for 1993 and members and alternates of the Sub-Commission for 1992/93, the text of ECOSOC resolution 1296 on NGO consultative status, a sample application for NGO consultative status, a sample letter requesting credentials at a particular session, lists of studies of the Sub-Commission and for Centre for Human Rights staff and a telephone list.

Zwaak, L. *International Human Rights Procedures: Petitioning the ECHR, CCPR and CERD.* **Nijmegen, Netherlands: Ars Aequi Libri, 1991. 168 pp.**

Step-by-step information needed to lodge complaints under the European Convention for the Protection of Human Rights and Fundamental Freedoms, the International

Covenant on Civil and Political Rights, and the Convention on the Elimination of All Forms of Racial Discrimination. Includes illustrative cases which have been brought before international bodies.

VII. Country Conditions: Handbooks and Current Awareness Publications

A.   Handbooks Providing Basic Information on Foreign Countries

Arnold, G., et al., eds. *Revolutionary and Dissident Movements of the World: An International Guide.* 3d ed. Harlow, Essex, U.K.: Longman Current Affairs, 1991. 480 pp.

> Provides lists of handbooks, manuals and other materials which discuss resistance movements against governments.

Countries of the World and Their Leaders Yearbook. 2 vols. Detroit: Gale Research Inc., 1980-.

> An annual, with a supplement in mid-year. Compilation of most recent releases of the U.S. State Department's "Background Notes on Countries of the World," its Travel Advisories, and reports on foreign government personnel, policies, and political and economic conditions.

The Europa World Yearbook [year]. 2 vols. London: Europa Publications Limited, 1926-.

> An annual publication which contains excellent brief descriptions of intergovernmental organizations, followed by an alphabetical survey of the countries of the world. Each country's entry includes an introductory survey, with information on climate, language, religion, recent history, government, defense, economic affairs, social welfare, education, public holidays, and weights and measures.
>
> This is followed by statistical tables. A directory section includes a brief description of the constitution, the structure of government, current government officials, political organizations, a list of press and periodical organizations, etc. More detailed treatments of countries are provided in the six regional books of the series: The Middle East and North Africa, Africa South of the Sahara, The Far East and Australasia, South America, Central America and the Caribbean, Western Europe and the United States and Canada.

Szajkowski, B. ed. *New Political Parties of Eastern Europe and the Soviet Union.* Harlow, Essex, U.K.: Longman, 1991. 404 pp.

> Includes directories of political parties in Eastern Europe, 1989 to the present, and in the former Soviet Union 1985-1991.

Some other useful handbooks include: *World Almanac and Book of Facts*; *World Factbook*; and *The Statesman's Year-Book*. For more detailed (if conventional) introductions, the *Area Handbook* and *Country Study* series produced by Foreign Area Studies of American University and the Library of Congress provide one-volume information on topics such as the history, politics, economics, and religions of many countries.

B.   Current Awareness of Country Conditions

FBIS Daily Report [volume name]. **Foreign Broadcast Information Service (FBIS). Washington: U.S. Government Printing Office, 1941-.**

> Published Monday through Friday, containing excerpts from regional, national and local periodicals and broadcasts. There are eight volumes (divided according to region): "Central Eurasia," "China," "East Asia," "East Europe," "Near East & South Asia," "SubSaharan Africa," "Latin America," and "West Europe. "

> These contain political, military, economic, environmental, and sociological news, commentary and other information. FBIS reports are available through subscription; they are held at most U.S. government depository libraries.

Joint Publications Research Service (JPRS). Washington, DC: U.S. Government Printing Office, 1967-.

> Translations of unclassified materials. JPRS has functioned since the late 1960's under the Foreign Broadcast Information Service (FBIS), a part of the U.S. Central Intelligence Agency. Much of the material translated by JPRS originates in third world countries.

Transdex. **Wooster, OH: Bell and Howell Co., 1975-.**

> Lists and indexes all JPRS publications. Monthly paper issues; annual cumulations on microfiche.

VIII. General Compilations of Human Rights Instruments

Included here are general compilations. Those prepared by the United Nations are listed in that section; others are listed with their organizations or topics in the sections below.

Blaustein, A., R. Clark, and J. Sigler, eds. *Human Rights Sourcebook*. New York: Paragon House Publishers, 1987. 970 pp.

> Contains United Nations and regional documents, as well as human rights documents of the International Labour Organisation (ILO) and the United Nations Educational, Scientific and Cultural Organization (UNESCO); documents on procedures of the United Nations, specialized agencies, the ILO and UNESCO; the main texts of the laws of war and of the ECSCE; some harder-to-find documents such as the Lusaka Manifesto on Southern Africa and the Universal Islamic Declaration of Human Rights; and provisions on constitutional rights in several countries.

Brownlie, I., ed. *Basic Documents on Human Rights.* **3d ed. Oxford: Clarendon Press; New York: Oxford University Press, 1992. 631 pp.**

Standard compilation of documents.

Lillich, R., ed. *International Human Rights Instruments: A Compilation of Treaties, Agreements, and Declarations of Especial Interest to the United States.* **2d ed. Buffalo, NY: W.S. Hein Co., 1990-.**

Looseleaf volume. Contains the 42 principal international human rights treaties and agreements concluded under the auspices of the United Nations, the Organization of American States, the International Labour Organisation, and other international bodies and conferences. Also contains citations to U.S. cases which discuss international human rights standards, selected bibliographies, and references to U.S. executive and congressional documents.

Lillich, R. *International Human Rights: Documentary Supplement.* **Boston: Little, Brown, 1991. 197 pp.**

Document supplement to Lillich, R. *International Human Rights: Problems of Law, Policy and Practice.* Contains the text of the principal U.N.-sponsored human rights treaties, the three regional human rights treaties, a number of other international human rights instruments, a model communication using U.N. human rights procedures, and two U.S. statutes linking foreign assistance to the human rights records of recipient states.

Chapter Three.
Human Rights Materials on Intergovernmental Organizations (IGOs) and Basic Treaties

I.   General Information on IGOs and Their Documentation

A.   *Handbooks and Indices*

American Society of International Law. *International Legal Materials.* **Washington, DC: American Society of International Law, 1962-.**

For annotation, see pp. 14-15.

The Europa World Yearbook [year]. **2 vols. London: Europa Publications Limited, 1926-.**

Provides convenient access to brief descriptions of IGOs. Volume I contains descriptions of the United Nations, its principal components, its regional commissions, 15 other U.N. bodies, and all of the specialized agencies within the U.N. system. It also provides descriptions of some 55 other intergovernmental organizations, both universal and regional. An especially useful feature of these descriptions is a listing of the publications of each organization. The regional handbooks published by Europa contain descriptions of the intergovernmental organizations in these regions. See p. 84, above, for full annotation.

Government Publications Review. **Elmsford, NY: Pergamon Press, 1973-.**

Six issues per year. Issue Six has annual article "United Nations and Other International Organizations," which is especially useful for those seeking the publications of these organizations. Contains full bibliographic information, price, an abstract of contents, and information about how to place an order. Publications listed include substantial reports and studies by intergovernmental organizations such as the Council of Europe, European Communities, International Labour Organisation, General Agreement on Tariffs and Trade, World Bank, International Monetary Fund, Organization for Economic Cooperation and Development, North Atlantic Treaty Organization, Organization of American States, and the specialized agencies of the United Nations (e.g., World Health Organization, Food and Agricultural Organization, and United Nations International Children's Emergency Fund). Has subject index.

Hatfield, S., comp. *Indexes to Publications of Selected International Organizations.* **Washington, DC: Library of Congress, Serial and Government Publications Division, Government Publications Section, 1987. 34 pp.**

A useful list of major indices to some of the publications and documents of selected intergovernmental organizations. Omits indices dealing primarily with technical scientific literature, as well as indices to International Court of Justice decisions .

International Bibliography. **New York: UNIPUB, 1983-1991.**

Continues *International Bibliography, Information, Documentation* which was published between 1973 and 1982. A useful quarterly index, listing the publications of intergovernmental organizations. Entries are arranged by subject and provide full bibliographic information, and brief descriptions of contents. Contains detailed subject index, with human rights heading. Periodical entries include tables of contents of the publications. The bibliography excludes working documents, draft texts, press releases and internal material. The Congressional Information Service (CIS) is currently exploring the possibility of reviving and revising this publication.

B.   *Constitutional Documents*

There is no good source of current information on the charters, bylaws and regulations of intergovernmental organizations. For this reason, although it is dated, the following source is included here. Researchers may also contact the organizations in question for such information.

Peaslee, A., ed. *International Governmental Organizations: Constitutional Documents.* **3d ed. 5 vols. The Hague: M. Nijhoff, 1974-1979.**

Part one (2 volumes) contains the documents of most of the major intergovernmental organizations dealing with political, economic, social, legal, and defense matters. It includes regional organizations such as the Andean Group and the Council of Europe, as well as multilateral lending institutions such as the International Monetary Fund (IMF), the World Bank, and the regional development banks.

Part two treats organizations concerned with agriculture, commodities, fisheries, food and plants, and has the constitutional documents of the Food and Agriculture Organization. Parts three and four (covering education, culture, copyright, science and health) contain the documents of the World Health Organization, and United National Educational, Scientific and Cultural Organization (UNESCO). Part five contains the constitutional documents of organizations concerned with communications, transport and travel.

II.   United Nations and U.N.-Related Human Rights Treaties and Treaty-Based Mechanisms

A.   *General Information on United Nations Materials*

The researcher unfamiliar with the United Nations faces two main problems: first, understanding the basic role and structure of U.N. human rights bodies and second, grasping the structure of the documentation. The most comprehensive one-volume description and evaluation of U.N. human rights bodies is Alston, P., ed. *The United Nations and Human Rights: A Critical Appraisal.* New York: Clarendon Press, 1992. 765 pp. A useful chart in this book offers a schematic view of all U.N.-related human rights bodies and an excellent bibliography can guide the researcher to many of the key publications about human rights and the U.N. system.

A good overview of U.N. human rights bodies and procedures can be found in the relevant chapters of Hannum, H., ed. *Guide to International Human Rights Practice.* 2d ed. Philadelphia: University of Pennsylvania Press, 1992, 308 pp. Also useful is *United Nations Action in the Field of Human Rights.* 2d ed. New York: United Nations, 1993, which provides a thorough introduction to the relevant U.N. organs and specialized agencies, as well as detailed summaries of U.N. actions relating to human rights. Especially useful are the references to relevant U.N. documents, reports and Official Records, which help to put the documentation in an institutional framework. Another highly useful source when beginning research is the *Yearbook of the United Nations,* annotated later in this section. Additional background on U.N. human rights developments and documentation is available in the *Human Rights Monitor* (see p. 91), pre-1992 issues of the *Human Rights Internet Reporter* (see p. 69), and Internet's new magazine, *Human Rights Tribune* (see p. 55).

Researchers looking for an excellent account of the politics of human rights in the United Nations should consult Iain Guest's *Behind the Disappearances: Argentina's Dirty War Against Human Rights and the United Nations.* Philadelphia: University of Pennsylvania Press, 1990, 605 pp. Focused on the Argentine case during the late '70s and early '80s, Guest brings the reader behind the scenes, illuminating the significance of otherwise arcane processes and opaque documents.

For purposes of human rights research, it is useful to divide United Nations materials into four categories: **sales publications, periodicals, Official Records, and mimeographed documents. Sales publications** are easiest to access, since they are likely to be separately cataloged as books, and are accessible by author, title, subject or key word through library catalogs. Most sales publications are also indexed in the *International Bibliography.* Sales publications usually consist of material that has appeared earlier in document form. **Periodicals** such as the *U.N. Chronicle, Development Forum,* or the *Bulletin of Human Rights* are easily accessible, since they are usually separately cataloged by libraries.

Official Records are also relatively easy to access, since they form a discrete subset of those U.N. documents considered most important, and are published separately each year as a set of paperbound volumes. For example, the annual report of the Human Rights Committee appears as a bound volume, Supplement No. 40, to the Official Records of the U.N. General Assembly. Since *General Assembly Official Records* are not overly voluminous, and are organized by annual sessions, the appropriate volume can be located fairly easily. The annual reports of most U.N. human rights bodies appear as separate paperbound volumes in the *Official Records* of the General Assembly or the Economic and Social Council.

Documents are the most difficult to work with, since they are so numerous, so various, and may exist only in mimeographed form. U.N. documents, identified and often arranged in libraries by unique U.N. document symbols ("slash numbers"), include materials of a wide variety: records of meetings, reports of conferences, reports commissioned by various U.N. organs, information presented to the United Nations by member states, statements by NGOs, etc. Much of this documentation is not very useful for research purposes. Of potentially greatest use are the documents of the U.N. bodies with responsibility for human rights matters, but even here there is much of minimal importance.

The basic index to U.N. documents is the *UNDOC Current Index*. This quarterly index provides access to U.N. documents, Official Records, and sales publications by subject, country, title, author, and document number. Use of *UNDOC* is somewhat cumbersome, however, so other sources should usually be tried first. Annual cumulations are published in microfiche.

> *Online:* Readex produces the index on CD ROM: *UNDOC,Current Index*. Cum. ed. New
> York: United Nations, 1986-.

There are two additional complications regarding U.N. documents. Restricted documents are not made public, and are not listed in *UNDOC Current Index*. Limited distribution documents, which include an "L." in the document symbol, are listed in *UNDOC* but are not distributed to U.N. depository libraries. Because they are considered to be of importance only temporarily, and of relevance only to those attending the particular meeting, they are made available only at the time and place of that meeting. The U.N. does publish a "List of Documents Made Available at Headquarters" (commonly called the *Journal*), which references limited distribution documents, but the list itself is not widely available. In most cases, however, the researcher need not worry about limited distribution documents, since, to the extent that their content is significant, it is likely they will be reprinted in a form which is indexed in *UNDOC* and more widely available.

To locate current U.N. documents, it may be necessary to use *UNDOC Current Index*. The following tools however, are more convenient for locating documentation.

Centre for Human Rights, Geneva. *United Nations Action in the Field of Human Rights*. New York: United Nations, 1988. 359 pp.

> A very useful ready-reference tool for access to detailed summaries of human rights
> developments within the United Nations to date. Especially useful for references to U.N.
> documents and publications. Every U.N. human rights body is described. A new edition
> is forthcoming.

Commission on Human Rights. Sub-Commission on the Prevention of Discrimination and Protection of Minorities. *List of Studies and Reports Prepared Pursuant to Sub-Commission Decision 1989/103*. E/CN.4/Sub.2/[YEAR]/2.

> An annual list of human rights-related studies and reports prepared for the General
> Assembly, the Economic and Social Council, the Commission on Human Rights, the Sub-

Commission, and studies and reports under preparation by special rapporteurs or experts of the Sub-Commission. Does not include studies or reports which review human rights developments in particular countries, nor reports or studies prepared for other functional commissions of the Economic and Social Council. Provides title, author, and year when its final version was considered, and the document symbol. Includes U.N. sales number if study/report was issued as a U.N. publication.

HR Documentation DH. **Geneva: International Service for Human Rights, 1989-.**

Appearing irregularly, this publication provides lists of resolutions of the U.N. Commission on Human Rights and Sub-Commission on Prevention of Discrimination and Protection of Minorities, lists of documents of these and other human rights bodies, compilations of voting results of the Commission on Human Rights, and other current information.

This is an extremely useful complement to the *Human Rights Monitor,* because of its listings of documents of many United Nations human rights bodies. Documents for each session are listed by U.N. symbol. The date and a brief description of content are provided. Both publications are available from the International Service for Human Rights, 1, rue de Varembe, P.O. Box 16, 1211 Geneva 20 CIC, Switzerland.

Human Rights Monitor. **Geneva: International Service for Human Rights, 1988-.**

About 6 times per year. Filling a major void in the literature, the *Monitor* is essential for current awareness of human rights developments within the United Nations. Describes recent meetings of U.N. human rights bodies, and provides information on forthcoming meetings. Gives information on meetings and activities of other U.N. bodies relevant to human rights issues. Summarizes meetings of the U.N. specialized agencies and other institutions, such as the International Labour Organisation and the Conference on Security and Cooperation in Europe. Provides information on NGO activities, ratifications of human rights instruments, and human rights-related awards.

Human Rights Newsletter. **Geneva: U.N. Centre for Human Rights, 1988-.**

Public relations document which provides brief accounts of the sessions of U.N. human rights bodies, information on activities of the Centre, and occasional information on NGO events. As is unfortunately the case with many U.N. publications, its accounts are formalistic, it is not published in a timely fashion, and it is not very useful to the researcher.

United Nations Chronicle. **New York: U. N. Office of Public Information, 1964-.**

For developments occurring recently, the *United Nations Chronicle,* now a quarterly, can sometimes be helpful, although coverage is selective, descriptions are sketchy, and document references are usually not provided.

Online: The *U.N. Chronicle* is online in NEXIS (in the UNCHRN file in the INTLAW, ITRADE, EXEC, WORLD, or NEXIS libraries) from January 1983.

United Nations. *United Nations Juridical Yearbook*. New York: U.N., 1962-.

> Editions include legislative texts, treaty provisions, discussions of legal activities (including selected legal opinions and judicial and administrative decisions) and an extensive bibliography concerning the legal status of the United Nations and related intergovernmental organizations.

Yearbook of the United Nations. Lake Success, NY: U.N. Office of Public Information, 1947-.

> Although published with a three- to four-year time lag, because of its excellent subject index the *Yearbook* is often the source to begin with. It provides good summaries of U.N. action on all matters before it, with references to relevant U.N. documents.

B.   U.N. Human Rights Instruments: Compilations and Status of Ratifications

1.   U.N. Compilations of Human Rights Instruments

International Human Rights Instruments of the United Nations, 1948-1982. Pleasantville, NY: UNIFO Publishers, 1983. 175 pp.

> Provides the final texts of instruments developed in the United Nations during this period.

U. N. Centre for Human Rights. *Human Rights: A Compilation of Human Rights Instruments*. New York: U.N., ST/HR/1/Rev.3. 1988. 416 pp.

> A basic reference tool which contains the texts of 67 conventions, declarations, recommendations, resolutions and other instruments adopted by the United Nations, the International Labour Organisation, and United Nations Educational, Scientific and Cultural Organization concerning human rights. Includes the dates of conventions' entry into force and a chronological list of instruments in the order of adoption. The compliation is being updated. Volume I covers the universal instruments and was issued in two parts in June 1993. Volume II, on the regional instruments, is expected.

2.   Status of U.N. Instruments

Human Rights Law Journal. Kehl am Rhein; Arlington, VA: N.P. Engel, 1980-.

> See p. 50 for full annotation. First issue of each year provides a list of the current ratification status of U.N. and other international human rights instruments.

Multilateral Treaties Deposited with the Secretary-General: Status as at 31 December [year]. New York: U.N., 1982-.

> Appearing annually, this is an important source for citations to U.N. treaties. Also provides information on the status of treaties, including date of entry into force, list of

states parties, dates of signature, accession or acceptance, and, importantly, the texts of declarations and reservations made by states parties. Covers United Nations and League of Nations treaties (but not regional instruments, International Labour Organisation conventions, or treaties on armed conflict).

Statement of Treaties and International Agreements Registered or Filed and Recorded with the Secretariat during the Month of [month and year]. **New York: U. N. Legal Department of the Secretariat, 1946-.**

Monthly. Includes current number of ratifications, accessions, subsequent agreements concerning treaties and international agreements registered with the Secretariat. Has cumulative alphabetical index by subject terms and parties. Less useful than publications listed above, since status of treaties is shown as of one to two years prior to the publication.

U. N. Centre for Human Rights. *Human Rights: Status of International Instruments.* **New York: U.N., ST/HR/5. 1987. 336 pp.**

Covers the ratification status and declarations, reservations, objections and derogations by states parties to 22 international human rights instruments. Annual updates to the chart of ratifications in this paperback publication are published by the United Nations as a small pamphlet, with the designation, *Human Rights. Status of International Instruments as at [date].*

C. Commentaries and Legislative History of the United Nations Charter and the Universal Declaration of Human Rights

1. U.N. Charter

Cot, J.-P. and A. Pellet, eds. *La Charte des Nations Unies: Commentaire Article par Article.* **2d ed., rev. et augm. Paris: Economica, 1991. 1571 pp.**

Article-by-article commentary in French.

Goodrich, L., E. Hambro, and A. Simons. *Charter of the United Nations: Commentary and Documents.* **3rd rev. ed. New York: Columbia University Press, 1969. 732 pp.**

Several chapters on the background and history of the Charter, followed by an article-by-article commentary, incorporating the practice of the first three sessions of the General Assembly. The text of several major documents are provided. Contains subject index and list of references to articles.

Simma, B., ed. *Charta der Vereinten Nationen. Kommentar.* **Munchen: C.H. Beck'sche Verlagsbuchhandlung, 1991. 1217 pp.**

German-language commentary on the Charter. An English translation was published in late 1993: Simma, B., ed. *Charter of the United Nations: A Commentary.* Oxford: Clarendon Press.

2.   Universal Declaration of Human Rights

Eide, A., et. al. *The Universal Declaration of Human Rights: A Commentary.* London; New York: Scandinavian University Press; Oxford: Oxford University Press, 1992. 474 pp.

> Article-by-article study of UDHR by human rights scholars and activists from five Nordic countries. Covers UDHR history, normative development, measures to ensure compliance, and performance of Nordic countries.

Verdoodt, A. *Naissance et signification de la declaration universelle des droits de l'homme.* Louvain: Nauwlaerts, 1964. 356 pp.

> Not a commentary on the Universal Declaration, but a summary account of the meetings, negotiations, and delegates' positions during the period of its elaboration. In French.

D.   *Human Rights Bodies Based on the United Nations Charter*

1.   Commission on Human Rights ("Commission") and the Sub-Commission on Prevention of Discrimination and Protection of Minorities ("Sub-Commission")

The types of documents which may be useful to the researcher include the proceedings themselves (e.g., resolutions condemning human rights violations in certain countries or the adoption of a new draft convention) or reports on specific countries or types of human rights violations. Both bodies designate individuals as Special Rapporteurs or Special Representatives to compile substantive reports which may deal with the human rights situation in a particular country — past reports have dealt with Chile, El Salvador, Iran, Haiti, Afghanistan, among others — or with particular "themes," such as human rights and mass exodus, states of emergency, slavery, human rights and disability, and human rights and the environment.

Country reports can be politically significant, and are cited by human rights advocates and government officials as evidence of improvement or deterioration in human rights conditions. Theme reports can be useful sources, since they often gather a lot of information relevant to a particular topic. These reports are published as U.N. documents of the E/CN.4/[year] or E/CN.4/Sub.2/[year] series, and are occasionally reproduced as U.N. sales publications.

Perhaps the easiest way to find documents from the Commission and Sub-Commission is to consult the relevant annex to the annual report for that session. These annexes contain comprehensive lists, by symbol number, of all the documents issued for the session. Document symbols and basic bibliographic information on these reports can also be located by using UNDOC, the *U.N. Yearbook* (for older reports), *Human Rights Monitor,* or *HR Documentation DH.* These publications are described above, in Section II.A. of this chapter.

Informative accounts of the highlights of Commission and Sub-Commission sessions, with some political background, usually appear in the *Human Rights Quarterly* or the *Review of the International Commission of Jurists*. Summaries of sessions of the Commission, the Sub-Commission and other U.N. human rights bodies appear in the *Human Rights Monitor*.

(a)   Documents of the Commission on Human Rights

United Nations. Economic and Social Council. *Official Records.* **Lake Success, NY: The Council, 1946-.**

> Annual report of the Commission on Human Rights, containing draft resolutions and decisions for adoption by ECOSOC, Commission resolutions and decisions adopted at the session, discussion and voting on agenda items. The annexes contain a list of Commission members, states represented by observers, nongovernmental organizations in consultative status, and a list of documents issued for the session.

> The symbols of Commission documents have recently become more systematized. Since 1978, documents released by the Economic and Social Council (ECOSOC) have the symbol, E/[year]/.... Documents produced by the Commission on Human Rights have been numbered by year since 1982. Prior to these years, the numbering system varied. For a consolidated reference source, consult the above-mentioned bibliography to Alston, P., *The United Nations and Human Rights,* which provides a list of document symbols. (See pp. 88-89 for discussion of bibliography.)

For detailed discussions of the evolution and work of the Commission, the following are useful.

> Alston, P. "The Commission on Human Rights," in *The United Nations and Human Rights,* edited by P. Alston, 126-210. Oxford: Clarendon Press, 1992.

> Tolley, H. *The U.N. Commission on Human Rights.* Boulder, CO: Westview Press, 1987. 300 pp.

*(b)   Documents of the Sub-Commission on Prevention of
        Discrimination and Protection of Minorities*

Like the Commission, the Sub-Commission has produced a number of useful reports and studies through its rapporteurs and special representatives. The suggestions about locating documents mentioned above apply. The categorizing system for Sub-Commission documents recently has also become more systematized. They now appear under the symbol E/CN.4/Sub.2/[year]/.... For a list of recent documents, consult the Alston bibliography mentioned above. Relevant documents can be located by using UNDOC, or if very recent, through *HR Documentation DH* and *Human Rights Monitor*. All three tools have been described in Section II.A. of this chapter.

2.   Commission on the Status of Women

Commission on the Status of Women. *List of Resolutions and Decisions on the Status of Women Adopted by the General Assembly and the Economic and Social Council 1946-1990.* **Vienna: U. N. Division for the Advancement of Women, 1991. 88 pp.**

> Contains a chronological list of all resolutions and decisions, and a keyword index covering those adopted 1974-1990.

E.   *Human Rights Treaties and Treaty-Based Mechanisms*

1.   International Covenant on Civil and Political Rights

(a)   *Commentary on and Legislative History of the International Covenant on Civil and Political Rights*

Bossuyt, M. *Guide to the "Travaux Preparatoires" of the International Covenant on Civil and Political Rights.* **Dordrecht; Boston: M. Nijhoff, 1987. 851 pp.**

> Provides access to the preparatory work of the International Covenant on Civil and Political Rights and its Optional Protocol. There are a series of helpful annexes: Annex II (bibliography on the International Covenant and Optional Protocol); Annex III (chronological list of principal documentation); Annex IV (table of roll-call votes in the Commission on Human Rights); Annex V (table of roll-call votes in the Third Commission of the United Nations General Assembly).

Henkin, L., ed. *The International Bill of Rights: The Covenant on Civil and Political Rights.* **New York: Columbia University Press, 1981. 523 pp.**

> Not a table of article-by-article annotations, but a series of related essays on particular rights or groups of rights in the Covenant. Includes essays on the background of the development of the Covenant, derogations from the Covenant, permissible limitations on rights, the obligation to implement the Covenant domestically, the international implementation system, and on the rights of self-determination, life, physical integrity and liberty, due process of law, freedom of movement, legal personality, privacy and the family, freedom of conscience and expression, equality and nondiscrimination and minorities.

Nowak, M. *CCPR Commentary: Commentary on the U.N. Covenant on Civil and Political Rights.* **Arlington, VA: N.P. Engel, 1993. 948 pp.**

> In-depth analysis of the substantive, organizational and procedural provisions of the Covenant and its two Optional Protocols. Covers practice and case law of the Human Rights Committee. Organized by article and paragraph numbers of the international instruments. Appendices include index of key words and relevant texts.

(b)   *Status of the International Covenant on Civil and Political Rights*

The *Report of the Human Rights Committee,* issued annually as a *Supplement of the Official Records of the U.N. General Assembly,* contains a list of current ratifications of the International Covenant on Civil and Political Rights and its Optional Protocol. The *Report* is described in the section below. The following resource also provides information on the ratification status of the covenant.

Reservations, Declarations, Notifications and Objections Relating to the International Covenant on Civil and Political Rights and the Optional Protocol Thereto. Geneva: United Nations, CCPR/C/2/Rev.2. [year].

> Produced periodically, the document contains the texts indicated in the title. This document is based on *Multilateral Treaties Deposited with the Secretary-General: Status as at [date]* . For a full description of the latter document, see pp. 92-93.

(c)   *The Human Rights Committee*

The Human Rights Committee has three major functions: (1) supervisory—receiving and studying states parties' periodic reports on their actions to give effect to the Covenant, questioning states' representatives, and making suggestions and general recommendations to states parties; (2) normative—elaborating the meaning of provisions of the Covenant through "general comments" which are general interpretations of the meaning of individual articles and paragraphs of the Covenant by the Committee acting in consensus; and (3) quasi-adjudicatory—under the Optional Protocol, considering communications from individuals claiming to be victims of violations of the Covenant (it may also consider inter-state complaints), and producing "decisions" and "views."

All of these activities are recorded in mimeographed documents in the CCPR/C/... series. They contain the texts of periodic reports of states. The summary records (CCPR/C/SR...) of sessions contain summaries of the discussion of periodic reports with states' representatives. "Decisions" of the Committee refer to admissibility determinations of individual complaints; "views" refer to determinations by the Committee on the merits of individual complaints. Both are also published as mimeo documents of the Committee in the CCPR/C/ series, as are the "general comments" of the Committee.

The *Selected Decisions* and the *Yearbooks,* although they bear U.N. document symbols, are not mimeographed documents, but sales publications. They provide convenient access to Committee documents, but are published with a considerable time lag, which limits their usefulness for current research.

The Yearbook of the Human Rights Committee is published in two-volume pairs with, at present, about a seven-year time lag. Volume I contains the summary records of Committee meetings. Volume II contains "documents"—primarily the texts of states' periodic reports—and "reports"—primarily the annual reports of the Committee to the U.N. General Assembly.

Human Rights Committee. *Report of the Human Rights Committee, [session no.].* **UN GAOR Supp.(No. 40), A/[session no.]/40 ([year]).**

This annual report to the U.N. General Assembly is the most convenient way to access information on current Committee activities. It includes summaries of most of the important Committee documents (except for the summary records of sessions). The *Report* is issued as a Supplement to the Official Records of the General Assembly, and includes: (1) summaries of the periodic reports submitted by states parties, and of the questions put to and answers given by the states' representatives by the Committee; (2) texts of the general comments of the Committee; (3) information on changes in procedure and organization; (4) a list of current ratifications of the Covenant and the Optional Protocols; (5) final views of the Committee; (6) decisions of the Committee; and (7) a list of Committee documents issued during the reporting period. These annual reports are reproduced, with some time lag, in the *Yearbook of the Human Rights Committee,* described below.

In addition, two compilations of decisions and views have been produced covering the years 1977 to 1988.

Human Rights Committee. *Selected Decisions Under the Optional Protocol.* **New York: U.N. CCPR/C/OP/1. 1985. 167 pp.**

Contains interlocutory decisions on communications prior to admissibility decision, decisions on admissibility, decisions to discontinue or suspend consideration, and views of the Human Rights Committee under article 5(4) of the Optional Protocol. Annexes contain the text of the Optional Protocol, provisional rules of procedure for the consideration of communications, a list of states parties to the Protocol as of December 31, 1984, and a statistical survey of status of communications as of July 31, 1982. Indexed by articles of the Covenant, by article of the Optional Protocol and by subject.

Human Rights Committee. *Selected Decisions under the Optional Protocol. Volume 2. Seventh to thirty-second sessions (October 1982-April 1988).* **New York: U. N., CCPR/C/OP/2. 1990. 246 pp.**

Contains interlocutory decisions, final decisions, and views. Annexes contain responses received from States parties after the adoption of views by the Committee; list of States parties to the Optional Protocol as of September 30, 1988; lists of Committee members, 1976-87; and statistical survey of the status of communications as of June 30, 1988. Indexed by articles of the Covenant, by articles of the Optional Protocol, by subject, and by author and victim.

Human Rights Committee. *Yearbook of the Human Rights Committee 1977-78.* **2 vols. New York: U. N., 1986.**

Volume I (UN Doc. CCPR/1) contains the summary records of the meetings of the first to fifth sessions. Volume II (UN Doc. CCPR/1/Add.1) contains the states parties' periodic reports to the Committee and the Committee's annual reports to the General Assembly for these sessions.

Human Rights Committee. *Yearbook of the Human Rights Committee 1979-1980.* **2 vols. New York: U. N., 1988.**

> Similar format to the 1977-78 *Yearbook*, described above. The 1979-80 *Yearbook* covers the sixth to the tenth sessions. Volume I is numbered as UN Doc. CCPR/2; Volume II as CCPR/2/Add.1.

Human Rights Committee. *Yearbook of the Human Rights Committee 1981-1982.* **2 vols. New York: U. N., 1989.**

> Covers the eleventh to the sixteenth sessions. Volume I is numbered as U.N. Doc. CCPR/3; Volume II as CCPR/3/Add.1.

Human Rights Committee. *Yearbook of the Human Rights Committee 1983-1984.* **2 vols. New York: U. N., 1991.**

> Covers the seventeenth to twenty-second sessions. Contains a list of records and documents published in all of the *Yearbooks* of the Committee (for the first to 22nd sessions).

McGoldrick, D. *The Human Rights Committee.* **Oxford: Clarendon Press; New York: Oxford University Press, 1991. 576 pp.**

> Contains chapters on the origins, drafting and significance of the International Covenant on Civil and Political Rights; the membership and work of the Committee; the system of periodic reporting; the Optional Protocol; selected articles of the Convention; and appraisals. Also contains an extensive bibliography.

2. International Covenant on Economic, Social and Cultural Rights

The researcher should also see Chapter Four, Section II.A. for additional sources.

Alston, P. and G. Quinn. "The Nature and Scope of States Parties' Obligations under the International Covenant on Economic, Social and Cultural Rights." *Human Rights Quarterly* **9 (May 1987): 156-229.**

> A suggested guide to the interpretation of the Covenant.

United Nations. Committee on Economic, Social and Cultural Rights. *Official Records.* **Lake Success, NY: The Council, 1946-.**

> Annual report of the Committee. Summarizes the activities of the Committee during the current year. An annex contains a list of documents of the Committee for the current session.

3.   Convention against Torture and other Cruel, Inhuman or Degrading Treatment or Punishment

Burgers, J. and H. Danelius, eds. *The United Nations Convention Against Torture.* Dordrecht; Boston: M. Nijhoff, 1988. 271 pp.

> An article-by-article commentary on the convention and discussion of the drafting history of the convention.

4.   Convention on the Rights of the Child

Because the first session of the Committee on the Rights of the Child took place quite recently, in the fall of 1991, the Committee has produced little substantive documentation. Initial reports of states parties were due in 1993.

5.   International Convention on the Elimination of All Forms of Racial Discrimination (CERD)

International Convention on the Elimination of All Forms of Racial Discrimination: Official Records, Decisions. New York: United Nations, CERD/SP/40, 1970-.

> Provides the texts of decisions by the Committee on the Elimination of All Forms of Racial Discrimination.

International Convention on the Elimination of All Forms of Racial Discrimination. Summary Records of the [#] Meeting. New York: U. N., CERD/SP/SR [#], 1970-.

> A series of documents published for each session, which summarizes the discussions and comments of Committee members and representatives of states parties.

Report of the Committee on the Elimination of Racial Discrimination. General Assembly Official Records: [#] Session. Supplement No. 18. New York: U.N., 1969-.

> Annual report of the Committee to the General Assembly. Summarizes the work of the Committee, including the consideration of reports by states parties, and decisions adopted by the Committee.

United Nations. Centre for Human Rights. *Second Decade to Combat Racism and Racial Discrimination: Global Compilation of National Legislation Against Racial Discrimination.* New York: U.N., HR/PUB/90/8, 1991. 201 pp.

> Not a Committee document, but a useful compilation. See annotation on p. 166.

6. Convention on the Elimination of All Forms of Discrimination against Women (CEDAW)

Report of the Committee on the Elimination of Discrimination against Women. ([#] Session) General Assembly. Official Records: [#] Session. Supplement No. [#]. . New York: U.N., [year].

> Annual report of the Committee to the General Assembly. Summarizes the work of the Committee, including the consideration of states parties' periodic reports to the Committee, and general recommendations of the Committee. Annexes include a list of states parties to the CEDAW, invitation and due dates for the submission of reports by states, and membership of the Committee.

United Nations. Committee on the Elimination of Discrimination Against Women. *The Work of CEDAW: Reports of the Committee on the Elimination of Discrimination Against Women (CEDAW).* Vol. 1, 1982-1985. New York: U.N., 1989. 744 pp.

> Contains reports of the Committee for its first four sessions. With the exception of the first session, for which there are no summary records, the report on each session is followed by the corresponding summary records. Summary records contain discussions and questions put to country representatives during the consideration by the Committee of reports by states parties to the Convention.

United Nations. Committee on the Elimination of Discrimination Against Women. *The Work of CEDAW: Reports of the Committee on the Elimination of Discrimination Against Women (CEDAW).* New York: U. N., 1989-.

> Contains information similar to that described above, but on sessions after 1985.

The Women's Watch. Minneapolis, MN: International Women's Rights Action Watch, Humphrey Institute of Public Affairs, 1987-.

> Quarterly newsletter on seminars, meetings, court decisions, legislative changes, and other developments in law and policy relating to the CEDAW.

III. International Labour Organisation (ILO)

A. Compilation of Instruments

International Labour Office. *International Labour Conventions and Recommendations 1919-1991.* 2 vols. Geneva: International Labour Office, 1992. 1481 pp.

> Contains full texts of ILO Conventions and Recommendations adopted by the International Labour Conference at its first 67 sessions, from 1919 to 1991. The texts adopted at subsequent sessions may be found in the *Official Bulletin*, Geneva: ILO, of the appropriate year, or in *Labour Law Documents*.

For information on the current status of ratifications, see International Labour Organisation. *Chart of Ratifications of International Labour Conventions.* Geneva: International Labour Office, 1991. See also the *Human Rights Law Journal.* (Annotations are on pp. 50 and 92.)

B.   *Official ILO Documents*

International Labour Office. *Special Report of the Director-General on the Application of the Declaration Concerning the Policy of Apartheid of the Republic of South Africa.* **Geneva: International Labour Office, 1965-1988.**

Published annually from 1965-1988, these reports deal with a broad range of issues connected with *apartheid* and its impact on labor and social matters in South Africa and South Africa-occupied Namibia.

International Labour Office. Committee of Experts on the Application of Conventions and Recommendations. *General Survey of the Reports on the Equal Remuneration Convention (No.100) and Recommendation (No. 90), 1951.* **Geneva: International Labour Office, 1986. 203 pp.**

Third in a series of surveys on the position of governments' law and practice on equal pay for men and women workers. Contains summaries of states' reports on the implementation of the instruments. Covers 128 states and six territories.

International Labour Office. Committee of Experts on the Application of Conventions and Recommendations. *Report of the Committee of Experts on the Application of Conventions and Recommendations (articles 19 and 22 of the Constitution).* **Geneva: International Labour Office, 1950-.**

Published annually as *Report III (Part 4A), Third item on the agenda: Information and reports on the application of Conventions and Recommendations.* Contains a general report on the activities of the Committee, including brief reports of complaints filed; followed by observations concerning particular countries' observance of Conventions and Recommendations. Does not cover freedom of association questions, which are handled by the Committee on Freedom of Association.

International Labour Office. Freedom of Association Committee. *Freedom of Association:Digest of Decisions and Principles of the Freedom of Association Committee of the Governing Body of the ILO.* **3d ed. Geneva: International Labour Office, 1985. 140 pp.**

Compilation of decisions by the Freedom of Association Committee in dealing with complaints of infringement of freedom of association submitted by governments or by workers or employers organizations. Decisions are arranged by subject categories. Annex contains a chronological list of cases.

International Labour Organisation. *Constitution of the International Labour Organisation and Standing Orders of the International Labour Conference.* **Geneva: International Labour Office, 1989. 87 pp.**

Besides the ILO constitution, the publication includes ILO rules and information about practice. Periodic updates issued.

Official Bulletin. **Geneva: International Labour Office, 1919-.**

Published since 1975 in two series, A and B. Series A, published three times a year, summarizes most of the activities of the ILO, and provides texts adopted by the International Labour Conference as well as other official documents. Series B contains the reports of the Freedom of Association Committee, which include cases and the Committee's conclusions and recommendations. Supplements to Series B contain the reports of Commissions of Inquiry appointed to examine complaints of violations of various ILO Conventions.

C.   Periodicals

Conditions of Work Digest. **Geneva: International Labour Office, 1986-.**

Two issues per year. Factual data on specific topics in conditions of work and quality of working life. Provides information on work in progress and annotated bibliographies. Worldwide coverage.

International Labour Review. **Geneva: International Labour Office, 1921-.**

Six times per year. Includes articles based on recent ILO (and other) research into economic and social topics relevant to international labor; also includes notices of new books received by the ILO.

Labour Law Documents. **Geneva: International Labour Office, 1990-.**

Three times per year, in English, French and Spanish editions. Important international instruments including new ILO Conventions and Recommendations, as well as principal national labor and social security laws and regulations, are published in full whenever feasible. The bibliographic information sections comprise indices of cases handled by ILO supervisory bodies and lists of recent legislation drawn from the LABORLEX database. Materials are arranged in an "international" section and a "national" section. The table of contents can be quickly scanned to determine which countries have passed what sort of legislation recently on labor or social security matters.

Legislative Series. **Geneva: International Labour Office, 1914-1989.**

Published under different names, and with different frequencies, since 1919. Continued by *Labour Law Documents* in 1990. (See entry above.) The series is a collection of important national labor and social security legislation and occasional excerpts from constitutions. Each issue contains some original English-language texts of legislation and some translations into English from other languages. Also available are many individual reports on specific topics such as employment, migration of labor, education, and income distribution. Cumulative chronological and subject indices are issued at irregular intervals.

Social and Labour Bulletin. **Geneva: International Labour Office, 1974-.**

Four issues and index each year. Brief analysis of current events and trends, both national and international, in the labor field: major labor legislation, industrial relations, collective agreements, job creation measures, impact of new technologies, efforts to improve the work environment, social security, equal opportunities, and training.

World Labour Report. **Geneva: International Labour Office, 1984-.**

Annual. A new series launched to survey major contemporary labour problems and issues throughout the world. Volume I (1984) treats the unemployment problem, incomes and wages, social security in industrialized countries, and the impact of information technology on employment, working conditions and industrial relations. Volume II (1985) deals with labor relations, trade unions and employers organizations, freedom of association, industrial relations, training for employment, and working conditions and women workers. Volume III (1987) includes discussions of recent trends in employment and hours of work, labor relations, social security and training as well as incomes from self-employment and from casual and regular wage employment.

D.   Bibliographies and Indices

ILO Publications and Documents: Title List, 1919-1987. **Geneva: International Labour Office, 1988.**

Useful for finding specific publications.

International Labour Documentation. **Geneva: International Labour Office, 1965-.**

Twelve issues per year. Very useful current awareness index in fields such as labor relations, labor law, employment, working conditions, social development, and rural development. Covers all ILO publications, and other books, journal articles, reports and technical documents held in the ILO library and specialized documentation units. Entries arranged by subject category. Some relevant categories are human rights, law, economic development, social problems, rural development, women, race, migration, and food and nutrition. Subject index in English, French and Spanish contains more specific headings, including countries. Issues contain the useful section, "New ILO Publications in English," and "International Labour Bibliography." The latter lists bibliographic publications of the ILO since 1987.

Online: International Labour Documentation is derived from information contained in the database LABORDOC produced by the ILO, and available online in Human Resource Information Network (LDOC) and in Orbit (LDOC).

Labour Information: A Guide to Selected Sources. Geneva: International Labour Office, 1991. 231 pp.

> An excellent annotated listing of over 500 publications in the labor field, covering reference materials and selected ILO publications in English. Part I lists and selectively annotates reference works arranged by format. Part II focuses on current ILO publications categorized by broad subject categories (e.g., employment, training) and subcategories. Contains title index.

Subject Guide to Publications of the International Labour Office, 1980-85. Geneva: International Labour Office, 1987. 614 pp.

> Lists English-language publications issued by the ILO between 1980 and 1985. Includes 2,719 sales publications, technical reports, working papers and other documents. Periodical articles and papers prepared for sessions of the ILO Governing Body are not included. Lists documents and publications by subject category.

IV.   World Health Organization (WHO)

A.   General

World Health Organization. *Basic Documents.* **7th ed. Geneva: WHO, 1956-.**

> Published irregularly. Contains the constitution, regulations, rules of procedure, and agreements of WHO; the rights and obligations of associate members and other territories; the principles governing relations between WHO and NGOs; and the financial regulations of WHO.

World Health Organization. *Handbook of Resolutions and Decisions of the World Health Assembly and the Executive Board.* **Geneva: WHO, 1973-.**

> Resolutions and decisions of WHO governing bodies.

World Health Organization. *International Digest of Health Legislation.* **Geneva: WHO, 1948-.**

> Four issues per year. Contains a selection of national and international health legislation, studies on current problems in health legislation, a "News and Views" section (including information on conferences and meetings), a "Book Reviews" section, and an "In the Literature" section (short book and journal notes). Official publications and other documents forwarded by member states constitute the principal source of material for the *Digest*. Texts of legislation are reproduced or translated in full or in extract form, and are summarized or mentioned by their title. Legislation is arranged under 22 subject headings. Each issue has a chronological index of legislation. Published also in French as *Recueil international de legislation sanitaire.*

World Health Organization. *Publications Catalog.* **Geneva: WHO, 1948-.**

Provides bibliographic data for all publications officially issued by WHO since its establishment in 1947. Includes over 2,000 books and reports. Also includes publications by five of the six regional offices of WHO: Africa, Eastern Mediterranean, Europe, South-East Asia, and Western Pacific. Entries are organized by author or editor, title, series, or subject.

B.   *Statistical Sources*

World Health Organization. *World Health Statistics Annual.* **Geneva: WHO, 1962-.**

Provides global, regional and national data.

World Health Organization. *World Health Statistics Quarterly.* **Geneva: WHO, 1967-.**

Contains articles in either French or English, with summaries in both languages. Detailed analysis of selected health topics of current interest.

V.   United Nations Educational, Scientific and Cultural Organization (UNESCO)

A.   *Texts of Instruments*

Blaustein, A., R. Clark and J. Sigler, eds. *Human Rights Sourcebook.* **New York: Paragon House Publishers, 1987. 970 pp.**

Contains human rights documents of UNESCO and texts on UNESCO procedures.

B.   *Other UNESCO Sources*

The Chronicle. **Paris: UNESCO, 1955-80.**

Bimonthly publication containing general interest, non-scholarly articles on children's issues.

The Courier. **Paris: UNESCO. 1984-.**

Monthly publication containing primarily general-interest, non-scholarly articles dealing with children's issues. Education and public health are consistent focuses. Continues *UNESCO Courier* (1954-1984), and an earlier version of *The Courier* (1948-1954).

Online: *The Courier* is available in selected full text in NEXIS (UNESCO file in the NEXIS or WORLD libraries) from 1983 to present.

Human Rights Teaching. **Paris: UNESCO, 1980-.**

> Although intended as a semiannual, just several issues have been published. Intended primarily for human rights teachers. Contains bibliographies listing basic books and articles concerned with human rights.

Report of the Director-General on the Activities of the Organization in [year]. **Paris: UNESCO, 1947-.**

> Annual. A summary review of the activities of UNESCO. Contains declarations, conventions, agreements and recommendations adopted under UNESCO auspices, a list of publications, and descriptions of the major programs of UNESCO.

VI.   Organization of American States (OAS)

A.   *Compilations of Instruments and Documents*

Buergenthal, T. and R. Norris. *Human Rights: The Inter-American System.* **5 vols. Dobbs Ferry, NY: Oceana Publications, 1982-.**

> Looseleaf, updated periodically. 5 volumes: Vol. 1 (Basic documents); Vol. 2 (Legislative History of the American Convention); Vol. 3 (Cases and Decisions); Vol. 4 (Cases and Decisions, Cont'd); Vol. 5 (Cases and Decisions, Cont'd and Inter-American System and Domestic Law). Brings together a wide variety of English-language documents, including the texts of instruments and basic documents, the legislative history of the American Convention, cases and decisions of the Inter-American Court of Human Rights and the Inter-American Commission on Human Rights, selected country reports of the Commission, and several Argentine and Costa Rican domestic court decisions of relevance to the American Convention. The organization and indexing of the volumes makes use of this collection difficult.

The Inter-American System: Treaties, Conventions and Other Documents: A Compilation. **A Compilation annotated by Garcia-Amador, F., Secretariat for Legal Affairs, General Secretariat, Organization of American States. London; New York: Oceana Publications, Inc., 1983. 505 pp.**

> A chronological compilation of the most important legal-political instruments of the Inter-American system from its inception to the present. It includes annotations. This volume is not confined to texts on human rights, but brings together a range of documents pertaining to the Inter-American system.

Inter-American Commission on Human Rights. *Annual Report — Inter-American Commission on Human Rights [year].* **Washington: General Secretariat, Organization of American States, 1975-.**

> The OAS statute and virtually all other OAS human rights documents and regulations are provided in this report.

Organization of American States. *Basic Documents Pertaining to Human Rights in the Inter-American System.* Washington, DC: General Secretariat, Organization of American States, 1988. 160 pp.

> Irregular. Published also in Spanish as *Manual de normas vigentes en materia de derechos humanos*. This is the official source containing the major instruments and regulations of the Inter-American human rights system, including the American Convention on Human Rights, the American Declaration of the Rights and Duties of Man, the statutes and regulations of the Inter-American Court of Human Rights and the Inter-American Commission on Human Rights, and the rules of procedure of the Inter-American Court of Human Rights. Gives a list of publications of the Court and the Commission, and a model complaint.

Zovatto, D., comp. *Los derechos humanos en el sistema interamericano:recopilacion de instrumentos basicos.* San Jose, Costa Rica: Instituto Interamericano de Derechos Humanos, 1987. 357 pp.

> Useful compilation in Spanish of treaties, declarations, statutes and regulations of Inter-American bodies. Also contains a convenient list of resolutions of the Organization of American States dealing with human rights. Contains a chronological index.

B.   Status of Ratifications of the American Convention on Human Rights

Human Rights Law Journal. Kehl am Rhein; Arlington, VA: N.P. Engel, 1980-.

> See annotations on pp. 50 and 92.

Inter-American Court of Human Rights. *Annual Report of the Inter-American Court of Human Rights.* Washington, DC: Inter-American Court of Human Rights, 1979-.

> An appendix shows the present status of signature/ratification of the American Convention and acceptance of the jurisdiction of the Court.

Lillich, R., ed. *International Human Rights Instruments.* 2d ed. Buffalo: W.S. Hein Co., 1990-.

> Lists parties to the American Convention, but the update of this looseleaf volume may lag by one year or more. See p. 86 for a full annotation.

C.   Commentaries and Legislative History of Inter-American Human Rights Instruments

Buergenthal, T. and R. Norris, eds. *Human Rights:The Inter-American System.* Vol. 2, *Legislative History of the American Convention.* Dobbs Ferry, NY: Oceana Publications, Inc. 1982-.

> Provides a detailed history of the American Declaration on the Rights and Duties of Man and the American Convention on Human Rights, as well as the human rights bodies of the Organization of American States.

Medina Quiroga, C. *The Battle of Human Rights: Gross, Systematic Violations and the Inter-American System*. Dordrecht; Boston: M. Nijhoff Publishers, 1988. 363 pp.

> Although its focus is on gross and systematic violations, the work provides a good account of the history and development of the Inter-American human rights system.

D.   *General Documents*

The following six volumes, covering the years indicated, contain the documents and information on the Organization of American States activities produced in each period. They also contain reports adopted by the Commission on individual cases in which petitioners alleged violations of human rights norms by member states of the OAS. Concludes with the 1987 OAS General Assembly resolutions concerning human rights.

> Inter-American Commission on Human Rights. *Inter-American Yearbook on Human Rights/Anuario Interamericano de Derechos Humanos 1968*. Washington, DC: General Secretariat of the Organization of American States, 1973. 428 pp.

> Inter-American Commission on Human Rights. *Inter-American Yearbook on Human Rights/Anuario Interamericano de Derechos Humanos 1969-70*. Washington, DC: General Secretariat of the Organization of American States, 1976. 547 pp.

> Inter-American Commission on Human Rights. *Inter-American Yearbook on Human Rights/Anuario Interamericano de Derechos Humanos 1985*. Washington, DC: General Secretariat of the Organization of American States, 1987. 917 pp.

> *Inter-American Yearbook of Human Rights/Anuario Interamericano de Derechos Humanos 1986*. Dordrecht;Boston;London: M. Nijhoff, 1988. 1051 pp.

> Inter-American Commission on Human Rights. *Inter-American Yearbook on Human Rights/Anuario Interamericano de Derechos Humanos, 1987*. London: M. Nijhoff, 1990. 500 pp.

> *Inter-American Yearbook on Human Rights/Anuario Interamericano de Derechos Humanos 1988*. Dordrecht; Boston; London: M. Nijhoff, 1991. 207 pp.

Organization of American States. General Assembly. *Indice tematico de las resoluciones de la Asamblea General, 1970-1982*. Washington, DC: Secretaria General de la Organizacion de los Estados Unidos, 1982. 33 pp.

> In Spanish. Subject index to OAS General Assembly resolutions.

Organization of American States. *Official Records*. Washington, DC: General Secretariat, Organization of American States, 1959-.

> Published annually since 1959. Lists documents of the eight organs of the OAS.

Organization of American States. Permanent Council. *Summary of the Decisions Taken at the Meetings and Texts of the Resolutions Approved.* Washington, DC: General Secretariat of the Organization of American States, OEA/Ser.G, 1971-.

> Official records of action taken at the OAS Permanent Council meetings. Continues Organization of American States. Council. *Decisions taken at the meetings of the Council of the Organization of American States* (1948-1970).

E.   *Inter-American Court of Human Rights*

1.   Texts of Decisions

Inter-American Court of Human Rights. *Series A — Judgments and Opinions.* San Jose, Costa Rica: Secretaria de la Corte, 1982-.

> Irregular. Provides the texts of the Court's several advisory opinions. Bilingual (Spanish/English).

Inter-American Court of Human Rights. *Series C — Decisions and Judgments.* San Jose, Costa Rica: Secretaria de la Corte, 1987-.

> Irregular. Provides opinions of cases decided under the Court's contentious jurisdiction. Bilingual (Spanish/English).

2.   Pleadings, Oral Arguments and Documents

Inter-American Court of Human Rights. *Series B — Pleadings, Oral Arguments and Documents.* San Jose, Costa Rica: Secretaria de la Corte, 1983-.

> Irregular. Bilingual (Spanish/English) texts of pleadings, briefs and other legal materials of the cases appearing in Series A.

Inter-American Court of Human Rights. *Series D.* (forthcoming).

> Will contain the principal documents of the judgments appearing in the C Series.

3.   General Resources and Documents

Davidson, S. *The Inter-American Court of Human Rights.* Aldershot, England; Brookfield, VT: Dartmouth Pub. Co. Ltd., 1992. 217 pp.

> Introductory treatise on the history, functions and jurisprudence of the Inter-American Court, with comparisons to the European Court of Human Rights, the International Court of Justice, and the Permanent Court of International Justice.

Inter-American Court of Human Rights. *Annual Report of the Inter-American Court of Human Rights to the General Assembly.* **Washington, DC: Inter-American Court of Human Rights, 1979-.**

> Contains a chapter on the origin, structure and competence of the court, and current membership. Provides a description of the activities of the Court. Appendices provide the texts of the Court's opinions, and the present status of signature/ratification of the American Convention and acceptance of the jurisdiction of the Court.

Inter-American Court of Human Rights. *Press Release.* **San Jose, Costa Rica: Inter-American Court of Human Rights, 1985-.**

> Irregular. Provides rapid information on recent judgments of the Court, on the dates and agenda of future sessions of the Court, on the current composition of the Court, and other activities.

F.   *Inter-American Commission on Human Rights*

Country Reports. **Washington, DC: General Secretariat, Organization of American States, 1979-.**

> The Commission issues reports on human rights in individual countries, whose titles are usually *Report on the Situation of Human Rights in [country name]/Informe Sobre la Situacion de los Derechos Humanos en [country name].* Perkins' research guide, cited below, lists the reports issued since 1980.

Inter-American Commission on Human Rights. *Archives, 1960-1984.* **Washington, DC: Organization of American States, 1986.**

> Microfiche collection which includes the *Commission Yearbook*, 1972-1982; reports of the work accomplished during its 1961-1975 sessions; *Annual Report*, 1970-1984; and reports on country conditions.

Inter-American Commission on Human Rights. *Ten Years of Activities, 1971-1981.* **Washington, DC: General Secretariat, Organization of American States, 1982. 403 pp.**

> This ten-year retrospective collection is available from the OAS as a sales publication.

Organization of American States. *Annual Report — Inter-American Commission on Human Rights [year].* **Washington, DC: General Secretariat, Organization of American States, 1975-.**

> Contains a general description of the activities of the Commission, including current membership. Provides accounts of on-site visits carried out, the texts of Commission reports on individual cases, and reports on the status of human rights in selected countries.

G.   Bibliographies

Perkins, S. "Latin American Human Rights Research 1980-1989: A Guide to Sources and a Bibliography." *Denver Journal of International Law & Policy* **19 (Fall 1990): 163-267.**

> A detailed guide and bibliography which focuses on legal materials. Good treatment of the human rights documents of the Organization of American States and the United Nations. Part V of the article is a bibliography of publications and articles on human rights in Latin America since 1980, arranged by region, by country and by topic. Part I of the article (Introduction) is an especially useful brief guide to Latin American legal materials generally.

Welch, T. *The Organization of American States: A Bibliography.* **Washington, DC: Columbus Memorial Library, Organization of American States, 1990. 87 pp.**

> Selected, annotated list of books and periodical articles treating the OAS, covering 1948-1989. Excludes official records and documents of the OAS. Title and subject index.

VII. The European Human Rights System

Strictly speaking, the European human rights system comprises those Council of Europe institutions responsible for supervising and enforcing human rights obligations of states under the European Convention on Human Rights. This section, however, also describes the human rights-related materials of two other institutions: (1) the "Helsinki Process," the documents and meetings of the Conference on Security and Cooperation in Europe (CSCE), and (2) the European Communities, historically not explicitly concerned with human rights, but whose activities necessarily affect human rights conditions in Europe and elsewhere.

A.   Council of Europe

The Council of Europe, established by western European states in 1949 and joined recently by Hungary, the Czech and Slovak Republics, and Poland, possesses three institutions directly concerned with supervising states parties compliance with the European Convention on Human Rights: the European Commission of Human Rights, the European Court of Human Rights, and the Committee of Ministers of the Council of Europe. The members of the Commission and the Court are elected by states but serve in their individual capacities. The Committee of Ministers is the political and executive arm of the Council of Europe. Its members are government officials of the member states.

Works providing a general introduction include the following:

> Gomien, D. *Short Guide to the European Convention on Human Rights.* Strasbourg: Council of Europe, 1991. 156p.

Robertson, A.H. and J.C. Merrils. *Human Rights in Europe*. 3d ed. Manchester, U.K.: Manchester University Press, 1993. 422 pp.

Four publications which review human rights activities of the Council of Europe, provide lists of publications, and summarize activity on cases include the following:

Council of Europe. Directorate of Human Rights. *Human Rights Information Sheet No. [#].* **Strasbourg: Council of Europe, 1978-.**

Irregularly published, these are substantial booklets which provide current information on cases, composition of the Court and Commission, on meetings and colloquies, new publications, activities of the Parliamentary Assembly, and other developments in the human rights system of the Council of Europe. Appendices contain texts of resolutions and recommendations of the Committee of Ministers and the Parliamentary Assembly, relevant resolutions of the European Parliament, and reports of colloquies.

Directorate of Human Rights. Human Rights Documentation Centre. *Documentation Sources in Human Rights.* **Strasbourg: Council of Europe, 1987. 38 pp.**

Irregular. These booklets are current catalogs of human-rights related publications of the Council of Europe. Publications listed include general documentation, reference books, Court judgments, Commission decisions on admissibility, Commission reports, resolutions of the Committee of Ministers, as well as other reports and studies.

Report on the Activities of the Council of Europe. **Strasbourg: Council of Europe, 1974-.**

Annual review of the activities of the Council of Europe, including a section on activities in the field of human rights.

Stock-Taking on the European Convention on Human Rights: A Periodic Note on the Concrete Results Achieved Under the Convention: the First Thirty Years: 1954-1984. **Strasbourg: European Commission of Human Rights, 1985. 333 pp.**

Provides a detailed survey of all of the cases handled in the European system, both inter-state and individual. Indicates which are considered significant. Summaries of individual cases in which a violation was found are organized by the type of violation. Cases in which a friendly settlement was achieved are listed, as are cases terminated in some other way. Both categories are arranged by issue raised under the Convention. Summaries of "cases of interest where no violation was established" are provided, as are "certain cases of special interest still pending." Annual supplements have been published since 1985. Every supplement covers the events of the year preceding publication.

Additional resources which give general information on Council of Europe activities include those listed below.

All-European Human Rights Yearbook. **Arlington, VA: N.P. Engel, 1991-.**

Annual. A new publication which intends to publish scholarly works from proceedings of international conferences, articles examining domestic and international human rights developments in Europe, and significant case law, and thereby strengthen human rights standards and implementation. The first volume provides the proceedings of a conference on the role of the Council of Europe, the CSCE and the European Communities in an all-European system of human rights protection.

Council of Europe. *Collection of Decisions of National Courts Relating to the European Convention on Human Rights.* **Strasbourg: Council of Europe, 1969-.**

Somewhat dated, but supplements bring series up to 1974. Provides summaries of Convention-related decisions of domestic courts of states parties to the European Convention.

Council of Europe. *Press Communique.* **Strasbourg: Council of Europe, 1985-.**

Irregular. Some issues are titled *Human Rights News*. Includes Resolutions of the Council of Europe Committee of Ministers and reports of cases before the European Commission of Human Rights and the European Court of Human Rights.

European Commission of Human Rights. *European Human Rights Reports.* **London: The European Law Centre Ltd., 1979-.**

Bimonthly. Provides summaries and extracts of cases. Includes all judgments of the European Court of Human Rights, selected decisions of the European Commission of Human Rights and summaries of other resolutions and settlements. Each issue is indexed by subject and by article of the European Convention on Human Rights. Court judgments are indexed by Series A number. Annual indices are also available: alphabetical, numerical, chronological, subject, and convention text.

Online: Contents of reporter are online in LEXIS (in the CASES file in the EURCOM library) from November 1960 to date. Good for quick access to recent decisions.

Human Rights Files. **Strasbourg: Council of Europe, 1978-.**

Each file deals with a particular aspect of human rights protection in relation to the European Convention on Human Rights. Below are the issues currently available.

No. 1. *Introduction to the European Convention on Human Rights: The Rights Secured and the Protection Machinery.* **Strasbourg: Council of Europe, 1978. 8 pp.**

Very basic, brief introduction to the Convention.

No. 2. *The Presentation of an Application before the European Commission of Human Rights.* Strasbourg: Council of Europe, 1978. 19 pp.

A practical guide, based on decisions of the European Commission on procedural questions.

No. 3. *Outline of the Position of the Individual Applicant before the European Court of Human Rights.* Strasbourg: Council of Europe, 1978. 8 pp.

Summarizes, up to 1978, the evolution of the position of the individual applicant before the European Court of Human Rights.

No. 4. *The Right to Liberty and the Rights of Persons Deprived of Their Liberty as Guaranteed by Article 5 of the European Convention on Human Rights.* Strasbourg: Council of Europe, 1981. 22 pp.

Summarizes the European Court's interpretation of Article 5, with respect to deprivation of liberty and conditions of detention.

No. 5. *Conditions of Detention and the European Convention on Human Rights and Fundamental Freedoms.* Strasbourg: Council of Europe, 1981. 38 pp.

Outlines the case law of the Court and Commission with respect to conditions of detention.

No. 6. Mendelson, M. *The Impact of European Community Law on the Implementation of the European Convention on Human Rights.* Strasbourg: Council of Europe, 1984. 43 pp.

Discusses (1) the legal consequences under the Convention if action is taken by a Community institution or member state in pursuance of a rule of Community law, but contrary to the Convention, and (2) the extent to which the interpretation of provisions in a Community instrument influences the interpretation of similar terms or the development of similar concepts under the Convention.

No. 7. Drzemczewski, A. *The Right to Respect for Private and Family Life, Home and Correspondence.* Strasbourg: Council of Europe, 1984. 29 pp.

Surveys the case law interpreting Article 8 of the European Convention on Human Rights.

No. 8. Drzemczewski, A. *The Position of Aliens in Relation to the European Convention on Human Rights.* Strasbourg: Council of Europe, 1985. 50 pp.

Review of historical background and Strasbourg case law on the rights of aliens under the Convention.

No. 9. Plender, R. *Problems Raised by Certain Aspects of the Present Situation of Refugees from the Standpoint of the European Convention on Human Rights.* **Strasbourg: Council of Europe, 1984. 38 pp.**

Argues that the European Convention on Human Rights is an indispensable and under-employed instrument for the protection of refugees in Western Europe.

No. 10. Boucaud, P. *The Council of Europe and Child Welfare: The Need for a European Convention on Children's Rights.* **Strasbourg: Council of Europe, 1989. 67 pp.**

Published before the adoption of the U.N. Convention on the Rights of the Child, this brochure reviews the scattered texts prepared by the Council of Europe to protect specific aspects of the life of children, and the decisions of the European Commission and the case law of the European Court of Human Rights.

No. 11. Sermet, L. *The European Convention on Human Rights and Property Rights.* **Strasbourg: Council of Europe, 1992. 55 pp.**

Analyzes property rights under the Convention, examining the issues of the definition of "possession," who can claim to be the victim of interference with his or her property (types of natural or legal persons), what constitutes interference with property, what form of control is exercised by Convention organs, and what forms of redress are available.

Yearbook of the European Convention on Human Rights/Annuaire de la Convention Europeenne des Droits de l'Homme. **The Hague: M. Nijhoff, 1960-.**

Annual in French and English. Best single source of information on the European human rights system. Major drawback is the 4-5-year time lag in publication. New format since Volume 28. Part 1 contains basic texts and information. Part 2 provides the case-law of the Commission, summaries of the judgments of the Court, and activities and Decisions of the Committee of Ministers. Part 3 provides texts of laws of member states relating to the Convention, extracts of decisions of national courts which refer to the Convention, and citations to motions and questions raised in the European Parliament with reference to the Convention. A bibliography and index are also provided.

1.   Compilations of Instruments

Council of Europe. *European Convention on Human Rights, Collected Texts.* **Strasbourg: Council of Europe, 1963-1986; Dordrecht; Boston: M. Nijhoff, 1987-.**

In French and English. Designed to give practicing lawyers and others clear and up-to-date information on all the instruments of the European human rights system, and on the texts relating to Convention bodies. Contains the texts of the Convention, eight Protocols, the Rules of Procedure of the Commission, the Rules of Court, the Rules of Procedure of the Committee of Ministers relating to the application of Articles 32 and 54 of the Convention, the Agreement on Persons participating in procedures before the

European Court and Commission of Human Rights and texts of declarations and reservations of signatory states. Provides the status of signatures and ratifications as well as declarations and reservations.

Miehsler, H. and H. Petzold, eds. *European Convention on Human Rights, Text and Documents.* **2 vols. Koln: Heymann, 1982.**

Vol. 1 contains Council of Europe treaties concerned with human rights, including the European Social Charter, and the subsequent rules of procedure adopted by the review bodies. Also contains the basic texts of the United Nations human rights system.

2.   Status of Instruments

Human Rights Law Journal. **Kehl am Rhein; Arlington, VA: N.P. Engel, 1980-.**

See annotations, pp. 50 and 92.

Minutes of the Plenary Session of the European Commission of Human Rights. **Strasbourg: Council of Europe, European Commission of Human Rights, 1954-.**

Published as booklets. Good sources for current status of instruments. Section on application of the European Convention on Human Rights provides information on deposit of instruments of ratification, signature, and entry into force of protocols. Texts of declarations and reservations to instruments are given in appendices.

Yearbook of the European Convention on Human Rights/Annuaire de la Convention Europeenne des droits de l'Homme. **The Hague: M. Nijhoff, 1960-.**

Annual. Comprehensive information on the status of ratifications, signatures, reservations, declarations; however, volumes appear with a substantial time lag.

3.   Commentaries and Drafting History

Council of Europe. *Collected Edition of the "Travaux Preparatoires" of the European Convention on Human Rights.* **8 vols. The Hague; Boston: M. Nijhoff, 1975-1985.**

In French and English. Contains the various documents that were used during the drafting of the European Convention on Human Rights and the first Protocol and reports of discussions in the Consultative Assembly of the Council of Europe and its Committee on Legal and Administrative Questions, and in the Committee of Ministers and certain of its committees of experts. This material was published during 1961-64 in an edition which was confidential and only for the use of governments, the European Commission of Human Rights and the European Court of Human Rights.

Vols. I and II contain the work of the Consultative Assembly in 1949; Vol. III contains the work of the Committee of Experts in 1950; Vol. IV, that of the Conference of Senior Officials in the same year; Vols. V and VI recount the discussions of the Committee of Ministers and of the Assembly in 1950; Vol. VII takes the reader down to the signature of the Convention in November 1950 and the beginning of the work on the First Protocol; Vol. VIII completes the account of the drafting of the Protocol and contains the general index.

Fawcett, J. *Application of the European Convention on Human Rights.* **Oxford: Clarendon Press; New York: Oxford University Press, 1987. 444 pp.**

Article-by-article and phrase-by-phrase commentary of the European Convention and its First, Fourth and Sixth Protocols, based on the reports and decisions of the Court and the European Commission.

Robertson, A.H. and J.C. Merrils. *Human Rights in Europe.* **3d ed. Manchester, U.K.: Manchester University Press, 1993. 422 pp.**

The third edition is substantially rewritten and updated. After an historical introduction, the authors provide a detailed analysis of the case law on the rights protected by the Convention and its Protocols. They then review the institutions responsible for supervising the Convention: the Commission and Court of Human Rights and the Committee of Ministers of the Council of Europe. Finally, they examine the relations between the Convention and other human rights arrangements, such as the new CSCE mechanism.

4.   European Commission of Human Rights

Ercman, S. *Guide to Case Law.* **Wien: Wilhelm Braumuller, 1981. 528 pp.**

Includes published decisions and reports of the Commission, European Court of Human Rights judgments, and sources of national court decisions. Arranged by article of the Convention. Covers case law up to 1979.

European Commission of Human Rights. *Collection of Decisions of the European Commission of Human Rights.* **46 vols. Strasbourg: Council of Europe, European Commission of Human Rights, 1960-1974.**

Contains a selection of important decisions between 1960 and 1974, in their original language only.

European Commission of Human Rights. *Collection of Decisions: Summary of Decisions Published in Volumes 1-30.* **Strasbourg: Council of Europe, European Commission of Human Rights, 1981. 472 pp.**

French and English. Brief summaries of the Decisions of the Commission from 1955-1970 are arranged according to articles, paragraphs and sub-paragraphs of the Convention and its Protocols. Citations to the relevant volume of the *Collection of Decisions* or to the *Yearbook* are provided.

European Commission of Human Rights. *Decisions and Reports.* **Strasbourg: Council of Europe, European Commission of Human Rights, 1975-.**

French and English. This series replaces *Collection of Decisions*. Includes complete texts or extracts from the "most significant" decisions on the admissibility of applications, as well as the Commission's Reports where they have been made public, except on cases which have been brought before the European Court of Human Rights (these Reports are published by the Court itself, in *Series B: Pleadings, Oral Arguments, Documents of the Court*).

European Commission of Human Rights. *Decisions and Reports: Summaries and Indexes. Volumes 1-20.* **Strasbourg: Council of Europe, European Commission of Human Rights, 1981. 333 pp.**

French and English. Brief summaries of Commission decisions between 1973-1980 are arranged according to European Convention article, paragraph, sub-paragraph, and key concept. Indices provide access by decision number, by name of applicant, by article and phrase within article, and by key word.

European Commission of Human Rights. *Minutes of the Plenary Session of the European Commission of Human Rights.* **Strasbourg: Council of Europe, European Commission of Human Rights, 1963-.**

These are good sources for information on the current status of cases and instruments. Published as booklets, each covering a session of several days, they contain the agenda for that session, briefly describe cases on admissibility and on the merits heard before the Commission, and provide the names of persons representing the Government and the applicant. Notes on the cases which describe their facts and status are given in the appendices.

A section on cases pending before the Commission and a section on cases pending before the Court provide recent developments. The section on the state of application of the European Convention on Human Rights provides information on deposit of instruments of ratification, signature, entry into force of protocols. Texts of declarations and reservations to instruments are given in appendices.

European Commission of Human Rights. *Survey of Activities and Statistics [year].* **Strasbourg: Council of Europe, European Commission of Human Rights, 1983-.**

Published annually as a mimeographed document. Reviews the activities of the Commission for the year indicated and includes statistics on Commission decisions and hearings. Lists citations.

5.   European Court of Human Rights

(a)   Texts of Judgments

European Court of Human Rights. *Judgments.* **Strasbourg: Council of Europe, 1960-.**

Irregular. Mimeographed version of judgments, produced rather quickly.

European Court of Human Rights. *Publications of the European Court of Human Rights. Series A, Judgments and Decisions.* **Strasbourg: Greffe de la Cour, Conseil de l'Europe, 1961-.**

Irregular. Official version of judgments, which first appear as mimeographed documents. (See publication cited above.)

European Court of Human Rights. *Publications of the European Court of Human Rights. Series B, Pleadings, Oral Arguments and Documents.* **Strasbourg: Greffe de la Cour, Conseil de l'Europe, 1962-.**

Irregular. Texts of pleadings and arguments before the Court. Appears with a substantial time lag.

Human Rights Law Journal. **Kehl am Rhein; Arlington, VA: N.P. Engel, 1980-.**

Monthly. Provides summaries or full texts of Court decisions. For full annotations, see pp. 50 and 92.

(b)   *Digests of Court Decisions*

Berger, V. *Case Law of the European Court of Human Rights.* **Vol. 1. 1960-1987. Dublin: Round Hall Press, 1989. 478 pp.**

Contains summaries of facts and law in each decision of the Court up to the end of 1987, arranged chronologically. Summaries are followed by a "summary bibliography" of books and articles dealing with the case, together with a note of the changes effected in the national law and procedure resulting from the decision. 110 cases are listed by name in the table of contents; there is a subject index, a table of cases, and an index of articles of the European Convention.

British Institute of Human Rights. *Human Rights Case Digest.* **London: British Institute of Human Rights, 1990-.**

Bimonthly. Summarizes decisions by the European Court of Human Rights and the European Commission of Human Rights as well as the texts of decisions of the Committee of Ministers. Contains summaries of Court judgments, decisions on admissibility by the Commission, and cases referred to the Court. Contains two indices: one of cases by name; the other by applicable article of the Convention.

British Year Book of International Law. **London: H. Frowde, 1920-.**

Annual. Contains a section with headnoted summaries of the judgments of the European Court of Human Rights.

Council of Europe. *Digest of Strasbourg Case Law Relating to the European Convention on Human Rights.* Koln: Heymanns, 1984-.

> Annual. An excellent index to decisions of the Court, covering the period 1955-1982. Provides relevant extracts of decisions (published and unpublished) and reports of the Commission of Human Rights, and of the Court. Vol. 6 is a general index to the first five volumes, which cover the Convention and its Protocols. Case law is analyzed and indexed according to each article of the Convention, and within each article according to individual phrases. Contains a subject index.

> Two looseleaf updates, covering Articles 1-6 are listed below. Both of the updates cover judgments of the Court from 1983 to the end of 1986, Opinions of the Commission from June 1982 to the end of 1985, and Decisions of the Commission from 1982 up to the end of 1984.

> Council of Europe. *Digest of Strasbourg Case Law Relating to the European Convention on Human Rights.* Update to Vol. 1 (Articles 1-5). Koln: Heymanns, 1988.

> Council of Europe. *Digest of Strasbourg Case-Law Relating to the European Convention on Human Rights.* Update to Vol. 2 (Article 6). Koln: Heymanns, 1989.

Ercman, S. *Guide to Case Law.* Wien: Wilhelm Braumuller, 1981. 528 pp.

> See p. 118 for annotation.

Vangeenberghe, F., ed. *Digest of Case Law Relating to the European Convention on Human Rights 1955-1967.* Heule, Belgium: Editions Administrative U.G.A., S.A., 1970. 523 pp.

> English and French. Dated, but still of some relevance for early period of the Convention.

6.   Committee of Ministers

Council of Europe, Committee of Ministers. *Collection of Recommendations, Resolutions and Declarations of the Committee of Ministers Concerning Human Rights, 1949-1987.* Strasbourg: Council of Europe, 1989. 214 pp.

> Presents in one volume the recommendations, resolutions and declarations of the Committee of Ministers which are the most relevant to the field of human rights. These provide a joint expression of the opinions of member states on matters relating to human rights from 1949 to 1987.

Council of Europe, Committee of Ministers. *Collection of Resolutions Adopted by the Committee of Ministers in Application of Article 32 and 54 of the European Convention for the Protection of Human Rights and Fundamental Freedoms, 1959-1983.* **Strasbourg: Council of Europe, 1984. 148 pp.**

> These collections contain the Committee of Ministers' Resolutions for cases that have not been referred to the European Court of Human Rights (Article 32), and for those made in supervision of the execution of a judgment of the Court (Article 54). Two supplements have been published: for 1984-85 (1986), and for 1986-87 (1989).

Miehsler, H. and H. Petzold, eds. *European Convention on Human Rights, Text and Documents.* **2 vols. Koln: Heymanns, 1982.**

> Volume 2 contains the decisions taken by the Committee of Ministers under Articles 32 and 54 of the European Convention, along with recommendations and resolutions of the Parliamentary Assembly of the Council of Europe, other documents, and statistics.

B. *European Communities*

The European Communities, an essentially economic structure based on the 1957 Treaty of Rome, is increasingly involved with human rights through the European Court of Justice and the European Parliament. EC law has direct effect in EC member states and prevails over inconsistent domestic law.

Bulletin of the European Communities. **Brussels: Secretariat General of the Commission, 1968-.**

> A monthly publication which reports on the activities of the Council and Commission. In addition to discussing legislation or proposals adopted or under consideration, there is usually information about the purpose of acts and citations to related documents such as Commission proposals, opinions of various bodies of the EC, and references to the *Official Journal* (OJ). (See description below.) Each issue is indexed and an annual index is published in the first issue of the following year. There is usually a nine-month time lag in publication of the issues.

Commission Documents. **Luxembourg: Office for Official Publications of the European Communities, 1967-.**

> Commission Documents, known as COM DOCS, are an excellent place to start EC research. These documents are the vehicle through which the Commission communicates with the Council, containing all proposals for new legislation, new policy initiatives and reports on actions. These documents are indexed in the *Catalogue of Documents*, now entitled *Documents* and published monthly with an annual cumulation.

Directory of Community Legislation in Force and Other Acts of the Community Institutions. **5th ed. (Position as of 1 Jan. 1984). Luxembourg: Office for Official Publications of the European Communities, 1984-.**

> Lists all legislation in force from 1952 to the present. The main volume lists legislation chronologically under broad subject headings. Under the principal citation, all modifications and the OJ citation are listed. (See below for a description of the *Official Journal*.)

Europe. **Brussels: Agence Europe, 1952-.**

> This daily bulletin is regularly consulted by EC functionaries in Brussels and others who want to keep current. It includes news of internal institutional developments and political events as well as articles on current topics of interest to the EC. It is an excellent way to track proposed legislation.

> *Online.* This publication is available on LEXIS in WORLD;TXTWE.

European Union - the Human Rights Challenge. **3 vols. Baden-Baden: Nomos Verlagsgesellschaft, 1991.**

> For an overview of human rights issues in the European Community, this is an excellent three-volume treatise which deals with most major issues. Vol. 1: Clapham, A. *Human Rights and the European Community: A Critical Overview.* 1991. Vol 2: Cassese, A., et al. *Human Rights and the European Community: Methods of Protection.* 1991. Vol. 3: Cassese, A., et al. *Human Rights and the European Community: The Substantive Law.* 1991.

General Report on the Activities of the Communities. **Brussels: The Commission, 1968-.**

> The annual required report of the European Commission to the Parliament. It gives a concise outline of the major actions, policy developments and activities of the year. There is usually a section dealing with human rights.

Official Journal of the European Communities. **Luxembourg: Office for Official Publications of the European Communities, 1973-.**

> The *Official Journal* (OJ) contains binding and non-binding legal acts of the EC. It is divided into four parts. For legal research the two most important sections are the L Series and the C Series. The L Series contains the regulations and directives adopted by the Commission and the Council. The C Series contains the resolutions of the Council, communications and notices of the Commission on such topics as proposals for legislation, and Court decisions.

> *Online.* CELEX is the full text, online version of the L series of the *Official Journal* and also offers bibliographic access to the C Series. In LEXIS this database is called ECLAW; in WESTLAW it is CELEX-LEG.

SCAD Bulletin. **Bruxelles: CECA; Washington, DC: European Community Informa-tion Service (distributor), 1985-.**

> This is the weekly paper edition of the SCAD databank which gives bibliographic references to the main Community acts, the publications of the European institutions, and articles from periodicals. (The Commission Library reviews over 1200 periodical titles for inclusion in this index.) References are broken down into 28 subject chapters and are then divided according to document type—Community instruments, official publications and documents, articles from periodicals dealing with the work of the Community and statements and opinions from industry. There is an author index and a keyword index (in French only). It is the most comprehensive index available to materials from the EC.

> *Online.* SCAD is available online through the EC but is not now offered by any commercial service.

C.   Helsinki Process

The "Helsinki Accords," the 1975 Final Act of the Conference on Security and Coopera-tion in Europe, contain human rights-related undertakings which have served as the basis for ongoing political dialogue and debate among participating states.

1.   Texts of Instruments

The text of the Final Act of the Conference on Security and Cooperation in Europe, signed in Helsinki in 1975, is found in *Department of State Bulletin* 73 (1975): 323, and *International Legal Materials* 14 (1975): 1292. (For a good source of human rights reports, the researcher should turn to Helsinki Watch, which has published numerous reports on human rights conditions in countries which have signed the Helsinki Final Act. The address is listed above, under Human Rights Watch, at p. 68.)

Barberini, G. *Codice della Conferenza sulla Sicurezza e la Cooperazione in Europa/* **C.S.C.E.** *Documents.* **Napoli: Edizion Scientifiche Italiane, 1990. 853 pp.**

> Bilingual (Italian and English). Contains the texts of the major documents: the Helsinki Final Act, the concluding documents of the Belgrade, Madrid, and Vienna conferences, reports of other meetings, collation of texts, and the rules of procedure of the CSCE. An appendix contains the major U.N. human rights instruments. Has a subject index.

Bloed, A., ed. *From Helsinki to Vienna: Basic Documents of the Helsinki Process.* **Dordrecht; Boston: M. Nijhoff, 1990. 285 pp.**

> The first publication in English of all of the substantive documents adopted by meetings in the framework of the Conference on Security and Cooperation in Europe until Spring 1990. Documents are preceded by a survey of the basic features of the Conference and the Helsinki process.

Kavass, I., et al., eds. *Human Rights, European Politics, and the Helsinki Accord: The Documentary Evolution of the Conference on Security and Cooperation in Europe, 1973-1975.* 6 vols. **Buffalo, NY: W.S. Hein, 1981.**

Compilation of human rights documents produced during the Helsinki Conference, July 1973-August 1975.

Kavass, I., and J. Granier, eds. *Human Rights, The Helsinki Accords and the United States Selected Executive and Congressional Documents.* **Buffalo, NY: W.S. Hein, 1982-.**

Annual. Series 1 reproduces the annual human rights reports submitted to Congress by the U.S. Department of State for the years 1976-1986. Series 2 reprints the semiannual reports by the President to the U.S. Commission on Security and Cooperation in Europe. Series 3 provides information on hearings before the Commission related to "Basket III" rights, and other Congressional hearings and prints.

2.   Commission on Security and Cooperation in Europe (CSCE)

A joint United States Congressional-Executive body set up the Commission on Security and Cooperation in Europe by statute in 1976 with the purpose of monitoring compliance with the Helsinki Final Act, the Commission has several publications: the *Activities Report*, 95th to 99th Congress; *Annual Report*, starting in 1987; fifteen special hearings on Basket III between 1977 and 1981; some 37 hearings and special reports on the implementation of the Helsinki Accords between 1980 and 1987, and numerous other reports, research articles and monographs. CSCE documents are available from the Commission on request (U.S. Congress, Washington, DC 20515).

A note to the researcher: the Commission is distinct from the Conference on Security and Cooperation in Europe (the "Helsinki Conference"), although both have the same acronym.

U. S. Congress. Commission on Security and Cooperation in Europe. *Annual Report of the Commission on Security and Cooperation in Europe for the Period Covering [year]: A Report to Congress.* **Washington, DC: The Commission, 1987-.**

Issued as a committee print, the report reviews the activities of the Commission, including CSCE follow-up activities, Commission delegations, and public hearings. A list of the reports and publications produced by the Commission during the relevant year is provided. Appendices give authorizing legislation, present and former Commission members, staff, and a list of meetings after the Vienna Conference.

U.S. Congress. Commission on Security and Cooperation in Europe. *CSCE Digest.* **Washington, DC: The Commission, 1977-.**

Monthly current awareness newsletter with information on activities of the Commission. Lists recent Commission publications.

3.   Research Guide

Louis-Jacques, L., and S. Nevin. *Human Rights in the Soviet Union and Eastern Europe: A Research Guide and Bibliography.* s.l.: s.n., 1989. 61 pp.

Good on the Helsinki Final Act and its literature. See p. 38 for a full annotation.

D.   *Inter-Parliamentary Union*

Outline of the Procedure in Force for the Examination of Communications Concerning Violations of the Human Rights of Parliamentarians. **Geneva: Inter-Parliamentary Union, 1985. 8 pp.**

An 8-page mimeo document with relevant resolutions and other documents attached as annexes.

Report of the Committee on the Human Rights of Parliamentarians. **[#] Interparliamentary Conference. Geneva: Inter-Parliamentary Union.**

Contains reports of cases submitted to the Inter-Parliamentary Council.

VIII.   Organization of African Unity (OAU)

A.   *Compilations of Instruments and Documents*

Hamalengwa, M., C. Flinterman and E. Dankwa, comps. *The International Law of Human Rights in Africa: Basic Documents and Annotated Bibliography.* **Dordrecht; Boston: M. Nijhoff, 1988. 427 pp.**

Provides basic documents and an annotated bibliography.

U.N. Centre for Human Rights. *The African Charter on Human and Peoples' Rights.* **New York: U.N. Centre for Human Rights, HR/PUB/09/1, 1990. 51 pp.**

Contains the text of the African Charter and the Rules of Procedure of the African Commission on Human and Peoples' Rights. An annex lists countries which have signed, ratified, or acceded to the African Charter.

B.   *Books, Periodicals and Articles*

African Commission on Human and Peoples' Rights. *Review of the African Commission on Human and Peoples' Rights.* **Banjul, The Gambia: OAU, 1991-.**

Scholarly articles in French and English; documentation section provides the text of the Convention and French and English versions of the activity report on the African Commission session. An annex gives a list of states parties, with dates of signature, ratification and deposit.

Organization of African Unity. African Commission on Human and Peoples' Rights. *Conference on the African Commission on Human and Peoples' Rights. June 24-26, 1991.* **New York: The Fund For Peace, 1991. 68 pp.**

Conference proceedings on the work of the Commission, human rights NGOs, states compliance with the African Charter, and U. S. human rights policy toward Africa.

Peter, C. *Human Rights in Africa: A Comparative Study of the African Human and Peoples' Rights Charter and the New Tanzanian Bill of Rights.* **NY: Greenwood, 1990. 145 pp.**

Historical background and comparison of the two instruments in title. Treats peoples' rights, legal enforcement mechanisms of the two instruments, and discusses the composition of the African Commission on Human and Peoples' Rights. Table of statutes and cases, bibliography and subject index included.

CHAPTER FOUR.
SELECTED HUMAN RIGHTS TOPICS, FIELDS AND THEMES

The materials discussed in this chaper are diverse. In order to make them accessible, they are organized by theme, by particular kinds of rights, and by particular groups. This chapter is not intended as a bibliography, but rather as an introductory guide to specific topics. Books and articles dealing with the substance of a right or issue appear first, and are followed by bibliographies or guides.

I.   Non-Western Traditions and Human Rights

An-Na'im, A. ed. *Human Rights in Cross-Cultural Perspectives: A Quest for Consensus*. Philadelphia: University of Pennsylvania Press, 1992. 479 pp.

Asked to address problems of the cultural legitimacy of international standards of human rights, the authors of several essays examine different ideological and cultural traditions, proposing reinterpretations to overcome the tensions and conflicts between those traditions and current international standards of human rights. Other essays present the views and priorities of specific indigenous perspectives in relation to national and international human rights regimes.

An-Na'im, A. *Toward an Islamic Reformation: Civil Liberties, Human Rights, and International Law*. Syracuse, NY: Syracuse University Press, 1990. 253 pp.

Based on the Meccan period of Muhammad's teachings, this work argues for an alternative intellectual foundation for a transformed Islamic law that will be appropriate for modern times.

An-Na'im, A. and F. Deng, eds. *Human Rights in Africa: Cross-Cultural Perspectives*. Washington, DC: The Brookings Institution, 1990. 399 pp.

Especially relevant are Howard, R. "Group versus Individual Identity in the African Debate on Human Rights," pp. 159-183; Donnelly, J. "Human Rights and Western Liberalism," pp. 31-55; and An-Na'im and Deng. "Introduction," pp. 1-11.

Blaustein, A., R. Clark, and J. Sigler, eds. *Human Rights Sourcebook*. New York: Paragon House Publishers, 1987. 970 pp.

Includes text of the Islamic Declaration of Human Rights. See p. 85 for full annotation.

Donnelly, J. *Universal Human Rights in Theory and Practice*. Ithaca: Cornell University Press, 1989. 295 pp.

Especially helpful are chapters 3, 4, 6 and 7.

Howard, R. *Human Rights in Commonwealth Africa*. Totowa, NJ: Rowman & Littlefield, 1986. 250 pp.

> See especially Chapter 2.

Lapeyre, A., F. de Tinguy and K. Vasak, eds. *Les Dimensions Universelles des Droits de l'Homme*. Bruxelles: Bruylant, 1990. 318 pp.

> In French. Contains several articles on human rights and Islam, Buddhism, Hinduism, and Christianity. Contains articles on "the Asiatic approach to human rights," "the foundations of human rights in Africa," "the Chinese approach to human rights," and "the socialist conception of human rights."

Mayer, A. *Islam and Human Rights: Tradition and Politics*. Boulder, CO: Westview Press, 1991. 258 pp.

> A comparative study of civil and political rights formulations which purport to embody Islamic principles. Deals well with issues of cultural relativism and universality from a universalist position. Based on case studies of Islamization in Pakistan, Sudan and Iran.

Schirmer, J., A. Renteln and L. Wiseberg. "Bibliography on Human Rights and Anthropology." In *Human Rights and Anthropology*, edited by T. Downing and G. Kushner, 121-200. Cambridge, MA: Cultural Survival, 1988.

> First attempt to bring together the dispersed literature on the anthropology of human rights. Unannotated, subject arrangement, limited primarily to works in English. See p. 162 for full annotation.

II.   Economic, Social and Cultural Rights

This section supplements the above section on the International Covenant on Economic, Social and Cultural Rights (Chapter Three, Section II.E.2).

A.   *General Works*

Alston, P. "The United Nations' Specialized Agencies and Implementation of the International Covenant on Economic, Social and Cultural Rights." *Columbia Journal of Transnational Law* 18 (1979): 79-118.

> Analyzes potential significance of entry into force of the International Covenant on Economic, Social and Cultural Rights, as well as role of four agencies in its implementation: the International Labour Organisation, the World Health Organization, the United Nations Educational, Scientific and Cultural Organization, and the Food and Agricultural Organization.

Alston, P. and G. Quinn. "The Nature and Scope of States Parties' Obligations under the International Covenant on Economic, Social and Cultural Rights." *Human Rights Quarterly* **9 (May 1987): 156-229.**

A suggested guide to the interpretation of the Covenant.

Eide, A. "Realization of Social and Economic Rights and the Minimum Threshold Approach." *Human Rights Law Journal* **10 (Winter-Spring 1989): 35-51.**

Analyzes the nature of and challenges to social and economic rights, and different possible approaches; also discusses states' obligations to respect the rights of other states to shared resources. Includes analysis of the right to food. Makes brief programmatic recommendations. See p. 134 for additional information.

Ganji, M. Special Rapporteur of the Commission on Human Rights. *The Realization of Economic, Social and Cultural Rights: Problems, Policies, Progress.* **New York: United Nations, E/CN.4/1131/Rev. 1, 1975. 326 pp.**

Divided into sections: national norms and standards; less developed countries; Socialist countries of eastern Europe; developed market-economy countries; international action for the protection and promotion of economic, social and cultural rights; and observations, conclusions and recommendations. Includes extensive tables, figures and maps. Emphasis placed on the countries of Africa, Asia and Latin America and the differing requirements of those countries for the attainment of economic, social and cultural rights.

Harris, D. *The European Social Charter.* **Charlottesville, VA: University Press of Virginia, 1984. 345 pp.**

Analysis focuses on labor laws and legislation, and social legislation in Europe. Discusses procedural aspects of international law.

Jacobs, F.G. "The Extension of the European Convention on Human Rights to Include Economic, Social and Cultural Rights." *Human Rights Review* **3 (Autumn 1978): 166-178.**

Study prepared for the Legal Affairs Committee of the Council of Europe Parliamentary Assembly for the Council's discussion. Analyzes the distinctions between rights and the arguments for and against extending the European Convention to include economic, social and cultural rights. Focuses on rights connected with employment; rights connected with health, social security and social welfare; educational and social rights; and rights connected with the environment.

"Limburg Principles on the Implementation of the International Covenant of Economic, Social and Cultural Rights." *Human Rights Quarterly* **9 (May 1987): 122-135.**

Statement on the current state of international law on economic, social and cultural rights by 29 international law experts who met to consider the implementation of the International Covenant of Economic, Social and Cultural Rights (Maastricht, the Netherlands, June 2-6, 1986).

Matscher, F., ed. *The Implementation of Economic and Social Rights: National, International and Comparative Perspectives.* **Kehl am Rhein; Arlington, VA: N.P. Engel, 1991. 517 pp.**

Series of essays, in English, German, and French, on implementation of economic and social rights in different types of legal systems and regions, and under different international organizations, such as the United Nations as a whole, and the International Labour Organisation.

Mower, A. G. *International Cooperation for Social Justice: Global and Regional Protection of Economic Social Rights.* **Westport, CT: Greenwood Press, 1985. 271 pp.**

Studies the efforts to protect economic and social rights at the global and regional levels. Focuses on the International Covenant on Economic, Social, and Cultural Rights and the the European Social Charter. Examines their origins, contents and implementation systems. Also explores the work of the International Labour Organisation and other specialized agencies .

Scott, C. "The Interdependence and Permeability of Human Rights Norms: Towards a Partial Fusion of the International Covenants on Human Rights." *Osgoode Hall Law Journal* **27 (Winter 1989): 769-878.**

Examines the extent to which human rights norms in the International Covenant on Economic, Social and Cultural Rights "permeate" the International Covenant on Civil and Political Rights (ICCPR), thereby subjecting them to the individual petition procedure under the ICCPR's Optional Protocol. Discusses conception of interdependence between rights and analyzes specific decisions by the Human Rights Committee.

Trubek, D. "Economic, Social and Cultural Rights in the Third World: Human Rights Law and Human Needs Programs." Chapter 6 in *Human Rights in International Law,* **edited by T. Meron. Oxford: Clarendon Press; New York: Oxford University Press, 1984.**

Argues that concept of minimum social welfare, or "programmatic obligations," is the basis for economic, social and cultural rights. Examines rights in existing international law and questions of implementation. Addresses questions of development doctrine. Focuses exclusively on the problems of realizing welfare obligations in the third world.

Turk, D. Special Rapporteur of the Sub-Commission on the Prevention of Discrimination and Protection of Minorities, "The Realization of Economic, Social and Cultural Rights," Final Report: UN doc. E/CN.4/Sub.2/1992/16.

This report was preceded by the following additional reports which are not subsumed by the final report: preliminary report: UN doc. E/CN.4/Sub.2/1989/19; first progress report: UN doc./CN.4/Sub.2/1990/19; and second progress report: UN doc. E/CN.4/Sub.2/1991/17.

U.N. Secretary-General. "Preliminary Study of Issues Relating to The Realization of Economic, Social and Cultural Rights." UN doc. E/CN.4/988 (1969). 80 pp.

Discusses development policies; safeguards for human rights; progressive implementation of economic, social and cultural rights; determination of priorities; prohibition of discrimination; role of public authorities and popular participation; national measures; international instruments; and procedures providing international review measures. Annex discusses international action and methods in regard to realization of economic, social and cultural rights.

B.   Right to Food

1.   Compilations of Instruments

Tomasevski, K., comp. *The Right to Food: Guide Through Applicable International Law.* Dordrecht; Boston: M. Nijhoff, 1987. 387 pp.

Contains excerpts from applicable international instruments which bear on the right to food, a chronological list of international instruments related to the right to food, and information on the legal nature and implementation of selected international instruments.

2.   Books, Articles and Journals

Alston, P. and K. Tomasevski, eds. *The Right to Food.* Boston: M. Nijhoff; Utrecht: Stichtung Studie- en Informatiecentrum Mensenrechten, 1984. 229 pp.

A collection of conference papers; topics range from philosophical foundations to the methodology of monitoring observance of the right to food.

Ball, N. *World Hunger: A Guide to the Economic and Political Dimensions.* Santa Barbara, CA: ABC-Clio, 1981. 386 pp.

International bibliography of over 3,200 books and periodical articles on problems of underdevelopment and problems of the rural sector, and questions about the food supply.

Centre for Human Rights. *Right to Adequate Food as a Human Right.* **Human Rights Study Series, no. 1. New York: United Nations, 1989. 73 pp.**

A report prepared by Asbjorn Eide, Special Rapporteur for the U.N. Sub-Commission on Prevention of Discrimination and Protection of Minorities. It deals with the causes of hunger; theoretical aspects of economic, social and cultural rights; existing recognition of the right to food in international law; state and international obligations; and monitoring and supervision.

Dreze, J. and A. Sen. *Hunger and Public Action.* **Oxford: Clarendon Press; New York: Oxford University Press, 1989. 373 pp.**

Part of series, Studies in Development Economics. Analyzes government policy affecting food supply, famine prevention and nutrition in developing countries. Particular focus is on how poor people are affected.

Eide, A. "Realization of Social and Economic Rights and the Minimum Threshold Approach." *Human Rights Law Journal* **10 (Winter-Spring 1989): 35-51.**

A revised version of a report given in December 1988. It draws heavily on Eide's study for the U.N. Sub-Commission on Prevention of Discrimination and Protection of Minorities on the right to food as a human right (presented in 1987). Includes analysis of the right and a section on implementation at the international level, as well as recommendations. See p. 131, above, for additional information.

Sen, A. *Poverty and Famines: An Essay on Entitlement and Deprivation.* **Oxford: Clarendon Press; New York: Oxford University Press, 1982. 257 pp.**

Focuses on the causation of starvation in general, and of famines in particular. Argues that traditional analysis of famines which focuses on the food supply is fundamentally defective and misleading; develops "entitlement approach," concentrating on ownership and exchange. Applies approach to case studies, including Great Bengal Famine of 1943, the Ethiopian famines of 1973 and 1974, the Bangladesh famine of 1974, and the famines in the Sahel African countries. Analyzes characterization and measurement of poverty. Accesssible to nontechnical reader.

***WHY (World Hunger Year)* Mineola, NY: World Hunger Year, 1989-.**

Bimonthly. Issued jointly by World Hunger Year (WHY) and the Institute for Food and Development Policy. Continues *Food Monitor*, 1977-89.

C.   Right to Health

1.   Books and Articles

Cohen, R. and L. Wiseberg. *Double Jeopardy - Threat to Life and Human Rights: Discrimination against Persons with AIDS.* Cambridge, MA: Human Rights Internet, 1990. 47 pp.

Reviews major initiatives by NGOs and IGOs, especially the elaboration of guidelines on the use of international human rights standards for the treatment of persons who are HIV+ or who have AIDS. Examines discrimination, censorship, compulsory testing/ screening, and restrictions on travel, among other issues.

Commission on Human Rights. Sub-Commission on Prevention of Discrimination and Protection of Minorities. *Discrimination against HIV-Infected People or People with AIDS.* Progress Report by Luis Varela Quiros, Special Rapporteur. E/CN.4/ Sub.2/1991/10, 24 July 1991. 68 pp.

Provides an analysis of discrimination associated with AIDS, and raises some of the conceptual and legal issues which relate to this discrimination. In addition, it surveys some of the regional, national and local strategies which have been successful in preventing or countering discrimination relating to AIDS and HIV. Preliminary conclusions and recommendations are offered.

Cook, R. "Human Rights and Infant Survival: A Case for Priorities." *Columbia Human Rights Law Review* 18 (Fall-Winter 1986): 1-41.

Explores the international human rights law obligating countries to be aware of preventable danger to their young populations, and subsequent obligations upon countries to deploy public resources to reduce infant mortality rates to an internationally acceptable level .

Cooper Weil, D. et al. *The Impact of Development Policies on Health: A Review of the Literature.* Geneva: World Health Organization, 1990. 165 pp.

Reviews the literature addressing the links between health conditions and development policies in five sectors: macroeconomics, agriculture, industry, energy and housing. It identifies the causes of ill health in each of these sectors, and highlights gaps in existing knowledge.

Dupuy, R.-J., ed. *The Right to Health and Human Rights.* Alphen aan den Rijn, The Netherlands: Sijthoff and Noordhoff, 1979. 500 pp.

Workshop papers are divided into three sections: fundamental concepts of the right to health, international action for the implementation of the right to health, and the right to health and the protection of the human environment.

Fuenzalida-Puelma, H. and S. Scholle Connor, eds. *The Right to Health in the Americas. A Comparative Constitutional Study.* **Scientific Publication no. 509. Washington, DC: Pan American Health Organization, 1989. 716 pp.**

Chapter 1 provides a conceptual background in international human rights and the right to health. Chapter 2 consists of 29 national analyses. Chapter 3 describes the constitutional history and evolution of the right in Latin America, North America and the Caribbean.

Gostin, L. and L. Porter, eds. *International Law and AIDS: International Response, Current Issues, and Future Directions.* **Washington, DC: Section of International Law and Practice, American Bar Association, 1992. 386 pp.**

Discusses AIDS and international law and legislation, and international cooperation. Contributors focus on public health law, programs and epidemiology; screening and international travel; discrimination, international labor law and U.S. workplace law; and particular issues for those who have used IV drugs. Extensive appendices include U.N. resolutions and other documents resulting from international conferences or organizations, international studies, and Council of Europe Committee of Ministers recommendations.

International Commission of Health Professionals for Health and Human Rights. *Health and Human Rights.* **Geneva: International Commission of Health Professionals for Health and Human Rights, 1986. 149 pp.**

A collection of short, policy-oriented articles dealing with various aspects of health and human rights.

International Institute for Human Rights Studies. *Le Medecin face aux Droits de l'Homme.* **Padova, Italy: CEDAM, 1990. 1485 pp.**

In French. Intended to provide physicians with a guide to existing groups of rules which relate to medicine and human rights: universal international conventions and treaties, European conventions and treaties, and national laws of the countries of the Council of Europe. Includes discussion of deontological and moral norms, as well as the moral teachings of Judaism, Islam, and Roman Catholicism. Contains articles on the concept of a right to health, with discussion of specific international norms. Provides a series of articles reporting on national legislation and practice in several Council of Europe countries. Contains articles on Judaic, Catholic and Islamic medical ethics. Provides texts on medical ethics produced by a variety of medical organizations. Concludes with a subject-classified presentation of a wide range of human rights and medical issues, relating each to the relevant positive law.

Jallow, H. and P. Hunt. *AIDS and the African Charter. Occasional Paper No. 3.* Banjul, the Gambia: African Centre for Democracy and Human Rights Studies, November 1991. 28 pp.

> The first section outlines the nature and extent of AIDS in Africa; a second section reviews African Charter provisions which are of particular relevance to AIDS. A conclusion suggests further areas of research and questions which might be asked by the African Commission when it considers the periodic reports of states parties. An appendix contains the African Charter.

"The Right to Health Care." Chapter 7 in *Philosophical Issues in Human Rights: Theories and Applications*, edited by P. Werhane, A.R. Gini, and D. Ozar, 286-323. New York: Random House, 1986.

> Contains four essays, two arguing for a right to health care, two objecting. Essays deal with issues such as medical care as a right, health care needs and distributive justice, what should count as basic health care, and public health as social justice.

Sida, Un Defi aux Droits: Actes du colloque organise a l'Universite Libre de Bruxelles les 10, 11, et 12 mai 1990. Bruxelles: Bruylant, 1991. 888 pp.

> In French. The proceedings of a three-day conference on human rights and AIDS. Contents are divided into several sections which deal with the following issues: the practice of international organizations, the protection of the most vulnerable, liability and private life, and moving towards a new body of human rights law and international solidarity concerning AIDS. An annex provides a chronological list of laws, directives, conventions, recommendations and other documents concerning AIDS.

Torrelli, M. *Le Medecin et les Droits de l'Homme.* Paris: Berget-Levrault, 1983. 466 pp.

> Treatise in French aimed at acquainting doctors and health personnel with the main international human rights instruments. The book discusses the social and legal implications of human rights for medical practice, and provides a series of texts on ethical or normative questions presented to encourage reflection on the roles and obligations of physicians and other health workers in the defense of fundamental rights and liberties of the person, in particular in the implementation of the right to health. Annexes contain the texts of major international documents of relevance to health and human rights.

United States. President's Commission for the Study of Ethical Problems in Medicine and Biomedical and Behavioral Research. *Securing Access to Health Care: A Report on the Ethical Implications of Differences in the Availability of Health Services.* 3 vols. Washington, DC: The Commission, 1983.

> Focuses on medical care (including the cost of care), ethics and policy, as well as accessibility to health services, in the United States.

World Health Organization. *Tabular Information on Legal Instruments Dealing with AIDS and HIV Infection, Part 1.* **s.l.: WHO, WHO/GPA/HLE/92.1, 1992. 151 pp.**

Alphabetical country listing with citations to legislative texts; each listing gives a brief description of the coverage and the purpose of the text, and provides references to the *International Digest of Health Legislation,* where appropriate. Includes all countries and jurisdictions, including the United States (other than State legislation).

2.   Newsletters and Periodicals

Annual Review of Population Law. **New York: U.N. Population Fund and Harvard Law School Library, 1974-.**

Annual. Deceptively titled, the *Review* indexes a wide range of international resolutions and agreements, national constitutions, laws and regulations, judicial pronouncements, and other legal texts which concern "population" issues. Excerpts, and sometimes entire texts, are provided. Arrangement is by country within subject categories, and by subject under each country. A selective bibliography is provided, and an editor's preface presents a summary of important developments in the field. Its coverage of a range of economic and social rights issues makes this periodical extremely useful.

Institute for International Health and Development. *International Health and Development.* **Washington, DC: Catholic University of America, Institute for International Health and Development, 1989-.**

Bimonthly. Short, policy-oriented articles on international health, hunger, and pharmaceuticals. Free market, private sector orientation.

3.   Indices, Guides and Bibliographies

Haselbauer, K. *A Research Guide to the Health Sciences: Medical, Nutritional and Environmental.* **New York: Greenwood Press, 1987. 655 pp.**

An annotated listing of 2,000 titles, predominantly published in the United States, in English. The aim is to describe the major reference works and information sources in the health sciences. It is intended for researchers at all levels. Entries are arranged in four major parts: general, basic science, social aspects, and medical specialties. Has a combined author/title/subject index.

Walters, L., ed. *Bibliography of Bioethics.* **Washington, DC: Kennedy Institute of Ethics, 1975-.**

An annual listing of English-language books, essays, journal and newspaper articles, court decisions, bills or laws, and other sources. Ethical aspects of health care, contraception, abortion, population, reproductive technologies, genetic intervention, mental health therapies, human experimentation, death and dying are covered.

D.   *Right to Housing*

Centre on Housing Rights and Evictions. *Legal Sources of the Right to Housing in International Human Rights Law.* Utrecht, The Netherlands: COHRE, February 1992. 18 pp.

Contains all codified bases of the right to adequate housing and related rights.

Centre on Housing Rights and Evictions. *Selected Bibliography on Housing Rights and Evictions.* Utrecht, The Netherlands: COHRE, 1993. 47 pp.

Unannotated bibliography of 350 sources on the rights to housing, including reports on professional research, NGO publications, U.N. documents and resolutions, fact-finding mission reports, and international and national laws. Contains sections on resettlement, structural adjustment and housing rights, as well as section providing general references on economic, social and cultural rights. Also contains contact addresses for NGOs.

Committee on Economic, Social and Cultural Rights. *"The Right to Adequate Housing (Art. 11 (1) of the Covenant)" General Comment No. 4.* In *Committee on Economic, Social and Cultural Rights: Report on the Sixth Session.* ECOSOC Official Records, 1992, Supplement No. 3, (UN Doc. E/1992/23) at pp. 114-120.

General comment aimed to draw attention to insufficent information provided by states parties on the right to housing and the gap between the international standards and the situation prevailing in many countries. Comment lists "principal issues" in the right to housing: legal security of tenure, availability of infrastructure, affordability, habitability, accessibility, location and cultural adequacy.

Commission on Human Rights. Sub-Commission on the Prevention of Discrimination and the Protection of Minorities. *The Right to Adequate Housing: Working Paper.* Submitted by Rajindar Sachar, expert appointed pursuant to resolution 1991/26 of the Sub-Commission on Prevention of Discrimination and Protection of Minorities. E/CN.4/Sub.2/1992/15, 12 June 1992. 25 pp.

Brief, but brings together some useful information.

United Nations Centre for Human Settlements (Habitat). *Developing a National Shelter Strategy: Lessons from Four Countries.* Nairobi: United Nations Centre for Human Settlements (Habitat), 1990. 43 pp.

Describes and analyzes policy implementation and institutional capacity in Brazil, Hungary, Kenya, and Mexico.

Habitat News. Nairobi: United Nations Centre for Human Settlements (Habitat), 1979-.

Published three times per year. Reports on the activities of the U.N. Centre for Human Settlements and related bodies.

Leckie, S. *From Housing Needs to Housing Rights: An Analysis of the Right to Adequate Shelter under International Human Rights Law.* Technical Report of the Human Settlements Programme of the International Institute of Environment and Development, app. 2. London: International Institute for Environment and Development, March 1992. 109 pp.

> Provides a detailed legal analysis of the linkages between the right to housing and various other human rights.

Leckie, S. "When Push Comes to Shove: Eviction's No Fiction." *Whole Earth Review* (Fall 1991): 88-89.

> Discussion of law and policy issues surrounding this increasingly common problem.

Newson, T. *Housing Policy: An International Bibliography.* London; New York: Mansell, 1986. 398 pp.

> Annotated listing of over 3,000 English-language sources. Over half of entries concern British housing policy. Cut-off date for material on Britain is 1985; for material on other countries, 1984. Entries arranged under 25 subject headings, within which materials are arranged geographically. Author and subject indices.

Ortiz, E. *The Right to Housing: A Global Challenge.* Mexico City, Mexico: Copevi, 1990. 331 pp.

> Documents the global housing crisis.

United Nations Centre for Human Settlements (Habitat). *Global Report on Human Settlements.* New York: Oxford University Press, 1987. 229 pp.

> Documents global human settlement conditions and trends, discusses key policy areas in settlement development, with emphasis on the third world, and presents conclusions on future strategies. Contains a lengthy statistical annex.

United Nations Centre for Human Settlements (Habitat). *The Global Strategy for Shelter to the Year 2000: As Adopted by the General Assembly of the United Nations at Its Forty-Third Session in Resolution 43/181 on 20 December 1988.* Nairobi: United Nations Centre for Human Settlements (Habitat), 1990. 57 pp.

> Contains guidelines for international action, conclusions and plan of action.

United Nations Centre for Human Settlements (Habitat). *Habitat Directory in the Field of Human Settlements.* Nairobi: United Nations Centre for Human Settlements (Habitat), 1986. 377 pp.

> Directory of U.N., other international, and regional, and national bodies conducting activities in the field of human settlements or which possess information on the subject. Includes information on 1,784 institutions.

United Nations Centre for Human Settlements (Habitat). *Human Settlements: Basic Statistics.* Nairobi: United Nations Centre for Human Settlements (Habitat), 1990-.

> Statistical information on four variables: population, land, housing, infrastructure and services.

United Nations Centre for Human Settlements (Habitat). *Operational Activities Report.* Nairobi: United Nations Centre for Human Settlements (Habitat). 1991-.

> Annual briefly describing the activities of the U.N. Centre: it focuses on technical cooperation programs and projects, country by country. For each country the projects, total cost, partners, background activities, goals and results are given.

E.   Labor Rights

This section does not discuss or provide specific sources on the work of the International Labour Organisation. Researchers interested in that topic should consult the section on the International Labour Organisation, Chapter Three, Section III. NGOs doing work on labor rights issues include the Lawyers Committee for Human Rights (listed above), which has analyzed the linkage between labor standards and international trade, and the International Labor Rights Education and Research Fund, 1828 L Street NW, Suite 801, Washington, DC 20036.

1.   Books and Articles

Alston, P. "Labor Rights Provisions in U.S. Trade Law: 'Aggressive Unilateralism'?" *Human Rights Quarterly* 15 (February 1993):1-35.

> An excellent overview. Provides many key citations to relevant provisions of U.S. and international labor law. Specific focuses include child labor, freedom of association, an analysis of the restrictions in the laws themselves, and the reactions of human rights groups.

Charnovitz, S. "International Trade and Worker Rights." *SAIS Review* 7 (1987): 185-198.

> An introduction to the concept of international worker rights, and to the discussion of the reemergence of worker rights in U.S. trade policy.

"Employee Rights in the Workplace." Chapter 6 in *Philosophical Issues in Human Rights: Theories and Applications,* edited by P. Werhane, A.R. Gini, and D. Ozar, 247-285. New York: Random House, 1986.

> Addresses accountability and employee rights, meaningful work, workplace democracy, and the question whether a human right to employment exists.

Encyclopedia of Occupational Health and Safety. **3d ed. 2 vols. Geneva: International Labour Organisation, 1985.**

Encyclopedia-style, illustrated articles on a broad range of topics. Intended to provide practical knowledge to those who have administrative or other responsibilities for safeguarding workers' health and safety. Matters which are of special interest to developing countries, but about which adequate knowledge is often lacking, are dealt with in detail. Some 200 new articles have been added covering new knowledge or subjects, particularly in the fields of toxicology and occupational hygiene, occupational cancer, occupational diseases of agricultural workers, occupational safety, psycho-social problems, and institutions and organizations active in the field of occupational health and safety. Subject index.

Evans, A. *Workers' Rights are Human Rights.* **Rome: International Documentation International, 1981. 112 pp.**

A handbook explaining the standards and procedures relevant to filing complaints of human rights violations.

Filippelli, R., ed. *Labor Conflict in the United States: An Encyclopedia.* **New York: Garland, 1990. 609 pp.**

254 alphabetically-arranged entries with brief bibliographies. Each entry is approximately 3-5 pages long. Entries cover significant strikes, lockouts, and boycotts. Encyclopedia includes a chronology of labor history.

International Convention on the Protection of the Rights of All Migrant Workers and Members of Their Families, U.N. Doc. A/RES/45./158, February 25, 1991 (45th Session).

Convention is the product of a working group established by the U.N. General Assembly in 1979 and has been opened for signature, ratification and accession. Text included in Annex to UN General Assembly resolution 45/158.

Leary, V. *International Labour Conventions and National Law: The Effectiveness of the Automatic Incorporation of Treaties in National Legal Systems.* **The Hague: M. Nijhoff, 1982. 190 pp.**

Empirical study which examines how effectively certain provisions of international labor conventions are incorporated in national law. Problems of national implementation of the labor conventions in Argentina, France, Mexico, the Netherlands, Switzerland and the United States are examined in detail; isolated examples from other countries such as Colombia, Guatemala, Italy and Liberia are also presented.

Ohshima, S. and C. Francis. *Japan Through the Eyes of Women Migrant Workers.* **Tokyo: Japan Women's Christian Temperance Union, 1989. 220 pp.**

Presents accounts about (mostly Asian) female workers in Japan who are victims of exploitation. Also describes the work of HELP Asian Women's Shelter. Appendices provide a list of other groups in Japan, the Philippines and Thailand which cooperate with HELP; the text of a petition to the U.N. Commission on Human Rights on the redress of the human rights of Asian women migrant workers in Japan; a proposal to revise the Japanese immigration law; and statistical charts.

Pease, E. *Occupational Safety and Health: A Sourcebook.* **New York: Garland, 1985. 279 pp.**

Annotated bibliographic guide to some 500 English-language publications including periodicals, reporters, databases, statistical sources, and reference books for the period 1970-1984. Directory gives information on government agencies, interest groups and private associations.

Wood, J. "International Labour Organisation Conventions—Labour Code or Treaties?" *International and Comparative Law Quarterly* **40 (July 1991): 649-657.**

Discusses problems of the judicial construction of ILO Conventions, when different conventions contain conflicting standards.

2. Bibliographies and Directories

Fenton, T. and M. Heffron, comps. and eds. *Transnational Corporations and Labor: A Directory of Resources.* **Maryknoll, NY: Orbis Books, 1989. 166 pp.**

Provides bibliographies and other sources on transnational corporations, the working class, and trade unions in developing countries.

Ferber, M. *Women and Work, Paid and Unpaid: A Selected, Annotated Bibliography.* **New York: Garland, 1987. 408 pp.**

See p. 181 for annotation.

International Labour Office. *Annotated Bibliography on Clandestine Employment.* **Geneva: ILO, 1987. 132 pp.**

Lists 213 monographs, journal articles, reports, and conference proceedings in a variety of languages, alphabetically by author. Contains a subject index.

3. Statistical Sources on Labor

International Labour Office. *Bulletin of Labour Statistics.* **Geneva: ILO, 1965-.**

Four main issues, October inquiry results and eight supplements. Includes articles on methodology and special topics; trilingual tables of current statistics on employment, unemployment, wages, hours of work, and consumer prices; and includes results of a detailed annual inquiry into wages, hours of work and retail prices. Continues in part: *International Labour Review.*

International Labour Office. *Yearbook of Labour Statistics.* **Geneva: ILO, 1936-.**

Annual. Trilingual comprehensive survey of annual data from all parts of the world relating to economically active population, employment, unemployment, hours of work, wages, labor cost, industrial disputes, occupational injuries, and consumer prices. Contains an index of countries, areas or territories included in each table.

F.   *General Statistical Sources and Other Materials Useful in Economic and Social Rights Studies*

1.   Statistical Sources

Congressional Information Service. *Index to International Statistics.* **Washington, DC: CIS, 1983-.**

Indexes the statistical publications of intergovernmental organizations.

Congressional Information Service. *Publications of International Intergovernmental Organizations.* **Washington, DC: CIS, 1983-.**

Monthly, with quarterly and annual cumulations. Master guide and index to current English-language statistical publications of the world's major intergovernmental organizations. 80-90 organizations are covered. Abstracts are arranged by issuing body and indexed by subject, name, geographic area, category, issuing source, title, and publication number.

International Monetary Fund. *International Financial Statistics.* **Washington, DC: IMF, 1948-.**

Monthly, with annual cumulations. Standard source of international statistics on international and domestic finance. Includes current data used for the analyses of problems in international payment and inflation and deflation, e.g., data on exchange rates, international liquidity, money and banking, international transactions, prices, production, government finance, and interest rates.

Jabine, T. and R. Claude, eds. *Human Rights and Statistics: Getting the Record Straight.* **Philadelphia: University of Pennsylvania Press, 1992. 458 pp.**

A useful discussion of many of the issues surrounding the use of statistical data in human rights research and advocacy is provided. The volume focuses on civil and political human rights, and contains a guide to human rights data sources, a listing and description of 29 databases that contain quantitative information on human rights, and related topics.

United Nations. Statistical Office. *Demographic Yearbook.* **New York: Department of Economic and Social Affairs, Statistical Office, U.N., 1948-.**

Annual compendium of international demographic data including official statistics from almost 250 geographic areas. Covers population (e.g., distribution, characteristics, natality, mortality, marriage and divorce).

United Nations. Statistical Office. *Statistical Yearbook.* **New York: Department of Economic and Social Affairs, Statistical Office, U.N., 1948-.**

Annual. Gives statistics on population, agriculture, mining, manufacturing, trade, education, etc.

U.S. Bureau of the Census. *Statistical Abstract of the United States.* **Washington: U.S. Government Printing Office, 1879-.**

Annual volume with quantitative summary statistics on political, social and economic organization of the United States.

World Bank. *World Tables.* **Baltimore: Johns Hopkins University Press, 1976-.**

Presents historical time series in absolute numbers for individual countries for the basic economic variables—population, national accounts, prices, balance of payments, external public debt, foreign trade indices, and central government finance—as well as economic and social indicators in a form suitable for cross-country analysis and comparison. Other useful International Monetary Fund statistical publications include *Balance of Payments Statistics* and *Direction of Trade Statistics.*

2. U.N. Regional Commissions

The various regional economic commissions of the U.N. Economic and Social Council produce a variety of publications on economic and social conditions, development strategies, and the like. The major commissions and some of their publications follow.

U.N. Economic Commission for Africa. *African Socio-Economic Indicators.* Addis Ababa: U.N. Economic Commission for Africa, 1986-.

U.N. Economic Commission for Africa. *Foreign Trade Statistics for Africa.* New York: U.N. 1977-.

U.N. Economic Commission for Africa. *Statistical Yearbook.* Addis Ababa: U.N. Economic Commission for Africa, 1970-1973.

U.N. Economic Commission for Africa. *Survey of Economic and Social Conditions in Africa.* New York: U.N.,1975-.

U.N. Economic and Social Commission for Asia and the Pacific. *Agricultural Information and Development Bulletin.* Bangkok: Agriculture Division, U.N. Economic and Social Commission for Asia and the Pacific, 1979-.

U.N. Economic and Social Commission for Asia and the Pacific. *Economic and Social Survey of Asia and the Pacific.* Bangkok: U.N. Economic and Social Commission for Asia and the Pacific, 1974-.

U.N. Economic Commission for Europe. Research Planning Division. *Economic Survey of Europe in [year].* Geneva: U.N., 1953-.

U.N. Economic Commission for Latin America. *CEPAL Review.* Santiago, Chile: U.N. Economic Commission for Latin America, 1976-.

U.N. Economic Commission for Latin America. *Economic Survey of Latin America.* New York: U.N. Economic Commission for Latin America, 1948-1981. Title since 1982 has been *Economic Survey for Latin America and the Carribean.*

U.N. Economic Commission for Western Asia. *Agriculture and Development; Studies on Selected Development Problems in Various Countries in the Middle East.* Beirut: U.N. Economic and Social Office, 1967-71.

U.N. Economic Commission for Western Asia. *Survey of Economic and Social Developments in ECWA Region* [s.l.]: The Commission, 1980-.

3.   Social and Economic Indicators

What follows is a selective listing of materials which contain information on social and economic indicators and measures of quality of life.

Anderson, V. *Alternative Economic Indicators.* London; New York: Routledge, 1991. 106 pp.

> Argues for a set of indicators to "dethrone" and replace the rate of GNP growth as the principal indicator. Topics include indicators concerned with living standards of the majority of the population, and indicators of the environment and natural resources. Presents statistics for 16 recommended priority indicators for 14 different countries.

Gilmartin, K. et al., eds. *Social Indicators: An Annotated Bibliography of Current Literature.* New York: Garland, 1979. 123 pp.

> Supplements Wilcox L. et al., *Social Indicators and Societal Monitoring,* 1972. Contains about 600 items, with a focus on literature published during 1972-78. Has author and subject indices.

Innes, J. *Knowledge and Public Policy: The Search for Meaningful Indicators.* **2d ed. New Brunswick, NJ: Transaction Publishers, 1990. 367 pp.**

Interesting discussion of the problems of creating and using social indicators.

Kurian, G. *The New Book of World Rankings.* **3d ed. New York: Facts on File, 1991. 324 pp.**

Compares the performance of states in more than 200 tables of rankings of various social and economic measures.

Morris, M. *Measuring the Condition of the World's Poor: the Physical Quality of Life Index.* **New York: Pergamon Press, 1979. 176 pp.**

Discussion of the need for a new indicator which measures progress in physical well-being more effectively than is possible with gross national product and other monetary indicators. Shortcomings of GNP and other measures are discussed, and the Physical Quality of Life Index (PQLI) is proposed as an alternative.

Oster, S. *The Definition and Measurement of Poverty.* **2 vols. Boulder, CO: Westview Press, 1978.**

Volume 1 provides a review of American literature since 1950; Volume 2 provides abstracts of books, articles, government documents and dissertations.

Sen, A., et al. *The Standard of Living.* **Cambridge; New York: Cambridge University Press, 1987. 125 pp.**

Analysis of the concept of standard of living which rejects economic interpretations in terms of utility or wealth and suggests an interpretation based on "capabilities and freedoms."

UNICEF. *The State of the World's Children.* **Oxford; New York: Oxford University Press, 1980-.**

Annual report focused on the status of children in developing countries. A particular focus is on health and hygiene. It also contains key statistics on child welfare in developing countries and world health.

United Nations Development Programme. *Human Development Report [year].* **New York: Oxford University Press, 1990-.**

See p. 150 for annotation.

United States. Bureau of the Census. *Social Indicators 1.* **Washington: U.S. Department of Commerce, Bureau of the Census, 1976-.**

> Triennial. Contains selected data on social conditions and trends in the United States: maps, charts and tables illustrating statistical measures of well-being and public perception in 11 major social areas, such as population, family, social security and welfare, health and nutrition, and public safety. International comparisons are presented for each social area.

United States Commission on Civil Rights. *Social Indicators of Equality for Minorities and Women: A Report of the U.S. Commission on Civil Rights.* **Washington, DC: The Commission, 1978. 136 pp.**

> Compares the level of well-being of the U.S. minority and female population to that of the majority male population, using measures in education, occupation, employment, income, poverty and housing.

III.   Human Rights, Development and International Trade

A.   Human Rights and Development

Proclaimed as a right by the U.N. General Assembly, the concept of development and its existence as a human right have been subject to sharply differing views. There is a large literature on human rights and development, spanning discussions of the concept of the right to development, strategies for local empowerment, dependency theory and the relationship between human rights and global economic processes. There is also an extensive development literature which may not use the language of rights. Sources of information on development and human rights include newspapers, the publications and documents of international organizations, and books and articles. Relevant books and articles are accessible through the general human rights bibliographies and research tools mentioned in Chapters One and Two. This section is intended merely to highlight some sources which may be especially useful.

1.   General Resources

"Bibliography. Symposium: Development as an Emerging Human Right." *California Western International Law Journal* **15 (Summer 1985): 639-646.**

> Entries arranged alphabetically in three sections: documents, articles and books.

Fenton, T. and M. Heffron, eds. *Transnational Corporations and Labor: A Directory of Resources.* **Maryknoll, NY: Orbis Books, 1989. 166 pp.**

> See pp. 78 and 143 for annotations.

Rehof, L. and C. Gulmann, eds. *Human Rights in Domestic Law and Development Assistance Policies of the Nordic Countries.* Vol. 12 of International Studies in Human Rights. Dordrecht; Boston: M. Nijhoff, 1988. 212 pp.

> Published by the Danish Center of Human Rights. Section on development assistance and human rights contains articles on the development assistance policies of Nordic and north European governmental aid agencies, and, generally, on the relation between development aid and human rights. A second section contains articles on the status of the European Convention of Human Rights in the Nordic countries

2. World Bank (International Bank for Reconstruction and Development)

Although much of their information is not made public, the publications of the World Bank and the International Monetary Fund are of interest to human rights researchers because they provide at least some data on policies which have profound effects on human rights, especially on the most vulnerable sections of the population. The Bank's many working papers and technical reports are separately catalogued as monographs, e.g., *World Bank Country Study, World Bank Country Economic Reports; World Bank Research News.* They are thus accessible by subject or by title.

World Bank. *Annual Report.* Washington, DC: The World Bank, 1955-.

> Summary of World Bank activities for the year.

World Bank. *Publications Update.* Washington, DC: The World Bank, 1984-.

> Current awareness bulletin which lists and describes all new titles published by the World Bank.

World Bank. *World Bank Catalog of Publications.* Washington, DC: The World Bank, 1979-.

> An annual catalog of sales and free publications arranged by subject.

World Bank. *World Development Report.* New York: Oxford University Press, 1978-.

> This annual includes a summary of recent developments in the world economy, and provides world development indicators, and 32 statistical tables giving data on social and economic development in 120 countries. See annotation of the United Nations Development Program's *World Development Report [year],* below, for comparison.

3. International Monetary Fund (IMF)

As mentioned above in the section on the World Bank, IMF publications may provide important data on policies which affect human rights, especially those of the most vulnerable sections of the population.

International Monetary Fund. *Annual Report of the Executive Board for the Financial Year Ended April 30, [year].* **Washington, DC: IMF, 1978-.**

> Summary of activities. An appendix lists publications issued by the IMF during the previous year. Titles are listed by type of publication, then alphabetically or chronologically by IMF identification number.

International Monetary Fund. *IMF Survey.* **Washington, DC: IMF, 1972-.**

> Newsletter published every two weeks, with general information about IMF activities.

4.   United Nations Development Program (UNDP)

United Nations Development Programme. *Human Development Report [year].* **New York: Oxford University Press, 1990-.**

> Very useful for cross-national comparisons based on a wide variety of indicators with relevance to human rights. The first half of the report consists of several chapters which discuss the concept of human development, the relation between human development and political freedom, widening gaps in opportunities, and strategies for the future. The report includes a Human Development Index (HDI), a single statistical measure with three components: life expectancy, educational attainment, and purchasing power.
>
> The report also includes a Human Freedom Index, which rates countries on their performance on 40 aspects of freedom, such as freedom of speech, travel, press, assembly, religion and unionization, along with less classic aspects like legal equality for women, legal tolerance of homosexuality, freedom from forced labor and capital punishment, and freedom for ethnic and national minorities. The second half contains statistical tables comparing countries on a wide range of matters, e.g., income, life expectancy, access to health services and safe water, sanitation, adult literacy, military expenditure, female-male gaps and rural-urban gaps. In contrast with the World Bank's *World Development Report*, this report emphasizes non-monetary measures of human welfare in its rankings.

B.   *International Trade*

For an overview of relevant U.S. legislation which relates international trade to human rights, see the discussion of the publications of Human Rights Watch and the Lawyers Committee for Human Rights, above, Chapter Two, Section IV., and below, Chapter Five, Section II. A.

Country Reports on Economic Policy and Trade Practices: Report submitted to the Committee on Foreign Affairs, Committee on Ways and Means of the U.S. House of Representatives, Committee on Foreign Relations, Committee on Finance of the U.S. Senate by the Department of State, in accordance with Section 2202 of the Omnibus Trade Competitiveness Act of 1988. **Washington, DC: U.S. Government Printing Office, 1989-.**

Published annually as mandated by statute, the report provides country-by-country reports on worker rights, and on several economic and trade-related matters: key economic indicators, macroeconomic trends, exchange rate policies, structural policies, debt management policies, significant barriers to U.S. exports and investment; and protection of U.S. intellectual property.

The Economist. **London: The Economist Newspaper, Ltd., 1843-.**

See p. 15 for annotation.

Economist Intelligence Unit Country Report. **London: The Unit, 1991-.**

On a country by country basis, these proprietary reports have the best country economic data to the current quarter, along with good political background. Not all libraries carry them because they are expensive, but they are standard for political risk assessment by business.

Encyclopedia of Business Information Sources. **Detroit: Gale Research, 1970-.**

Biennial, with periodic supplements. A bibliographic guide to more than 26,000 entries. Includes reference books, bibliographies and directories. Specific sub-topics include management and commerce in the United States.

The Financial Times. **London: MacRae, Curtice & Co., 1888-.**

Essential for international trade, especially defense issues.

Left Business Observer. **New York: Henwood, 1986-.**

Eleven issues a year. Comment and analysis on politics, business and economics. The focus is on the United States.

Lowenfeld, A. *Public Controls on International Trade.* **2d ed. Vol. 6 of** *International Economic Law.* **New York: M. Bender, 1983. 449 pp.**

Deals with the General Agreement on Tariffs and Trade (GATT), international trading system, and multilateral trade negotiations.

Multinational Monitor. **Washington, DC: Corporate Accountability Research Group, 1980-.**

> Monthly. Good source for information on corporate abuses, and efforts at improving corporate accountability.

Strauss, D. *Handbook of Business Information: A Guide for Librarians, Students and Researchers.* **Englewood, CO: Libraries Unlimited, 1988. 537 pp.**

> General guide to sources.

World Bank. *World Bank Annual Reports.* **Washington, DC: World Bank. 1982-.**

> Annual. The annual *World Development Report* is key for quantitative information.

The World Factbook. **Washington, DC: Central Intelligence Agency, U.S. Government Printing Office (distributor), 1981-.**

> For a current survey in a page or two of any given country, this is a very helpful encyclopedia. Published on a yearly basis in unclassified form by Brassey's Press (U.S.). The economic data are inferior to those of the *Economist Intelligence Unit* reports, discussed on p. 151.

C.   Arms Trade and Militaries

Anyone researching this area should check for any new publications released by the Stockholm International Peace Research Institute (SIPRI), Pipers vag 28, S-171 73 Solna, Sweden.

Anthony, I., ed. *Arms Export Regulations.* **London; NY; Oxford: SIPRI, 1991. 267 pp.**

> Survey of arms export regulations from around the world based on a 1989 survey by SIPRI. Provides information on legislation, guidelines, and decision-making processes for arms export regulation in 24 countries. Also includes chapters on multilateral export controls, European Community arms export regulations, U.N. deliberations on the arms trade and U.N. embargoes against the Republic of South Africa.

Arms Control Today. **Washington, DC: Arms Control Association, 1974-.**

> Monthly by nonpartisan national membership organization founded in 1971, "dedicated to promoting public understanding of effective policies and programs in arms control and disarmament." Contains feature articles on subjects such as nuclear weapons, arms control government policies, the arms trade, international weapons conventions and disarmament. Also includes brief news updates and section on new publications.

Defense News. Springfield, VA: Times Journal Co., 1986-.

> Key U.S. weekly on defense.

Jane's Defence Weekly. London: Jane's Information Group, 1984-.

> Weekly. Essential for all aspects of defense industry and arms trade. Latest on defense news, technology, and deals. Standard source for the defense industry.

Jane's Intelligence Review. Coulsdon, Surrey, U.K.: Jane's Information Group, 1991-.

> Monthly. Standard source for the defense industry. Incorporates *Jane's Soviet Intelligence Review.* Provides detailed information on weapons systems used, primarily in Communist, or formerly Communist, countries. Also includes analyses of political and strategic factors in certain countries.

Jane's International Defence Review. London: Jane's Information Group, 1991-.

> Monthly. Essential for all military discussions. Standard source for the defense industry.

Laurance, E. *The International Arms Trade.* New York: Lexington Books, 1992. 245 pp.

> A highly regarded source on the defense and weapons industries, military assistance and arms transfers.   Part of Issues in World Politics Series.

Ohlson, T., ed. *Arms Transfer Limitations and Third World Security.* Oxford; NY; London: SIPRI, 1988. 260 pp.

> Assesses past attempts, current proposals and future possibilities for limiting the trade in weapons and weapons technology with third world countries. The third in a trilogy. Also useful are the two related SIPRI publications: *Arms Production in the Third World* (1986); and *Arms Transfers to the Third World, 1971-1985* (1987).

SIPRI Yearbook [year]: World Armaments and Disarmament. **Stockholm: Stockholm International Peace Research Institute, 1972-.**

> Annual. A major source of analysis and quantitative data on the world's armaments and military forces, and efforts at disarmament and arms control. Topics include nuclear weapons programs of the major nuclear powers, military use of outer space, chemical and biological warfare, military expenditures, the arms trade and armed conflicts, and conventional and nuclear arms control. Tables provide extensive quantitative data.

U.S. Arms Control and Disarmament Agency. *World Military Expenditures and Arms Transfers.* **Washington, DC: The Agency, 1976-.**

> Annual report, presenting a summary of major military developments, including statistical tables on military expenditures, armed forces, arms transfers, relative burden, and relative indicators.

U.S. Department of State. *Conventional Arms Transfers to the Third World.* **Washington DC: The Department of State, Bureau of Public Affairs, 1982-.**

Annual report. This is the standard U.S. Government nonclassified report on arms trade between the United States and third world countries.

IV.   Human Rights and the Environment

Because this is an emerging area, relevant international instruments and regulations may not be explicitly identified as human rights-related. The researcher will need to consult handbooks on international environmental law, general social science literature, and NGOs which are active in the field.

A.   *International Environmental Instruments*

Hohman, H. *Basic Documents of International Environmental Law.* **3 vols. London: Graham & Trotman Limited; Norwell, MA: Kluwer Academic Publishers Group, 1992.**

Vol. 1: Reproduces the important environmental resolutions, guidelines, decisions, recommendations and drafts of the principal international global and regional organizations and recording bodies. Vol. 2: Includes the important global and regional agreements on seas, rivers and lakes. Vol. 3: Compiles important global and regional agreements on soils, species, air and atmosphere, and nature generally. Also includes documents relating to the Earth Summit.

Ruster, B. and B. Simma, comps. and eds. *International Protection of the Environment: Treaties and Related Documents. Second Series.* **Dobbs Ferry, NY: Oceana Publications, 1990-.**

Looseleaf. Continues the 30-volume series covering the years 1754-1981, published under the same title. Contains the texts of a wide range of international documents, including treaties, agreements, resolutions, decisions and memoranda of understanding.

Weiss, E.B. *In Fairness to Future Generations.* **Tokyo: United Nations University; Dobbs Ferry, NY: Transnational Publishers, 1989. 385 pp.**

Contains listing and review of provisions of national constitutions dealing with the right to a healthy environment.

Weiss, E.B., et al. *International Environmental Law: Basic Instruments and References.* **Dobbs Ferry, NY: Transnational Publishers, 1992. 749 pp.**

Intended as a "convenient, broad-based, up-to-date compilation of basic international environmental instruments." It reproduces in whole or in part 85 instruments. A reference list provides basic information and citations for these and about 800 other instruments. Texts and references are organized by subject. An index of popular names is provided.

B.   Books, Articles and Reports

Birnie, P.W. and A.E. Boyle. *International Law and the Environment.* **Oxford: Clarendon Press; New York: Oxford University Press, 1992. 563 pp.**

> Chapters include focuses on international law and the environment, international organizations and the formulation of environmental law and policy, structure of international environmental law (rights and obligations of the states, enforcement, compliance and dispute settlement, and the role of national law). Topics discussed also include marine pollution, international control of hazardous waste, nuclear energy and conservation regimes. Includes tables of cases and major treaties and instruments.

Gormley, W. P. *Human Rights and Environment: The Need for International Co-operation.* **Leyden: Sijthoff, 1976. 255 pp.**

> Focuses on activities within the Council of Europe and the United Nations which deal with environmental issues. Addresses the question of whether individuals, groups and NGOs have a legal right to a clean environment.

Gormley, W. P. "The Legal Obligation of the International Community to Guarantee a Pure and Decent Environment: The Expansion of Human Rights Norms." *Georgetown International Environmental Law Review* **3 (Summer 1990): 85-116.**

> Interesting article focusing on development of human rights norm of safe environment which encompasses a concept of duty.

Kindt, J. "Environment, Economic Development and Human Rights: A Triangular Relationship?" In *Proceedings of the Annual Meeting, American Society of International Law, Annual 1988,* **40-63. Washington, DC: American Society of International Law.**

> Summary of the panel discussion on legal and policy issues.

Kiss, A. and D. Shelton. *International Environmental Law.* **Ardsley-on-Hudson, NY: Transnational Publishers, 1991. 541 pp.**

> Discusses the theory, objectives and historical evolution of international environmental law, as well as the major principles of international law which apply to the environmental field. Appendices provide the texts of major international environmental law instruments.

Kromarek, P. *Environnement et droits de l'homme.* **Paris: U.N. Educational, Scientific and Cultural Organization, 1987. 178 pp.**

In French. A series of articles by different authors on conceptual issues such as questions of monitoring and enforcement of a right to environment, and the relation of such a right to other human rights.

Sand, P., ed. *The Effectiveness of International Environmental Agreements: A Survey of Existing Legal Instruments.* **Cambridge: Grotius, 1992. 539 pp.**

A series of essays on the effectiveness and validity of international environmental law.

Sand, P. "Environmental Law in the United Nations Environment Program." In *The Future of the International Law of the Environment,* **edited by R. Dupuy, 51-66. Dordrecht; Boston: M. Nijhoff, 1985.**

Discussion of the role of the U.N. Environment Program (UNEP) in encouraging national legislation and administration of international pollution problems.

Shuktin, W. "International Human Rights Law and the Earth: The Protection of Indigenous Peoples and the Environment." *Virginia Journal of International Law* **31 (Spring 1991): 479-511.**

Good article on the critical intersection between these two specialized areas.

Sohn, L. "The Stockholm Declaration on the Human Environment." *Harvard International Law Journal* **14 (Summer 1973): 423-515.**

Discussion of 1972 Conference on the Human Environment in Stockholm and resulting declaration.

Thorme, M. "Establishing Environment as a Human Right." *Denver Journal of International Law & Policy* **19 (Winter 1991): 301-342.**

Doctrinal law review article arguing for the creation of a human right to environment through the filing of environment-related complaints in human rights fora.

Uibopuu, H-J. "The Internationally Guaranteed Right of an Individual to a Clean Environment." *Comparative Law Yearbook* **1 (1977): 101-120.**

Brief article discussing the special status international environmental law provides to individuals, and the existing provisions in international law supporting a right to a clean environment. There is also a brief overview of fora for individual claims.

United Nations. Commission on Human Rights. Sub-Commission on the Prevention of Discrimination and the Protection of Minorities. Forty-third session. *Human Rights and the Environment.* Preliminary Report prepared by Fatma Zohra Ksentini, Special Rapporteur, pursuant to Sub-Commission resolutions 1990/7 and 1990/27. E/CN.4/Sub.2/1991/8, 2 August 1991. 29 pp.

> Reviews the provisions of various international instruments on human rights which relate to the environment, lists constitutional provisions, discusses the right to the environment in relation to indigenous peoples' rights and to the right to development. Reviews some of the current ways in which the environment is being assaulted, and the effects of environmental degradation on human rights. Discusses procedural and implementation questions.

C.   *Indices, Guides and Bibliographies*

Buckley-Ess, J., and M. Hathaway, eds. *A Directory of Natural Resource Management Organizations in Latin America and the Caribbean.* 1st ed. s.l.: Partners of the Americas, 1988. 205 pp.

> Lists public and private organizations working in each country. Also describes their activities, whom they work with, their funding sources and contact people. Lists materials, such as reports or brochures, available to the public.

Gates, J. "The Bhopal Chemical Gas Leak Incident: A Research Guide and Bibliography." *International Journal of Legal Information* 19 (Spring 1991): 11-33.

> Lists bibliographies, articles, monographs, and video programs. Section on research guides provides information on Library of Congress subject headings, and suggests terms to use when searching printed and online sources.

Nordquist, J., comp. *Environmental Issues in the Third World: A Bibliography.* Santa Cruz, CA: Reference and Research Services, 1991. 72 pp.

> Unannotated list of English-language books, pamphlets, documents, and articles in periodicals and books. Entries arranged in seven broad subject categories, including deforestation, multinational corporations, the World Bank, and toxic waste dumping. A final section lists bibliographies, directories and environmental organizations.

Templeton, V. *World Environment Law Bibliography: Non-Periodical Literature in Law and the Social Sciences Published since 1970 in Various Languages with Selected Reviews and Annotations from Periodicals.* Littleton, CO: F.B. Rothman, 1987. 480 pp.

> Includes commercially produced monographs and treatises, as well as documents of international organizations and of some foreign governments. Subject index.

D.   *Periodicals*

The following are some of the publications which regularly provide useful articles on environmental law, policy and human rights.

Colorado Journal of International Environmental Law and Policy. Niwot, CO: University Press of Colorado, 1990-.

Georgetown International Environmental Law Review. Washington, DC: Georgetown International Environmental Law Review, 1988-.

International Environmental Affairs. Hanover, NH: University Press of New England for the Trustees of Dartmouth College, 1989-.

International Environmental Law and Policy. Series. Boston: Graham & Trotman; Norweu, MA: Kluwer Academic Publishing Group: 1989-.

International Environment Reporter. Washington, DC: Bureau of National Affairs, 1978-.

IUCN Bulletin. Morges, Switzerland: International Union for the Conservation of Nature and Natural Resources. 1961-.

U.N. International Children's Emergency Fund. *The State of the World's Children.* New York: Oxford University Press. 1980-.

    See annotation on p. 184.

University of Southern California Journal of Law and the Environment. Los Angeles: Students of the Gould School of Law, 1985-1987.

World Bank. *World Development Report.* New York: Oxford University Press, 1978-.

    See annotation on p. 149.

Yearbook of International Environmental Law. London; Boston: Graham & Trotman, 1991-.

    Features a bibliography in every volume and an extensive documents supplement.

V.   Indigenous Peoples' Rights

A.   Books and Articles

Bennett, G. *Aboriginal Rights in International Law*. Occasional Paper of the Royal Anthropological Institute of Great Britain and Ireland, no. 37. London: Anthropological Institute for Survival International, 1978. 88 pp.

> A lawyer's view of the rights to which aboriginal people are currently entitled under international law, and of the prospects of successfully enforcing these rights through the international system. Now somewhat dated.

Brownlie, I. *Treaties and Indigenous Peoples*. Edited by F.M. Brookfield. Oxford: Clarendon Press; New York: Oxford University Press, 1992. 105 pp.

> Collection of four lectures focused on the Treaty of Waitangi and the rights of the Maori people in New Zealand. Specific focus is question of group rights within context of equitable relations with Pakeha. Concepts of self-determination, minority rights and indigenous peoples are examined.

Human Rights Internet. *For the Record: Indigenous Peoples and Slavery in The United Nations*. Human Rights Internet Reporter, suppl. to Vol. 14. Ottawa: Human Rights Internet, 1991. 48 pp.

> Synthesis of four issues of a newsletter published during recent sessions of the U.N. Working Groups on Indigenous Populations and Contemporary Forms of Slavery. Highlights the issues and gets behind the scenes.

Indian Rights, Human Rights: Handbook for Indians on International Human Rights Complaint Procedures. Washington, DC: Indian Law Resource Center, 1984. 129 pp.

> Provides a general discussion of human rights law and institutions. Body of the book is devoted to international complaint procedures. An appendix contains the texts of international instruments and relevant documents a select list of NGOs, and addresses to which complaints should be sent.

Sanders, D. "The Re-Emergence of Indigenous Questions in International Law." *Canadian Human Rights Yearbook* 3 (1983): 3-30.

> Describes indigenous rights movements that have fought for legal rights in international fora in the 19th and 20th centuries.

Sanders, D. "The U.N. Working Group on Indigenous Populations." *Human Rights Quarterly* 11 (August 1989): 406-433.

> An informative account of the evolution, politics and activities of this important body.

Thompson, R., ed. *The Rights of Indigenous Peoples in International Law: Selected Essays on Self-Determination.* Saskatoon: University of Saskatchewan Native Law Centre, 1987. 68 pp.

> Includes articles by G. Alfredsson, A. Eide, D. Shelton, R. Falk, and D. Opekokew. Focuses on indigenous peoples, international law and the United Nations.

United Nations. Sub-Commission on Prevention of Discrimination and Protection of Minorities. *Study of the Problem of Discrimination Against Indigenous Populations.* 5 vols. New York: United Nations, E/CN.4/Sub.2/1986/7/Add.4, 1986.

> Comprehensive compilation of information. Vol. 5, "Conclusions, Proposals and Recommendations," is especially useful.

Vermeer, B., ed. *Archive of the Fourth Russell Tribunal on the Rights of the Indians of the Americas.* Zug, Switzerland: Inter Documentation Co., 1984.

> Microfiche collection of documents by and about Amerindians and other indigenous peoples, presented to the jury of the tribunal and distributed during the tribunal. Includes accusations of violations of human rights and descriptions of the cases presented. Also contains documents about the organization of the Tribunal. Includes indices of countries and areas, peoples and tribes, descriptors, periodicals.

B.   *Newsletters and Periodicals*

Cultural Survival Quarterly. Cambridge, MA: Cultural Survival, 1981-.

> Policy-oriented articles. Most issues focus on a specific theme.

Ethnies: Droits de l'Homme et Peuples Autochtones. Paris: Survival International, 1985-.

> Three times a year.

Fourth World Bulletin: Issues in Indigenous Law and Politics. Denver, CO: University of Colorado at Denver, Fourth World Center for the Study of Indigenous Law and Politics, 1988-.

> Published three times a year. Short articles on legal and political developments in indigenous affairs around the world. Aims to provide forum for indigenous perspectives on domestic and international law and politics.

IWGIA Document. Copenhagen: International Work Group for Indigenous Affairs, 1971-.

> Monographic series. A series of over 70 reports on indigenous peoples. Each report deals with a different group or issue.

IWGIA Newsletter. Copenhagen: International Work Group for Indigenous Affairs, 1978-.

Contains brief articles on indigenous peoples worldwide.

IWGIA Yearbook. Copenhagen: International Work Group for Indigenous Affairs, 1986-.

In-depth studies of indigenous problems, human rights, race discrimination and civil rights.

Indigenous Peoples and Development Series. London: Anti-Slavery Society, 1983-.

A series of reports released about once a year on various topics. Topics of current reports include multinational corporations and ancestral lands in the Philippines; the Chittagong Hill Tracts in Bangladesh; Papua New Guinea; the Hmong of Thailand; land and justice issues for Australian aborigines; and West Papua.

Minority Rights Group. *MRG Reports.* **London: MRG, 1970-.**

A series on minorities. Each report deals with a single group. See p. 167 for full annotation.

Survival: The International Newsletter of Survival International. London: Survival International, 1990-.

Brief articles on current developments. Continues *Survival International News.*

C.   Bibliographies, Guides and Indices

1.   General Bibliographies

Knight, D., and M. Davies. *Self-Determination: An Interdisciplinary Annotated Bibliography.* **New York; London: Garland Publishing, Inc., 1987. 254 pp.**

Contains section, "The Fourth World: Indigenous Peoples."

Narby, J. and S. Davis. *Resource Development and Indigenous Peoples: A Comparative Bibliography.* **Boston: Anthropology Resource Center, 1983. 32 pp.**

Comparative bibliography emphasizing materials on large-scale resource development projects which have demonstrable effects on the environments, economies, social structures and cultures of native communities. Does not include materials on Africa, the Middle East, or most of Asia. Excludes rural social trends in the highland Indian areas of South and Central America. Over 300 entries are arranged by geographic region and by country, and indexed under eight rubrics.

Roy, B. and D. Miller. *The Rights of Indigenous Peoples in International Law: An Annotated Bibliography.* Saskatoon: University of Saskatchewan Native Law Centre, 1985. 97 pp.

Roy, B., and R. Thompson.*The Rights of Indigenous Peoples in International Law: An Annotated Bibliography. Supplement - 1986.* Saskatoon: University of Saskatchewan Native Law Centre, 1986. 33 pp.

> The bibliography and its supplement are restricted to general materials dealing with the general application of international law to indigenous peoples. Specific attention is given to the position in international law of the indigenous nations or peoples living in Canada, the United States and Australia. Useful annotations of the reports of each session of the Working Group on Indigenous Populations. Also includes the Sub-Commission on the Prevention of Discrimination and Protection of Minorities *Study of the Problem of Discrimination Against Indigenous Populations*, by Special Rapporteur Jose Martinez Cobo. Includes relatively recent books, journal articles, dissertations, unpublished papers and U.N. documents. Subject index, followed by alphabetical listing of annotated entries.

Schirmer, J., A. Renteln and L. Wiseberg. "Bibliography on Human Rights and Anthropology." In *Human Rights and Anthropology*, edited by T. Downing and G. Kushner, 121-200. Cambridge, MA: Cultural Survival, 1988.

> Preponderance of sources in this extensive unannotated bibliography are in English. Material is organized by topic, and generally falls into two categories: (1) anthropological and philosophical debates over cultural relativism and legal comparability; and (2) particular problems and issues (such as race, caste, warfare, indigenous peoples).

"Select Bibliography." In *The Rights of Peoples*, edited by J. Crawford, 213-232. Oxford: Clarendon Press; New York: Oxford University Press, 1988.

> Unannotated. Does not include the general human rights literature, unless it is relevant to the debate over peoples' rights.

2.   Bibliographies — Indians of the Americas

Fritz, L. *Native Law Bibliography.* Saskatoon: University of Saskatchewan Native Law Centre, 1984. 100 pp.

> Based almost entirely on the holdings of the Native Law Centre Library, entries are arranged under subject headings. Strong emphasis on Canadian materials, but includes material on North American, Australian, and New Zealand native peoples. The subject fields are divided by country: Australia, Canada, New Zealand, and the United States.

Fritz, L. *Native Law Bibliography.* 2d ed. Saskatoon: University of Saskatchewan Native Law Centre, 1990. 167 pp.

> Organized in the same way as the first edition, but includes a greater range of subject headings.

Hoxie, F. *Native Americans: An Annotated Bibliography.* Pasadena, CA: Salem Press, 1991. 325 pp.

> Focus is on recent scholarly books; less emphasis is given to hard-to-get scholarly journals. Arrangement of entries is by geographic region and subject. Author index.

Martin, M. *Ethnographic Bibliography of North America: 4th Edition. Supplement 1973-1987.* 3 vols. New Haven: Human Relations Area Files Press, 1990.

> Intended to provide basic coverage of literature on the native peoples of North America.

National Indian Law Library. *National Indian Law Library Catalogue: An Index to Indian Legal Materials and Resources.* Boulder, CO: Native American Rights Fund, 1982-.

> The Catalogue contains materials on rights of native peoples in the United States: references to cases, briefs, pleadings, orders and decisions, books, journal articles, reports and studies, and legal opinions and memoranda. A subject index, table of cases, and numerical index are provided. Two supplements have been issued: in 1987, the December 1985 supplement came out; in 1990, the 1989 supplement was released.

3.   Guides —Indians of the Americas

Carter, N. "American Indian Law: Research and Sources." *Legal Reference Services Quarterly* 4 (Winter 1984/1985): 5-71.

> Attempts to bring together all of the major bibliographic and substantive sources on American Indian law. The guide assumes no expertise in American Indian law or history. Basic research instructions and background explanations are given along with the sources. Materials are broadly categorized under primary, secondary and collateral subdivisions.

Haas, M. *Indians of North America: Methods and Sources for Library Research.* Hamden, CT: Library Professional Publications, 1983. 163 pp.

> For the beginning researcher.

Hirschfelder, A., et al. *Guide to Research on North American Indians.* Chicago: American Library Association, 1983. 330 pp.

> Another guide for the beginning researcher, but more in-depth and extensive than the above publication.

D.   *International Labour Organisation (ILO) Indigenous and Tribal Populations Convention*

International Labour Office. *Partial Revision of the Indigenous and Tribal Populations Convention, 1957 (no.107).* **Report VI(1). Geneva: International Labour Office, 1987-1988. 127 pp.**

> This document is the ILO preliminary report which served as a basis for subsequent discussions. It summarizes the background to the ILO Governing Body's decision to consider partial revision of the Convention, presents an analysis of the law and practice on the subject in various countries as well as an overview of recent developments. It also includes, as an appendix, extracts from the report of the Meeting of Experts called by the Governing Body in 1986 for advice on this question. The report, which concluded with a questionnaire, was communicated to the governments of the ILO member states, which were invited to send their replies.

International Labour Office. *Partial Revision of the Indigenous and Tribal Populations Convention, 1957 (no.107).* **Report VI(2). Geneva: International Labour Office, 1987-1988. 112 pp.**

> Contains the replies from member states or employers or workers organizations to the preliminary report.

International Labour Office. *Partial Revision of the Indigenous and Tribal Populations Convention, 1957 (no.107).* **Report IV(1). Geneva: International Labour Office, 1988-1989. 127 pp.**

> Contains the text of a proposed convention concerning indigenous and tribal peoples in independent countries; as well as analyses about international action in the U.N. and ILO; the role of indigenous peoples' organizations and non-indigenous NGOs in international action; and rights issues concerning land, environment and natural resources, and labor and conditions of employment.

International Labour Office. *Partial Revision of the Indigenous and Tribal Populations Convention, 1957 (no.107).* **Report IV(2A). Geneva: International Labour Office, 1988-1989. 68 pp.**

> Contains replies and commentaries of member states to the proposed Convention.

International Labour Office. *Partial Revision of the Indigenous and Tribal Populations Convention, 1957 (no.107).* **Report IV (2B). Geneva: International Labour Office, 1988-1989. 27 pp.**

> Contains the text of a proposed convention concerning indigenous and tribal peoples in independent countries.

VI.   Ethnic and Minority Rights

A.   Books and Articles

Capotorti, F. *Study on the Rights of Persons Belonging to Ethnic, Religious and Linguistic Minorities.* New York: United Nations, 1991. 114 pp.

A comprehensive review of international legal regimes governing ethnic, religious and linguistic minorities, and of discrimination against such minorities. Report appeared originally in 1977 as U.N. Doc. E/CN.4/Sub.2/384, and Add. 1-7, as the final report of the rapporteur appointed by the Sub-Commission on Prevention of Discrimination and Protection of Minorities.

Dinstein, Y., ed. *The Protection of Minorities and Human Rights.* Dordrecht; Boston: M. Nijhoff, 1992. 537 pp.

Collection of essays which grew out of international legal colloquium at the Faculty of Law at Tel Aviv University in March 1990. Topics of essays include conceptual problems of rights of minorities, general issues and specific problems. The book also contains relevant judicial decisions, an index of cases, a name index and subject index.

Hannum, H. *Autonomy, Sovereignty and Self-Determination: The Accommodation of Conflicting Rights.* Philadelphia: University of Pennsylvania Press, 1990. 503 pp.

Part I provides an international legal background to issues of sovereignty, self-determination, minority rights, indigenous rights and human rights. Part II examines claims for autonomy in nine different contexts. Part III offers a survey of contemporary and historical autonomous entities. A concluding chapter analyzes ways in which apparent conflicts among individual, group and state rights can be reconciled.

Horowitz, D. *Ethnic Groups in Conflict.* Berkeley: University of California Press, 1985. 697 pp.

Comprehensive treatment of the importance of ethnic affiliations, the sources of ethnic conflict, interethnic accommodation, and the relation of ethnicity to military politics.

Lerner, N. *Group Rights and Discrimination in International Law.* Dordrecht; Boston: M. Nijhoff, 1991. 181 pp.

A summary and brief analysis of provisions of international law regarding group rights, discrimination and related matters. Part I is an historical overview; Part II treats racial and religious discrimination; Part III deals with protection of specific groups; and Part IV with the protection of specific rights.

Sigler, J., ed. *International Handbook on Race and Race Relations.* New York: Greenwood Press, 1987. 483 pp.

A collection of articles dealing with racial problems in 20 countries.

Steiner, H., ed. *Ethnic Conflict and the U.N. Human Rights System.* Cambridge, MA: Harvard Law School, Human Rights Program, forthcoming 1994.

Nine essays by scholars and activists from different regions on aspects of the U.N. human rights system that bear on ethnic conflicts. Topics include minority issues and group claims in the U.N.; U.N. action on the Sri Lankan and South African conflicts; the role of the Security Council; U.N. development strategy and ethnic conflict; U.N. regulation of autonomy regimes for minorities; and U.N. activity with respect to indigenous peoples.

Thornberry, P. *International Law and the Rights of Minorities.* Oxford: Clarendon Press; New York: Oxford University Press, 1991. 451 pp.

A comprehensive review of minority rights and related problems and issues, including the rights of indigenous peoples, and the protection of minorities under international law.

Thornberry, P. *Minorities and Human Rights Law.* MRG Report No. 73. London: Minority Rights Group, 1991. 37 pp.

An excellent summary, one of many first-rate reports produced by the Minority Rights Group. Most MRG reports deal with a specific group, and discuss the legal, historical and social situation of the group.

Thornberry, P. *World Directory of Minorities.* Chicago: St. James Press, 1990. 427 pp.

Contains over 160 entries covering hundreds of named minorities: provides brief updated versions of Minority Rights Group's reports and other publications, and adds a large number of new entries not previously published. Arranged by geographic region, with a brief introduction to each region. Appendices contain extracts from international instruments of relevance to minority issues. Subject index.

United Nations. Centre for Human Rights. *Second Decade to Combat Racism and Racial Discrimination: Global Compilation of National Legislation Against Racial Discrimination.* New York: U.N., HR/PUB/90/8, 1991. 201 pp.

Contains the text of constitutional or legal provisions governing equality and non-discrimination, specific institutions for the promotion of racial tolerance and harmony, recourse procedures, remedies, penalties and the struggle against *apartheid*. Materials are based on responses of governments to questionnaires sent by the Secretary-General to states around 1985.

Van Dyke, V. *Human Rights, Ethnicity and Discrimination.* Westport, CT: Greenwood Press, 1985. 259 pp.

Author argues that human rights are and should be associated not only with individuals but with groups. Chapters examine groups based on language, religion and race.

B.   Newsletters and Periodicals

Canadian Ethnic Studies. Calgary: Research Centre for Canadian Ethnic Studies at the University of Calgary, 1969-.

> Semiannual, interdisciplinary journal on ethnicity, immigration, inter-group relations and the history and cultural life of ethnic groups in Canada.

Ethnic Studies Report. Kandy, Sri Lanka: International Centre for Ethnic Studies, 1983-.

> Semiannual. Scholarly articles on ethnic studies, with emphasis on South and Southeast Asia.

Europa Ethnica. Vienna: W. Braumuller, 1961-.

> Quarterly. In German, with occasional articles in English and French. Focus on ethnic/ national issues in Europe. Scholarly articles, book reviews, and brief notes on recent developments.

Immigrants and Minorities. London: F. Cass, 1982-.

> Three issues a year. Scholarly articles on immigrants and minorities worldwide.

Minority Rights Group. *MRG Reports.* London: MRG, 1970-.

> A series of over 70 reports, most focused on the legal and social issues facing a single minority group. MRG reports are succinct, accurate, and usually of high quality. Titles vary.

Nationalities Papers. Charleston, IL: Association for the Study of the Nationalities, 1972-.

> Semi-annual publication of the Association for the Study of the Nationalities of the former USSR and Eastern Europe.

C.   Indices, Guides and Bibliographies

Baer, G. "Minorities and Refugees." Chapter 12 in *International Organizations 1918-1945: A Guide to Research and Research Materials*, 145-152. Wilmington, DE: Scholarly Resources, 1991.

> Annotated list of books and articles on the protection of minorities and refugees under the League of Nations.

Bentley, G. *Ethnicity and Nationality: A Bibliographic Guide.* Seattle: University of Washington Press, 1981. 381 pp.

> Lists English-language materials published through 1979. First section contains annotated entries, followed by a larger section of unannotated works. Has an index by geographic area and by contents.

Gilbert, V. "Current Bibliography of Immigrants and Minorities: Monographs, Articles and Theses, 1982-1984: Part I." *Immigrants & Minorities* 6 (July 1987): 212-254.

Gilbert, V. "Current Bibliography of Immigrants and Minorities: Monographs, Periodical Articles and Theses, 1982-1984: Part II." *Immigrants & Minorities* 6 (November 1987): 369-388.

> Both of the bibliographies above are unannotated, but entries are arranged in detailed subject or geographical categories.

Horak, S. *Eastern European National Minorities, 1919-1980: A Handbook.* Littleton, CO: Libraries Unlimited, 1985. 353 pp.

> Annotated bibliography of 982 items.

Institute of Race Relations. *Sage Race Relations Abstracts.* London; Beverly Hills: Sage Publications, 1975-.

> Quarterly which abstracts European and U.S. periodical literature on immigration and race relations.

Kinloch, G. *Race and Ethnic Relations: An Annotated Bibliography.* New York: Garland, 1984, 250 pp.

> English language books and articles published between 1960 and 1980 on inter-group relations, primarily in the United States.

Knight, D., and M. Davies. *Self-Determination: An Interdisciplinary Annotated Bibliography.* New York: Garland, 1987. 254 pp.

> The authors selected major works and interpretations in English across a wide range of disciplines. Includes a selection of the *Selbstbestimmungsrecht* literature in German, and a few pertinent French sources. Articles in newspapers and magazines are not included. Entries are arranged in six thematic chapters: "practice and interpretations," "theoretical considerations: identity, territory and power," "world regional perspectives and state case studies," "the fourth world: indigenous peoples," and "future directions." Annotations are detailed, excellent short expositions of the positions taken in, and the significance of, each work cited. Contains an index of authors.

Newman, R., comp. *Black Access: A Bibliography of Afro-American Bibliographies.* Westport, CT: Greenwood Press, 1984. 249 pp.

Unannotated listing of books and articles. Includes subjects of slavery and Reconstruction in the United States, but excludes works on the U.S. Civil War, the Caribbean, Latin America and Africa. Subject index.

Palley, C. *Minorities and Autonomy in Western Europe.* London: Minority Rights Group, 1991. 32 pp.

Brief case studies of minority groups in seven countries: Italy, Finland, Denmark, Germany, Belgium, Switzerland, and the Netherlands.

Potgieter, P.J. *Index to Literature on Race Relations in South Africa, 1910-1975.* Boston: G.K. Hall, 1979. 555 pp.

Detailed subject index and author index to books and periodical articles on *apartheid*, its implementation, and *apartheid*-centered society; problems posed by South African multiracialism and multinationalism; and racial and cultural differences in other countries. Does not include newspaper reports or unpublished documents. Selection is limited to items in Afrikaans, English, Dutch and German. U.N. documents/publications not included, nor are most South African government publications.

Rupesinghe, K. and B. Verstappen. *Ethnic Conflict and Human Rights in Sri Lanka: An Annotated Bibliography.* London; New York: Hans Zell, 1989. 565 pp.

Attempts to record the literature on the escalation of internal conflict, with emphasis on 1983-1988. Includes scholarly articles, documents and statements from the parties to the conflict.

"Select Bibliography." In *The Rights of Peoples*, edited by J. Crawford, 213-232. Oxford: Clarendon Press; New York: Oxford University Press, 1988.

Unannotated. Does not include the general human rights literature, unless it is relevant to the debate over peoples' rights. Entries are listed under the following headings: (1) General and Miscellaneous, (2) African Charter on Human and Peoples' Rights, (3) Right to Communication, (4) Cultural and Linguistic Rights, (5) Right to Development, (6) Rights to Environment, (7) Right to Existence, (8) Rights of Indigenous Peoples, (9) Right to International Peace, (10) Rights of Minorities, (11) Permanent Sovereignty over Natural Resources, (12) Right to Self-Determination.

Sigler, J. *Minority Rights: A Comparative Analysis.* Westport, CT: Greenwood Press, 1983. 245 pp.

Focuses on the legal status of and laws affecting minorities. Contains an annotated bibliography of minority rights, pp. 215-237.

VII. Refugees and Population Movements

A.   Compilations of Instruments and Documents

Office of the United Nations High Commissioner for Refugees. *Collection of International Instruments Concerning Refugees.* **2d ed. Geneva: UNHCR, 1979. 335 pp.**

> Includes texts of international instruments, but contains no information on which states have ratified them. Includes universal and regional instruments and the Statute of the Office of the U.N. High Commissioner for Refugees (UNHCR).

Office of the United Nations High Commissioner for Refugees. *Handbook on Procedures and Criteria for Determining Refugee Status under the 1951 Convention and the 1967 Protocol Relating to the Status of Refugees.* **Geneva: UNHCR, 1979. 93 pp.**

> Authoritative handbook on terms and procedures. U.S. immigration and federal courts, as well as courts in other countries, have looked to this handbook for assistance in interpreting the Convention and Protocol.

Office of the United Nations High Commissioner for Refugees. *United Nations Resolutions and Decisions Relating to the Office of the United Nations High Commissioner for Refugees.* **1989 ed. Geneva: UNHCR, HCR/INF/.49, 1989-.**

> Looseleaf. Published irregularly. Provides the texts of all resolutions and decisions of the U.N. General Assembly and the Economic and Social Council relating to the Office of the U. N. High Commissioner for Refugees.

Plender, R. ed. *Basic Documents on International Migration Law.* **Dordrecht; Boston: M. Nijhoff, 1988. 411 pp.**

> Provides excerpts or full texts of the principal legal instruments governing migration. 77 instruments are included. Provides a list of states parties to each instrument.

Takkenberg, A. and C. Tahbaz, eds. *The Collected Travaux Preparatoires of the 1951 Geneva Convention Relating to the Status of Refugees.* **3 vols. Amsterdam: Dutch Refugee Council, 1990.**

> Reprints of U.N. documents pertaining to the drafting history of the Convention, organized chronologically. Detailed tables of contents in each volume indicate subject areas or articles discussed in summary records.

B.   Books

Anker, D. *The Law of Asylum in the United States: A Guide to Administrative Practice and Caselaw*. 2d ed. Washington, DC: American Immigration Law Foundation, 1991. 191 pp.

> A comprehensive treatment of U.S. asylum jurisprudence and practice with useful resource appendices.

Bhabha, J., and G. Coel. *Asylum Law and Practice in Europe and North America*. 1st ed. Washington, DC: Federal Publications, 1992. 239 pp.

> A comparative analysis by leading experts. Important issues addressed from a comparative perspective.

Goodwin-Gill, G. *The Refugee in International Law*. Oxford: Clarendon Press; New York: Oxford University Press, 1983. 318 pp.

> Good survey and introduction to Refugee Convention concepts. A particularly useful discussion of *nonrefoulement* principle.

Grahl-Madsen, A. *The Status of Refugees in International Law*. 2 vols. Leyden: A.W. Sijthoff, 1966-1972.

> Classic treatise on refugee law. Cited as authority by U.S. courts and international scholars. Good starting point for researchers.

Hathaway, J. *The Law of Refugee Status*. Toronto: Butterworths, 1991. 252 pp.

> Good introduction to and comprehensive treatment of the refugee definition, with emphasis on Canadian jurisprudence.

Lawyers Committee for Human Rights. *The Human Rights of Refugees and Displaced Persons: Protections Afforded Refugees, Asylum Seekers, and Displaced Persons under International Human Rights, Humanitarian and Refugee Law*. New York: Lawyers Committee for Human Rights, 1991. 28 pp.

> Examines the extent to which human rights law supplements and extends existing refugee law protection afforded refugees, asylum seekers, and displaced persons under refugee law and humanitarian law.

Plender, R. *International Migration Law*. 2d ed. Dordrecht; Boston: M. Nijhoff, 1988. 587 pp.

> Two chapters give the historical background of the concept of nationality and the exclusionary power of the state. Subsequent chapters treat the right to leave and return; freedom of movement in the European Community; Council of Europe conventions; migration for employment; temporary migration; and refugees and the expulsion of aliens.

C.   Newsletters and Periodicals

Berliner Institut fur Vergleichende Sozialforschung. *Archiv Migration.* **Berlin: Berliner Institut fur Vergleichende Sozialforschung, 1986-.**

Monthly. Chiefly in German with some parts in Turkish and English. A collection of photocopied newspaper articles, gathered monthly from newspapers in German, English and Turkish, and journals dealing with international migration movements and discrimination.

Center for Migration Studies. *International Migration Review.* **New York: Center for Migration Studies, 1964-.**

Quarterly containing scholarly articles, research notes, conference reports, book reviews, review of reviews (brief annotations of books and articles), international newsletter on migration, and list of books received.

International Journal of Refugee Law. **Oxford: Oxford University Press, 1989-.**

A quarterly journal, aiming to stimulate research and thinking on refugee law and its development. A special 350-page issue is a supplement to Vol. 2. Part I contains selected papers presented at the Lowenstein Symposium on International Human Rights Law at Yale Law School in April 1990. Part II provides a series of government working papers, and perspectives from international organizations and nongovernmental organizations.

Refugee Studies Programme. *Journal of Refugee Studies.* **Oxford: Oxford University Press, 1988-.**

Quarterly of Oxford's Refugee Studies Programme. Contains scholarly articles, field reports, interviews, conference reports, book reviews and announcements.

Refugee Settlement Information Exchange Project. *Refugee Reports.* **Washington, DC: Refugee Resettlement Information Exchange Project, 1979-.**

A current awareness newsletter published biweekly. Includes a feature article, a recent developments section, an update section, information on new programs and projects, current research, and short sections entitled "Job Board," "Meetings and Conferences," and "Statistics."

U.N. High Commissioner for Refugees. *Refugees.* **Geneva: UNHCR, 1984-.**

Monthly magazine of the U.N. High Commissioner for Refugees. Brief, general articles for the nonspecialist.

U.S. Committee for Refugees. *World Refugee Survey.* **New York: U.S. Committee for Refugees, 1980-.**

> Annual containing articles, statistical tables and graphs, country reports, directory of refugee organizations, and a bibliography.

World Refugee Report. **Washington, DC: U.S. Department of State. Bureau for Refugee Programs, 1985-.**

> Annual. Continues *Country Reports on the World Refugee Situation.* Reviews the situation of refugees worldwide. Provides statistical data.

D.   *Indices, Guides and Bibliographies*

Allard, D. *A Selected and Annotated Bibliography on Refugee Children.* **Geneva: Centre for Documentation on Refugees, U.N. High Commissioner for Refugees, 1988. 138 pp.**

> Annotated list of 258 items, arranged according to nine categories. Contains subject and author indices.

International Refugee Integration Resource Centre, U.N. High Commissioner for Refugees. *International Bibliography of Refugee Literature.* **Working Ed. Geneva: IRIRC, 1984. 153 pp.**

> Lists books, articles, documents and reports published (mainly after 1979). Access by region, broad subject heading, author. Uses the same categories as used in the journal *Refugee Abstracts*: International, Origins, Exodus, Asylum, Resettlement, and Integration. Entries are arranged by subcategories under these rubrics. A list of book and journal publishers' addresses is provided. Most entries in English, some in French and German.

Larson, C. "Refugees: Information Sources." Paper Presented at the Seventh National Third World Studies Conference, Omaha, NB: October 18-20, 1984. 27 pp.

> Covers indices and abstracts, periodicals, resource and research centers, and recent bibliographies. Good discussion of online databases.

Luca, D. "The 1951 Convention Relating to the Status of Refugees, A Selected Bibliography." *International Journal of Refugee Law* **3 (1991): 633-663.**

> Contains 72 entries referencing sources in English, Spanish, German and French. Focus is on items which deal with the 1951 Convention Relating to the Status of Refugees at the international level, not the level of national implementation. Each entry has an abstract.

Office of the U.N. High Commissioner for Refugees and the Refugee Policy Group. *A Selected and Annotated Bibliography on Refugee Women.* **Geneva: U.N. High Commissioner for Refugees, 1985. 69 pp.**

Lists articles, books, documents, conference papers, arranged by four categories: international, exodus, countries of asylum, and countries of resettlement. Author and subject index, and publishers' addresses are provided.

Peace Palace Library. *Right of Asylum: Selective Bibliography.* **The Hague: Peace Palace Library, 1989. 74 pp.**

Selective bibliography compiled from materials at the Peace Palace Library. Closing date is July 1989. Entries arranged by subject and geographical categories.

Refugee Abstracts. **Geneva: Centre for Documentation on Refugees, U.N. High Commissioner for Refugees, 1982-.**

Quarterly. Essential source, containing the following sections: an annotated bibliography of scholarly books, articles, reports, and documents; an annotated list of practice-oriented manuals and documents; book reviews; the texts of resolutions and other documents of international organizations; and information on upcoming conferences, meetings and courses.

Rumbaut, R., comp. *Refugees in the Contemporary World: A Selected Bibliography.* **San Diego, CA: San Diego State University, Indochinese Health and Adaptation Research Project, 1985. 34 pp.**

Unannotated. Entries organized in a broad subject arrangement, followed by a "case study" section listing works by region.

"Selected Works on the Rights and Status of Refugees Under United States and International Law, 1960-1980." *Michigan Yearbook of International Legal Studies Annual.* **1982: 589-630.**

Well-annotated entries are arranged under several headings. Includes books, periodical articles, U.S. government publications, and a list of serial publications relating to refugees.

E. Directories and Thesauri

Aitchison, J. *International Thesaurus on Refugee Terminology.* **Dordrecht; Boston: M. Nijhoff, 1989. 476 pp.**

Intended for use by organizations active in documentation work concerning refugees. The thesaurus is to be published in French and Spanish as well. It is in five parts, having a systematic display, an alphabetical display, a permuted index, and two indices of language concordance, where terms are listed in French, English and Spanish equivalents, with references to their class codes in the systematic display.

Honsey, D., S. Rosen and D. Weissbrodt. *Guide to Documentation Resources for Asylum Applications.* **Minneapolis, MN: Amnesty International, USA, 1991. 38 pp.**

Lists organizations which have documentation centers or publish information about human rights conditions in various parts of the world. Intended to be used by legal practitioners.

Refugee Studies Program. *The Directory of Current Research on Refugees and Other Forced Migrants.* **Oxford: Oxford University Press, 1987. 119 pp.**

Four sections. "Directory" lists alphabetically the most important details for some 150 researchers; Appendix I lists the major output of these researchers, both published and unpublished. Two other appendices are classified listings of the researchers: Appendix II, according to academic discipline, and Appendix III, according to the area of the world which has been their primary focus.

Schorr, A. *Refugee and Immigrant Resource Directory 1990-1991.* **Juneau, AK: Denali Press, 1990. 349 pp.**

Includes information on 958 local, regional, national and a few international organizations, research centers, academic programs, and foundations, etc. that offer services or provide information and/or policy analysis about refugees and immigrants. Organizations are arranged by state. Appendices contain U.S. Immigration and Naturalization Service office listings, tables and charts on current and historical trends in immigration and refugee admissions to the United States.

VIII. Women's Rights

A. Books and Articles

Change International Reports. **London: Change, 1980-.**

About 20 short reports on the status of women in different countries or under special circumstances have been produced, usually authored by a woman from the country concerned. "Thinkbooks" on themes such as "Violence and Violation: Women and Human Rights" (1986) have also been produced.

Charlesworth, H., ed. *What Are Women's International Human Rights?* **Philadelphia: University of Pennsylvania Press, forthcoming, 1994.**

A series of essays about women's rights as international human rights. Extensive footnotes and bibliographic information will be provided.

Connors, J.F. *Violence Against Women in the Family.* **New York: United Nations, 1989. 120 pp.**

A survey of available literature, and an analysis of research findings on the issue of violence against women in the family. Chapters explore the causes and consequences of violence against women in the home, types of responses to violence, and strategies for the future.

Department of International Economic and Social Affairs, Statistical Office, and International Research and Training Institute for the Advancement of Women. *Improving Concepts and Methods for Statistics and Indicators on Women.* **New York: United Nations, 1984. 70 pp.**

This work has two stated aims: (1) to identify gaps and problem areas where reconceptualization of indicators is critical, and (2) to propose long-range goals for improving the quality and relevance of data on the condition of women.

Distribution of Seats Between Men and Women in National Parliaments: Statistical Data from 1945 to 30 June 1991. **Reports and Documents Series, no. 18. Geneva: Inter-Parliamentary Union, 1991. 175 pp.**

Bilingual (French and English).

Forward-Looking Strategies for the Advancement of Women to the Year 2000. **A/CONF.11/28, September 15, 1985. 89 pp.**

Report of the World Conference held in Nairobi, Kenya to review and appraise the achievements of the United Nations Decade for Women. Focuses on progress in the areas of equality, development and peace.

Hevener, N. *International Law and the Status of Women.* **Boulder, CO: Westview Press, 1983. 249 pp.**

Examines the more than 20 international legal instruments dealing specifically with women.

International Labour Office. Committee of Experts on the Application of Conventions and Recommendations. *General Survey of the Reports on the Equal Remuneration Convention (No.100) and Recommendation (No. 90), 1951.* **Geneva: International Labour Office, 1986. 203 pp.**

See p. 102 for annotation.

Inter-Parliamentary Union. *Women and Political Power.* **Geneva: Inter-Parliamentary Union, 1992. 191 pp.**

Cross-country objective and subjective data on a number of questions relating to political participation: the right to vote and be elected, exercise of voting rights, political awareness, women in political parties, affirmative action, women in government, the image of women politicians, etc.

Isaacs, S. et al. *Assessing the Status of Women: A Guide to Reporting Using the Convention on the Elimination of All Forms of Discrimination Against Women.* New York: International Women's Rights Action Watch, 1988. 44 pp.

> Manual designed to assist individuals and groups assess and report on the status of women in their country using the Convention as a framework. Committee on the Elimination of Discrimination Against Women (CEDAW) guidelines and suggestions are provided, as is a series of questions under each of the 16 substantive Convention articles. An appendix gives information on past reports of CEDAW and on the International Research and Training Institute for the Advancement of Women (INSTRAW).

LAWASIA. *Women and the Law.* Kuala Lumpur: LAWASIA Human Rights Standing Committee, 1986. 245 pp.

> Report of a seminar, including papers on a number of issues concerning women in Asia and the Western Pacific. A sampling of the papers contained in the report: "Human Rights and Family Law," "Women and Employment in Malaysia," "Women and the Law in Singapore," "Positive Glances at Thai Women's Rights," "Women and the Law in the Republic of Korea," and "Women and the Law in Australia."

Ohshima S. and C. Francis. *Japan Through the Eyes of Women Migrant Workers.* Tokyo: Japan Women's Christian Temperance Union, 1989. 220 pp.

> See pp. 142-143 for annotation.

Rhoodie, E. *Discrimination against Women: A Global Survey of the Economic, Educational, Social and Political Status of Women.* Jefferson, NC: McFarland, 1989. 618 pp.

> Gives surveys of the major regions of the world, with country case studies. Chapter 31, "Data: Guide to Information Sources" provides an overview of the availability of source material on women's progress toward equality. Subsequent sections cover comparative or international studies, sources by region, and law and other journals and newspapers which regularly contain articles about women's status and women's rights. An unannotated alphabetical bibliography appears on pp. 587-599.

Schmittroth, L., comp. and ed. *Statistical Record of Women Worldwide.* Detroit; Gale Research, 1991. 763 pp.

> Coverage is approximately 50% U.S. and 50% international. Data about men, data by race/ethnicity, and about girls are also presented whenever feasible, as is information on historical changes from 1970 (for U.S. data). Statistics are arranged according to topic, e.g. income, spending and wealth; crime, law enforcement and legal justice; the military; and health and medical care. Contains a subject and geographic index.

Sicherl, P. *Methods of Measuring Disparity between Men and Women: A Technical Report.* Santo Domingo, Dominican Republic: International Research and Training Institute for the Advancement of Women, 1989. 178 pp.

> Discusses techniques for the analysis of gender disparities over time.

Taubenfeld, R. and H. Taubenfeld, eds. *International Treaties, Declarations, and Other Acts Concerning Sex-Based Discrimination and the Rights of Women in International Law.* 4 vols. Dobbs Ferry, NY: Oceana Publications, 1978-.

> Looseleaf containing the texts of documents relating to the rights of women: treaties and other international agreements, major declarations of international bodies, and national constitutional provisions.

United Nations. Division for the Advancement of Women. *Directory of National Machinery for the Advancement of Women, 1991.* Vienna: United Nations Division for the Advancement of Women, 1991. 170 pp.

> Contains entries from 110 countries on organizational structures established with particular responsibility for the advancement of women and the elimination of discrimination against women at the central or national level. These include governmental, non-governmental or joint bodies.

United Nations. Statistical Office. *Compiling Social Indicators on the Situation of Women.* New York: United Nations, 1984. 94 pp.

> Not primarily concerned with the development of new data collection programs, but with developing reliable indicators on the situation of women from existing censuses, household surveys and registration systems. Has some discussion of the underlying methods and concepts of existing sources. Part One reviews basic methods, objectives, and sources for social indicators on the situation of women. Part Two presents and discusses illustrative indicators in a series of areas. See companion publication, *Improving Concepts and Methods for Statistics and Indicators on Women,* described on p. 176.

United Nations. Statistical Office. *The World's Women 1970-1990: Trends and Statistics.* New York: United Nations, 1991, ST/ESA/STAT/SER.K/8. 120 pp.

> Intended to enable a better understanding of which conditions have changed for women — and which have not. Tries to reach women, women's advocates and the media. Provides concise statistical information and analysis on the following topics: (1) women, families and households; (2) public life and leadership; (3) education and training; (4) health and child-bearing; (5) housing, human settlements and the environment; and (6) women's work and the economy.

Women, Law and Development in Africa. *WILDAF: Origins and Issues.* **Washington, DC: OEF International, 1990. 276 pp.**

> Part II contains status reports from 16 countries on critical legal problems for women and local and national initiatives for confronting them. Part III contains papers which explore a series of issues on women and the law: rights awareness, organizing, access to economic resources, and violence toward women.

B. *Newsletters and Periodicals*

HELP Asian Women's Shelter. *Network News No.[#].* **Tokyo: HELP Asian Women's Shelter.**

> Newsletter of the HELP shelter, providing information on the current situation of women migrant workers in Japan, current activities of the shelter, and statistical information on women migrant workers in Japan. Three times per year.

ISIS International. *Book Series.* **Rome: ISIS International, 1987-.**

> Continues *ISIS International Women's Journal* (see below).

ISIS International Women's Journal. **Rome: ISIS International, 1984-1986.**

> Articles on international feminism and women in developing countries. Continued by *Book Series.* Each issue of the journal is usually devoted to a single theme.

International Research and Training Institute for the Advancement of Women. *INSTRAW News.* **Santo Domingo, Dominican Republic: United Nations International Research and Training Institute for the Advancement of Women, 1984-.**

> Brief articles on the activities of INSTRAW, including descriptions of workshops, seminars and projects. In English, French, and Spanish.

International Women's Tribune Centre. *Tribune: A Women and Development Quarterly.* **New York: International Women's Tribune Centre, 1981-.**

> Quarterly. Focus is building a global network of activists working on international women's rights.

Women in Action. **Rome: ISIS International, 1984-.**

> Semiannual newsletter on the activities of women's groups, international feminism, and the social situation of women. Appears in Spanish as *Mujeres en Accion.*

Women Living under Muslim Laws/Femmes sous Lois Musulmanes. Dossiers. **Grabels (Montpellier), France: Women Living under Muslim Laws/Femmes sous Lois Musulmanes, International Solidarity Network, 1986-.**

Occasional, in French or English. Dossiers include articles, reports and campaign material on the situation of women subject to Islamic law.

Women's International Network. *News — Women's International Network.* **Lexington, MA: WIN, 1974-.**

Quarterly. Lists documentation, reports, conferences, organizations, and publications.

Women's World. **Geneva: ISIS-Women's International Cross-Cultural Exchange, 1984-.**

Quarterly. Each year the publication is issued twice as dossier and twice as a newsletter. Dossiers are organized around a single theme. Issued in English and Spanish.

C.   Indices, Guides and Bibliographies

Annual Review of Population Law. **New York: U.N. Fund for Population and Harvard Law School Library, 1974-.**

See p. 138 for annotation.

Byrne, P. and S. Ontiveros, eds. *Women in the Third World: A Historical Bibliography.* **Santa Barbara, CA: ABC-Clio Information Services, 1986. 152 pp.**

600 abstracts and citations of journal articles published between 1970-1985. Entries arranged alphabetically by author within geographic chapters.

Commission on the Status of Women. *List of Resolutions and Decisions on the Status of Women Adopted by the General Assembly and the Economic and Social Council 1946-1990.* **Vienna: U.N. Division for the Advancement of Women, 1991. 88 pp.**

Part One lists in chronological order all such resolutions and decisions since the establishment of the United Nations. Part Two is an alphabetical list of keywords in the resolutions and decisions of 1974-1990.

Cook, R. "Women's International Human Rights: A Bibliography. "*New York University Journal of International Law and Politics.* **24 (Winter 1992): 857-888.**

An extensive listing of published works on the right to nondiscrimination on the basis of gender established by the Convention on the Elimination of All Forms of Discrimination Against Women, and other international and regional human rights instruments. Focuses on international law. Articles are not annotated, but the bibliography lists and annotates cases heard by the Human Rights Committee, the Permanent   Court of

International Justice, the European Commission and Court of Human Rights, and the Inter-American Court of Human Rights. Cook updates the bibliography on an ongoing basis.

Ferber, M. *Women and Work, Paid and Unpaid: A Selected, Annotated Bibliography.* **New York: Garland, 1987. 408 pp.**

Lists and critically annotates 1,031 monographs and journal articles, most published since 1960. Entries are arranged in four major chapters.

International Refugee Integration Resource Centre, U.N. High Commissioner for Refugees. *International Bibliography of Refugee Literature.* **Working Ed. Geneva: IRIRC, 1984. 153 pp.**

Contains sections on women and children (including unaccompanied minors), pp. 55-60; 100-101. (See p. 173 for full annotation.)

Nordquist, J., comp. *The Feminization of Poverty.* **Santa Cruz, CA: Reference and Research Services, 1987. 64 pp.**

Bibliography on female poverty, sex discrimination, employment discrimination, and women heads of households. Focus is on the United States.

Nordquist, J., comp. *Rape: A Bibliography.* **Santa Cruz, CA: Reference and Research Services, 1990. 72 pp.**

Lists books, articles, documents and pamphlets that pertain to rape. Includes a list of resources.

Studies on Women Abstracts. **Abingdon, Oxfordshire: Carfax Pub. Co., 1983-.**

Quarterly. Abstracts theoretical and empirical materials from major international journals and books. Each issue has author and subject index.

Watson, G. and J. Sentner. *Feminism and Women's Issues: An Annotated Bibliography and Research Guide.* **2 vols. New York: Garland, 1990. 1710 pp.**

A very useful compilation of more than 7,300 entries covering English-language books and articles on a broad range of women's issues. Most sources were published between 1970-1985. Table of contents functions as an index, but is somewhat difficult to use.

Women Studies Abstracts. **Rush, NY: Rush Pub. Co., 1972-.**

Quarterly, with annual index. Abstracts articles from a wide range of periodicals, including foreign-language journals. Abstracts are arranged in broad subject categories. There is good cross-referencing, and a detailed subject index. This is an especially useful tool because of its broad geographic scope, and the range of publications—academic, policy and activist—that it indexes.

IX.   Children's Rights

A.   Books and Articles

Alston, P. et al., eds. *Children, Rights and the Law.* Oxford: Clarendon Press; New York: Oxford University Press, 1992. 268 pp.

> Using the U.N. Convention on the Rights of the Child as a framework, contributors examine the advantages and disadvantages of approaching children's rights from a "rights" perspective.

Application of International Standards Concerning the Human Rights of Detained Juveniles. **Report prepared by the Special Rapporteur, Mary Concepcion Bautista, pursuant to U.N. Sub-Commission Resolution 1991/16, E/CN.4/Sub.2/1992/20. 3 June 1992. 20 pp.**

> Provides an overview of pertinent international standards, efforts to implement them, observations and recommendations.

Cohen, C. P. and H. Davidson, eds. *Children's Rights in America: U.N. Convention on the Rights of the Child Compared with United States Law.* Chicago: American Bar Association Center on Children and the Law, 1990. 344 pp.

> A collection of essays by specialists in various areas of U.S. law, who analyze the extent to which U.S. national and state laws and social policies conform to the Convention's standards.

Commission on Human Rights. *Sale of Children.* **Report submitted by Vitit Muntarbhorn, Special Rapporteur appointed in accordance with U.N. Resolution 1990/68 of the Commission on Human Rights, E/CN.4/1991/51. 28 January 1991. 18 pp.**

> Describes situation of the "sale of children," including adoption, child labor, organ transplantation, child prostitution, and child pornography. Briefly discusses issues of causation, the international legal framework on the issue of the sale of children, and tools for assessing national contexts. Indicates areas where action is needed, and ends with conclusions and recommendations.

Detrick, S., ed. and comp. *The United Nations Convention on the Rights of the Child: A Guide to the Travaux Preparatoires.* Dordrecht; Boston: M. Nijhoff, 1992. 712 pp.

> Provides complete overview of drafting process of the U.N. Convention on the Rights of the Child. Includes compilation of the main U.N. documents by the Convention Working Group and the Commission on Human Rights.

Freeman, M. and P. Veerman, eds. *The Ideologies of Children's Rights.* International Studies in Human Rights, vol. 23. Dordrecht; Boston: M. Nijhoff, 1992. 369 pp.

> Analysis of moral foundations and theoretical underpinnings of children's rights. Questions addressed include universality of rights of child, relevance of theories of natural law and legal positivism, and attitudes toward and by children. Also addresses applications of rights in specific countries and areas of protection (e.g., welfare rights, education, health, prevention of child abuse, juvenile justice, protection of children in armed conflict).

Veerman, P. *The Rights of the Child and the Changing Image of Childhood.* Dordrecht; Boston: M. Nijhoff, 1992. 655 pp.

> A comprehensive review of attempts in the 20th century to define the rights and needs of the child with reference to more than 40 declarations and conventions relevant to children's rights.

B.   *Newsletters and Periodicals*

Anti-Slavery Society for the Protection of Human Rights. *Child Labour Series.* London: Anti-Slavery Society, 1978-.

> Irregular. Each report is devoted to a specific issue.

The Children's Tribune. New York: Defense for Children International-USA, 1988-.

> A bulletin to the U.S. Congress on DCI-USA concerns. Also provides news of DCI activities and publications.

Defence for Children International. *International Children's Rights Monitor.* Geneva: DCI, 1983-.

> Quarterly. Current awareness publication on children's rights issues and advocacy at the national and international levels.

International Journal of Children's Rights. Dordrecht: M. Nijhoff; Boston: Kluwer Academic Publishers, 1993-.

> Quarterly. Critical scholarship and practical policy development. Journal uses insights and methodologies of relevant social science, medical, public health, social work, humanities, and legal disciplines.

United Nations International Children's Emergency Fund. *Assignment Children.* Geneva: UNICEF, 1979-.

> Semi-annual. Multidisciplinary journal concerned with major social development issues, with particular reference to children, women and youth. Cumulative index 1979-1982, published in 1983. Author and subject index.

United Nations International Children's Emergency Fund. *The State of the World's Children.* Oxford; New York: Oxford University Press, 1980-.

> Annual. Contains 21 brief articles reviewing the situation of children internationally. Economic and social statistics, with particular reference to children's well-being, are presented. Includes statistics on nutrition, health and education; basic, demographic and economic indicators; basic indicators on less populous countries; and the rate of progress.

C.   Indices, Guides and Bibliographies

Corcos, C. "The Child in International Law: A Pathfinder and Selected Bibliography." *Case Western Reserve Journal of International Law* 23 (Spring 1991): 171-196.

> Provides a broad range of information related to children's rights: books, articles, bibliographies, databases, materials by and about NGOs. The author's commentary provides useful background on the evolution, current debates and status of the rights of the child.

International Labour Office. *Annotated Bibliography on Child Labour.* Geneva: International Labour Office, 1986. 69 pp.

> Lists monographs, journal articles, reports, conference proceedings, and chapters of books. Most of the references are documents that are widely accessible.

X.   Rights of Sexual Minorities

A.   Books and Articles

Adam, B.D. *The Rise of a Gay and Lesbian Movement.* Boston: Twayne, 1987. 203 pp.

> Provides an overview of the emergence of lesbian and gay subcultures and political movements throughout the Western world, and indicates prospects for further expansion in Western as well as non-Western countries.

Batchelor, E. Jr., ed. *Homosexuality and Ethics.* New York: Pilgrim, 1980. 261 pp.

> Collection of essays representing the entire range of Christian attitudes toward homosexuality — from hostility to acceptance — written by prominent theologians.

Baumgardt, M., et al. *Die Geschichte des §175: Strafrecht gegen Homosexuelle.* Berlin: Rosa Winkel, 1990. 175 pp.

> Collection of essays examining the history of legal prohibitions of homosexual conduct in Germany.

Blackwood, E., ed. *Anthropology and Homosexual Behavior*. New York: Haworth, 1986. (Originally published as *Journal of Homosexuality*, Vol. 11, Nos. 3/4, Summer 1985). 217 pp.

Collection of essays examining non-heterosexual identities and experiences in a number of cultures.

Cohen-Jonathan, G. "Respect de la vie privée et familiale." In *Juris Classeur: Vol.5, Traité de droit européen*, Fasc. 6521, 3-16. Paris: Editions Techniques, 1992.

Homosexuality, transsexualism, and the right to privacy under the European Convention.

Crane, P. *Gays and the Law*. London: Pluto Press, 1982. 244 pp.

An account of the law on homosexuality in England, Wales, Scotland and Northern Ireland. The author attempts to bring together and analyze the laws affecting gay men and lesbian women in these regions, and demonstrates how these laws reflect and reinforce popular prejudices. Contains a list of gay rights organizations in the United Kingdom.

Darty, T. and S. Potter, eds. *Women-Identified Women*. Palo Alto: Mayfield, 1984. 316 pp.

Collection of essays on various aspects of lesbian life, including discrimination, self-image, and social adjustment.

Duberman, M., M. Vicinus, and G. Chauncey, Jr. *Hidden from History: Reclaiming the Gay and Lesbian Past*. New York: Penguin, 1990. 579 pp.

Comprehensive collection of essays on the history of homosexuality.

Dyer, K., ed. *Gays in Uniform*. Boston: Alyson, 1990. 135 pp.

Examines discrimination against homosexuals in military service in the United States.

Fernand-Laurent, J. "Les problèmes juridiques et sociaux des minorités sexuelles." (Trans., "The Legal and Social Problems of Sexual Minorities.") U.N. doc. E/CN/Sub.2/1988/31.

First United Nations treatment of sexual minorities. Reflects little knowledge of the subject.

Girard, P. "The Protection of the Rights of Homosexuals under the International Law of Human Rights: European Perspectives." *Canadian Human Rights Yearbook* (*Annuaire Canadien des droits de la Personne*) 1986: 3-24.

Reflections on European human rights law in the wake of *Dudgeon*.

Gonsiorek, J. C. and J. D. Weinrich, eds. *Homosexuality: Research Implications for Public Policy.* **Newbury Park: Sage, 1991. 295 pp.**

Collection of essays surveying social, political, and theoretical issues germane to the study of homosexuality. Important work. Essay on international perspective.

Greenberg, D. *The Construction of Homosexuality.* **Chicago: University of Chicago, 1988. 635 pp.**

Historical and anthropological survey of non-heterosexual orientation and behavior, and of the emergence of a distinctly homosexual identity. Important work.

Harvard Law Review, eds. *Sexual Orientation and the Law.* **Cambridge, MA: Harvard, 1990. 170 pp.**

Survey and analysis of legal discrimination against homosexuals in the United States.

Hasbany, R., ed. *Homosexuality and Religion.* **New York: Haworth Press, 1989. 231 pp. (Originally published as** *Journal of Homosexuality,* **Vol. 18, Nos. 3/4, 1989/90.)**

Collection of essays on attitudes toward homosexuals within the contemporary Judeo-Christian tradition.

Heinze, E. *Sexual Orientation: A Human Right.* **Doctoral dissertation for the University of Leiden, The Netherlands, forthcoming, 1994.**

Detailed argument for recognition of rights for sexual minorities under international human rights law.

Helfer, L. R. "Lesbian and Gay Rights as Human Rights: Strategies for a United Europe." *Virginia Journal of International Law* **32 (1991): 157-212.**

Approaches to anti-discrimination measures in the European community.

Helfer, L.R. "Finding a Consensus on Equality: The Homosexual Age of Consent and the European Convention on Human Rights." *New York University Law Review* **65 (1990): 1044-1100.**

Discriminatory age of consent laws in the European Community.

Hunter, N.D., S.E. Michaelson, and T.B. Stoddard. *The Rights of Lesbians and Gay Men.* **3d ed. Carbondale, IL: Southern Illinois University Press, 1992. 220 pp.**

Survey and analysis of legal discrimination against homosexuals in the United States. Good companion piece to *Harvard Law Review* publication listed above.

ILGA (International Lesbian and Gay Association; formerly the IGA, International Gay Association). *Second Pink Book.* **Utrecht: University of Utrecht, 1988.**

Systematic survey of the situation of homosexuals in various countries. The first edition appeared in 1985: *1985 IGA Pink Book.* Amsterdam: COC. The third was scheduled to appear in 1993: Tielman, R., A. Hendriks, and E. van der Veen, eds. *The Third ILGA Pink Book.* Buffalo, NY: Prometheus.

Jeffery-Poulter, S. *Peers, Queers and Commons: The Struggle for Gay Law Reform from 1950 to the Present.* **London; New York: Routledge, 1991. 296 pp.**

Historical account of the post-war gay movement for full legal equality in Britain. Presents a critical assessment of the effects of Thatcherism on the gay movement in the 1980s. Contains a list of gay advocacy groups in the United Kingdom, and subject and name indices.

Magnuson, R. J. "Civil Rights and Sexual Deviance: The Public Policy Implications of the Gay Rights Movement." *Hamline Journal of Public Law and Policy* **9 (1989): 217-235.**

Important for understanding arguments against recognizing rights for homosexuals under U.S. equal protection doctrine.

Michelman, F. "Law's Republic." *Yale Law Journal* **97 (1988): 1493-1537.**

Examines the necessity of equal rights for homosexuals, particularly with reference to the rights to privacy and intimate association, within a pluralistic, constitutional democracy.

Mirabet i Mullol, A. *Homosexualidad Hoy.* **Barcelona: Editorial Herder, 1985. 498 pp.**

Important reference book in Spanish on homosexuality; provides an encyclopedic overview of changing theories, as well as a precis of the emergence of a gay movement in post-Franco Spain, especially in Barcelona. In Spanish and Catalan.

Mohr, R. *Gays/Justice: A Study of Ethics, Society and Law.* **New York: Columbia, 1988. 357 pp.**

Ethical reflections on anti-homosexual discrimination in the United States, with emphasis on legal issues.

Plant, R. *The Pink Triangle: The Nazi War against Homosexuals.* **New York: Henry Holt, 1986. 257 pp.**

Detailed history of Nazi persecution of homosexuals.

Stein, E., ed. *Forms of Desire: Sexual Orientation and the Social Constructionist Controversy.* **New York: Garland, 1990. 365 pp.**

Collection of essays examining the current debate between "essentialist" and "social constructivist" understandings of sexual orientation.

Stumke, H. and R. Finkler. *Rosa Winkel, Rosa Listen.* **Hamburg: Rowohlt, 1981. 512 pp.**

The most comprehensive treatment of the gay movement in Germany, this book carefully documents the early period, the destruction of gay people and their movement in the Holocaust, and the persecution of the 1950s and 1960s in the Federal Republic of Germany.

Tatchell, P. *Europe in the Pink: Lesbian and Gay Equality in the New Europe.* **London: Gay Men's Press, 1992. 158 pp.**

Overview of the social and political situation of homosexuals in post-communist Western and Eastern Europe.

Waaldijk, K., and A. Clapham, eds. *Homosexuality: A European Community Issue.* **Dordrecht; Boston: Martinus Nijhoff Publishers; Norwell, MA, 1993. 426 pp.**

Collection of essays on the possibilities and prospects for expanding lesbian and gay rights within the European Community.

Wasserstrom, R. A. *Morality and the Law.* **Belmont, CA: Wadsworth, 1971. 149 pp.**

Collection of essays on the debate between Lord Devlin and H.L.A. Hart concerning the State's right to regulate morals, with specific attention to homosexuality.

Weeks, J. *Against Nature: Essays on History, Sexuality and Identity.* **London: Rivers Oram, 1991. 224 pp.**

Collection of the author's past and recent writings on sexuality and sexual orientation.

B.   Newsletters and Periodicals

Law and Sexuality. **New Orleans: Tulane University School of Law, 1991-.**

Annual. Includes articles, review essays and comments on family and sexual orientation issues.

Lesbian-Gay Law Notes. **New York: Bar Association for Human Rights of Greater New York, 1984-.**

Monthly. Provides information on jurisprudence, state practice and newsbriefs relating to gay, lesbian and AIDS legal issues; also annotates relevant publications.

C.   *Indices, Guides and Bibliographies*

Dynes, W. *Homosexuality: A Research Guide.* **New York: Garland Pub., 1987. 853 pp.**

> Interdisciplinary, multi-language bibliography with commentary introducing sections and detailed annotations. Entries arranged by subject; bibliography also has personal names index.

Malinowsky, H., comp. *International Directory of Gay and Lesbian Periodicals.* **Phoenix, AZ: Oryx Press, 1987. 226 pp.**

> Lists about 500 titles. Contains subject, geographic and publisher/editor indices.

Parker, W. *Homosexuality: A Selective Bibliography of Over 3,000 Items.* **Metuchen, NJ: Scarecrow Press, 1971. 323 pp.**

> The 1971 bibliography contains over 3,002 annotated items, arranged by form of publication (e.g., books, pamphlets, articles in books, newspaper articles, etc.). It is followed by two supplements listed below, which follow the same format. All contain author and subject indices.

> Parker, W. *Homosexuality Bibliography. Supplement, 1970-1975.* Metuchen, NJ: Scarecrow Press, 1977. 337 pp.

> Parker, W. *Homosexuality Bibliography. Second Supplement, 1976-1982.* Metuchen, NJ: Scarecrow Press, 1985. 395 pp.

Ridinger, R., comp., *The Homosexual and Society: An Annotated Bibliography.* **New York: Greenwood Press, 1990. 444 pp.**

> Takes as its subject seven areas of homophobia: adoptive and foster care, child custody, the military, employment discrimination, censorship, religion, and police attitudes and actions. Entries are drawn primarily from the journals of the mainstream U.S. homosexual community, legal journals, and popular periodicals such as *Time* and *Newsweek*. Some monographs are also included.

D.   *Cases*

The researcher may also wish to consult a number of cases brought under the European Convention of Human Rights. Key cases involving homosexuality include the *Dudgeon* case, judgment of 22 October 1981, Series A no. 45; and the *Norris* case, judgment of 26 October 1988, Series A no. 142. Key cases involving transsexualism include *B. v. France*, judgment of 25 March 1992, Series A no. 232-C; the *Cossey* case, judgment of 27 September 1990, Series A no. 184; and the *Rees* case, judgment of 17 October 1986, Series A no. 106.

XI.   Laws of Armed Conflict

A.   Texts of Instruments

International Committee of the Red Cross. *International Law Concerning the Conduct of Hostilities: Collection of Hague Conventions and Some Other Treaties.* **Geneva: International Committee of the Red Cross, 1989. 195 pp.**

> Compilation of one of the key bodies of law on the conduct of warfare, the Hague Conventions .

Levie, H. S. *The Code of International Armed Conflict.* **2 vols. London; New York: Oceana Publications, 1986. 1099 pp.**

> Subject-matter arrangement of rules of armed conflict which have been formally stated in international documents. Excludes rules of customary international law which are not so stated.

Paenson, I. *Manual of the Terminology of the Law of Armed Conflicts.* **Netherlands: Bruylant Nijhoff, 1989. 844 pp.**

> Defines terminology of the law of war, comparing the various treaty languages (English-French-Spanish-Russian).

Roberts, A. and R. Guelff, eds. *Documents on the Laws of War.* **2d ed. Oxford: Clarendon Press, 1989. 509 pp.**

> Provides treaty texts, lists of states parties, and other texts which are authoritative expositions of the law (if not formal international agreements). Contains index and select bibliography.

Schindler, D. and J. Toman, eds. *The Laws of Armed Conflict.* **3d rev. ed. Scientific Collection of the Henry Dunant Institute. Dordrecht: M. Nijhoff; Norwell, MA: Kluwer Academic Publishers, 1988. 1033 pp.**

> Best single collection of documents on the laws of armed conflict. Comprehensive and well indexed. Helpful brief annotations describing the instruments.

Solf, W. and J. Roach. *Index of International Humanitarian Law.* **Geneva: International Committee of the Red Cross, 1987. 283 pp.**

> Detailed subject index of articles of the various instruments.

U.S. Department of the Army. *The Law of Land Warfare.* **Washington, DC: U.S. Government Printing Office, 1985.**

> U.S. Army field manual giving interpretation of international laws of war.

B. Commentaries

Commentaries are article-by-article discussions of particular legal instruments. Those following are some of the most prominent about the laws of war.

Bothe, M., et al. *New Rules for Victims of Armed Conflicts: Commentary on the Two 1977 Protocols Additional to the Geneva Conventions of 1949.* **The Hague; Boston: M. Nijhoff, 1982. 746 pp.**

> Article-by-article commentary based on the drafting history of the two 1977 Protocols. Written by two delegates to the Diplomatic Conference of 1974-1977.

Levie, S., ed. *The Law of Non-International Armed Conflict: Protocol II to the 1949 Geneva Conventions.* **Dordrecht; Boston; M. Nijhoff, 1987. 635 pp.**

> History of the provisions of Protocol II and the views of those involved in its negotiation.

Pictet, J. *The Geneva Conventions of 12 August 1949.* **4 vols. Geneva: International Committee of the Red Cross, 1952-60.**

> One of the major commentaries of the 1949 Conventions. A comprehensive, article-by-article commentary on the 1949 Geneva Conventions.

Sandoz, Y., C. Swinarski and B. Zimmerman, eds. *Commentary on the Additional Protocols of 8 June 1977 to the Geneva Conventions of 12 August 1949.* **Geneva: International Committee of the Red Cross: M. Nijhoff, 1987. 1625 pp.**

> Article-by-article commentary by the International Committee of the Red Cross.

C. Books and Articles

American University Journal of International Law and Policy. **Washington, DC: Washington College of Law, 1986-.**

> Publishes each year the proceedings of the school's workshop on international humanitarian law — frequently very interesting, in part because it often attracts senior government lawyers from different countries. Topics vary from year to year; the 1993 workshop dealt with proposals for a war crimes tribunal to try international law violations committed in the former Yugoslavia.

Bailey, S. *Prohibitions and Restraints in War.* **London: Oxford University Press for the Royal Institute of International Affairs, 1972. 194 pp.**

> Considered a classic work on the laws of war.

Best, G. *Humanity in Warfare: the Modern History of the International Law of Armed Conflicts.* **London: Metheun, 1983. 408 pp.**

A brief history of the development of the laws of war, with a discussion of the legislative foundations of 1815-1914. Includes an unannotated bibliography of books the author considers particularly important or to which he referred in his footnotes.

Cassese, A., ed. *Current Legal Regulation on the Use of Force.* **Dordrecht; Boston; M. Nijhoff, 1986. 536 pp.**

A series of essays which examine how the use of force by individual states and liberation movements is currently regulated by international law. It also covers the operations of regional organizations and questions not purely legal, such as military security, nuclear weapons and the current political order.

Dinstein, Y. "Human Rights in Armed Conflict: International Humanitarian Law." In *Human Rights in International Law: Legal and Policy Issues,* **edited by T. Meron, 345-368. Oxford: Clarendon Press, 1984.**

Brief introduction. Discusses interplay of human rights in peacetime and wartime, the interplay of human rights and corresponding duties in armed conflict, and problems of implementation and supervision of the laws of war. Offers teaching suggestions, syllabus, minisyllabus, bibliography and minibibliography.

Kalshoven, F. *Constraints on the Waging of War.* **Geneva: International Committee of the Red Cross, 1987. 175 pp.**

Very useful introduction to the law of Geneva (developments concerning the Geneva Conventions and the International Committee of the Red Cross), the Hague (leading up to and resulting from the principles and rules embodied in the Hague Convention and Regulations on Land Warfare of 1899/1907) and New York (U.N. General Assembly and Security Council action).

Meron, T. *Human Rights and Humanitarian Norms as Customary Law.* **Oxford: Clarendon Press; New York: Oxford University Press, 1989. 263 pp.**

Attempts to clarify the status of international human rights and humanitarian norms in public international law. Two principal areas are addressed: (1) the relationship of human rights and humanitarian norms with customary law, and (2) the relationship of human rights and humanitarian norms with the general principles of international law (particularly with the principles governing the international responsibility of states for acts and omissions of their officials and organs).

Meron, T. *Human Rights in Internal Strife: Their International Protection.* **Cambridge: Grotius, 1987. 172 pp.**

Examines the intersection of human rights and humanitarian law norms in situations of "internal strife," where for various reasons the situation does not correspond to the classical models of civil and international wars. (These reasons could include the level of intensity, organization, duration, intent of the parties, or the collective or individual nature of the acts.) The author seeks to determine whether there exists a serious gap in protection where humanitarian law meshes with human rights law.

de Mulinen, F. *Handbook on the Law of War for Armed Forces.* **Geneva: International Committee of the Red Cross, 1987. 232 pp.**

ICRC training course for military officers; useful as a basic guide.

Shanor, C. A. and Terrell, T. P. *Military Law in a Nutshell.* **St. Paul: West Pub., 1980. 378 pp.**

Very useful summary of U.S. law pertaining to the military, including U.S. interpretation of the laws of war.

Walzer, M. *Just and Unjust Wars: A Moral Argument with Historical Illustrations.* **2d ed. NY: Basic Books, 1992. 361 pp.**

A conceptual discussion of the laws of war and just war theory by a philosopher.

Wilson, H. A. *International Law and the Use of Force by National Liberation Movements.* **Oxford: Clarendon Press, 1988. 209 pp.**

Good blackletter law discussion of national liberation wars, internal wars, and laws of armed conflict.

D.   *Newsletters and Periodicals*

Annual Report [year]. **Geneva: International Committee of the Red Cross, 1955-.**

Annual review of the activities conducted by the ICRC, including protection and assistance operations for military and civilian victims of armed conflict, work on international humanitarian law and ICRC principles. In 1990, the volume was published as *1990 Reference Report.*

Bulletin. **Geneva: Press Division of the International Committee of the Red Cross, 1976-.**

Monthly which reports current activities of the International Committee of the Red Cross.

International Review of the Red Cross. **English ed. Geneva: International Committee of the Red Cross, 1961-.**

Published in French since 1869, in English since 1961. Published monthly before 1978 and bimonthly thereafter. Official publication of the International Committee of the Red

Cross. Contains scholarly and policy articles, news of the Red Cross and the Red Crescent, information about ratifications of relevant instruments, and book reviews.

Military Law Review. **Charlottesville, VA: Judge Advocate General's School at University of Virginia, 1958-.**

Quarterly. Issues frequently carry articles on the laws of war.

Online: Indexed in the *Public Affairs Information Service , Social Sciences Citation Index* and LEXIS.

Yearbook. **International Institute of Humanitarian Law. San Remo: Villa Nobel, 1985-.**

Annual, in English and French.

E.   *Indices, Guides and Bibliographies*

Institut Henry-Dunant. *Basic Bibliography of International Humanitarian Law.* **Geneva: Henry Dunant Institute, 1985. 106 pp.**

An abbreviated version of the *Bibliography of International Humanitarian Law Applicable in Armed Conflicts,* described below.

Institut Henry-Dunant. *Index on the Teaching of International Humanitarian Law in Academic Institutions/Repertoire sur l'enseignement du droit international humanitaire dans les milieux academiques.* **2 vols. Geneva: IHD, 1987-.**

In English, French and Spanish. Looseleaf.

International Committee of the Red Cross. *Bibliography of International Humanitarian Law Applicable in Armed Conflicts.* **2d ed. rev. and updated. Geneva: International Committee of the Red Cross and Henry Dunant Institute, 1987. 605 pp.**

The most comprehensive bibliography of articles and books worldwide on humanitarian law. A good starting point for all researchers.

XII. Criminal Justice, Prisons and Rights of the Detained

NGO reports are a good source of information about these questions. For example, Amnesty International has published reports on prison conditions, the rights of the detained, and fair trials throughout the world. The various divisions of Human Rights Watch cover criminal justice questions and the rights of the detained on a regular basis; they have also published several recent reports on human rights in prisons, covering countries such as Czechoslovakia (1989); Indonesia (1990); Israel and the Occupied Territories (1991); Jamaica (1990); Mexico (1991); and Poland (1988). Human Rights Watch also recently set up a Prison Project to focus on the conditions in prisons around the world. In addition, many national NGOs monitor conditions within their own countries; one example is the Prison Project of the American Civil Liberties Union, which focuses on prison conditions in the United States.

A.   Compilations of Instruments

Hannum, H., et al. *Materials on International Human Rights and U.S. Criminal Law and Procedure.* Washington, DC: The Procedural Aspects of International Law Institute, 1989. 152 pp.

> Identifies and compares norms of U.S. criminal procedure with the basic instruments of international human rights. Focus is on U.S. constitutional requirements. Includes an introductory section on the impact of international human rights law in U.S. courts, followed by sections on topics such as liberty, arrest and bail, detention, habeas corpus, and fair trial.

Instruments and Resolutions Relating to the Administration of Justice and the Human Rights of Detainees. E/CN.4/Sub.2/1987/CRP.1 (1987).

> Contains the Minimum Rules for the Administration of Juvenile Justice (Beijing rules) adopted by the U.N. General Assembly on November 29, 1985, and other texts.

United Nations. Centre for Social Development and Humanitarian Affairs. *Compendium of United Nations Standards and Norms in Crime Prevention and Criminal Justice.* New York: United Nations, A/CONF.144/INF.2, 1992. 278 pp.

> Part I, "Crime Prevention and Criminal Justice," includes the texts of 22 norms and standards. In addition to the Minimum Standard Rules for the Treatment of Prisoners, Part I contains a number of declarations, codes, minimum rules, and other treaty and non-treaty instruments pertaining to the rights of the detained. Part II, "Human Rights," contains the texts of the major instruments.

B.   Books, Reports and Articles

Alderson, J. *Human Rights and the Police.* Strasbourg: Council of Europe, Directorate of Human Rights, 1984. 214 pp.

> A guide for use in training police officials. Emphasis is on the rules evolved through the case law of the European Convention on Human Rights.

Chernichenko, S. and W. Treat. *The Right to a Fair Trial: Current Recognition and Measures Necessary for Its Strengthening.* Third report prepared by Mr. Stanislav Chernichenko and Mr. William Treat. Commission on Human Rights. Sub-Commission on Prevention of Discrimination and Protection of Minorities. E/CN.4/Sub.2/1992/24, 12 May 1992. 12 pp.

> This report, which comments on and revises two earlier reports, contains three substantive addenda which are longer than the report itself:

Interpretations of International Fair Trial Norms by the European Commission and Court of Human Rights. E/CN.4/Sub.2/1992/24/Add.1, 15 May 1992. 59 pp.

Interpretations of International Fair Trial Norms by the Inter-American Commission on and Court of Human Rights. E/CN.4/Sub.2/1992/24/Add. 2, 27 May 1992. 22 pp.

Right to Amparo, Habeas Corpus, and Similar Procedures. E/CN.4/Sub.2/1992/24/Add. 3, 29 April 1992. 48 pp.

Frankowski, S. and D. Shelton, eds. *Preventive Detention: A Comparative and International Law Perspective.* **Dordrecht; Boston: M. Nijhoff, 1992. 302 pp.**

Contains an article on relevant international standards, and articles on the preventive detention laws and policies of seven countries: Japan, the United States, Sweden, Switzerland, Austria, the former USSR, and Poland.

Reynaud, A. *Human Rights in Prisons.* **Strasbourg: Council of Europe, Directorate of Human Rights, 1986. 218 pp.**

Intended for heads of prison establishments, this guide begins with a brief introduction on the development of human rights institutions and procedures. Next, Part I discusses the major international instruments applicable to prisons, and the European regional instruments. Part II discusses the protection mechanisms for prisoners under the European Convention on Human Rights, and analyzes a series of specific prisoner rights, based on decisions of the European Commission of Human Rights and the European Court of Human Rights. Several appendices set out the texts of relevant international and Council of Europe instruments. A bibliography appears on pp. 211-216.

Rodley, N. *The Treatment of Prisoners under International Law.* **Paris: U.N. Educational, Scientific and Cultural Organization; Oxford: Clarendon Press; New York: Oxford University Press, 1987. 374 pp.**

Traces the development of international and regional legislation aimed at eliminating the practices of torture and other ill-treatment. Examines the problems of defining torture, and those of establishing mechanisms for implementing newly developed legislation. Examines extrajudicial execution and "disappearance" and discusses legal or ethical safeguards to end the practices.

XIII. International Criminal Law, War Crimes, and Crimes against Humanity

Bassiouni, M. *Crimes Against Humanity in International Criminal Law.* **Dordrecht; Boston: M. Nijhoff; Norwell, MA: Kluwer Academic Publishers (Distributors), 1992. 820 pp.**

Overview of scholarly research on the Nuremberg trials. Explores the history and evolution of "crimes against humanity." Covers issues such as principles of legality, command responsibility, and obedience to superior orders. Excellent bibliography.

Bassiouni, M. *International Crimes: Digest/Index of International Instruments 1815-1985*. 2 vols. New York: Oceana, 1986.

> Does not contain texts of instruments, but rather citations to texts. Gives basic data: place and date of signature, signatories, states parties, and brief summaries of content.

Bassiouni, M., ed. *International Criminal Law*. 3 vols. Dobbs Ferry, NY: Transnational Publishers, Inc., 1986-1987.

> Series covers all aspects of international criminal law through essays by 40 contributors. Extensive appendices contain the texts of relevant documents.

Charny, I.W., ed. *Genocide, A Critical Bibliographic Review*. New York: Facts on File Publications, 1988. 273 pp.

> A series of essays purporting to present an authoritative, encyclopedia-like statement of the knowledge base in a given field or area of study of genocide. Also provides an annotated critical bibliography.

Dull, P. and M. T. Umemura. *The Tokyo Trials: A Functional Index to the Proceedings of the International Military Tribunal for the Far East*. Ann Arbor: University of Michigan Press, 1957. 94 pp.

> Index covers all material included in the Proceedings of the Military Tribunal for the Far East. Modelled on the Subject Index to the Nuremberg Military Tribunal, but contains more subjects and subdivisions.

Gilbert, G. *Aspects of Extradition Law*. International Studies in Human Rights, vol. 17. Dordrecht; Boston: M. Nijhoff; Norwell, MA: Kluwer Academic Publishers (Distributors), 1991. 282 pp.

> Examines those aspects of extradition law which reveal conflicts between different legal systems and areas in which there is a need for an improvement in procedures. Includes a case list, a discussion of mechanisms and procedures, and a bibliography.

International Military Tribunal. *Trials of War Criminals Before the Nuernberg Military Tribunals under Control Council Law No. 10. Nuernberg, October, 1946-April, 1949*. 15 vols. Washington, DC: U.S. Government Printing Office, 1949-1953.

> Indictments, judgments and other important parts of the record of the trials held in Nuremberg of the 12 major war criminals.

International Military Tribunal for the Far East. *The Tokyo War Crimes Trial*. Edited by R. J. Pritchard and S. M. Zaide. 22 vols. New York: Garland, 1981-1987.

> Complete transcripts of the proceedings of the International Military Tribunal of the Far East. Annotated by the editors.

International Military Tribunal for the Far East. *The Tokyo War Crimes Trial. Index and Guide.* **Edited by R. J. Pritchard and S. M. Zaide. 5 vols. New York and London: Garland, 1981-1987.**

A companion to the complete transcripts. Also annotated. Volumes I and II comprise an index of names and subjects. Volume III is a narrative summary of the proceedings and a document key (listing prosecution and defense documents). Volumes IV and V point to research aids selected from reference materials produced during the trial.

Kader, D. "Law and Genocide: A Critical Annotated Bibliography," *Hastings International and Comparative Law Review* **11 (Winter 1990): 381-390.**

Includes major writings since the end of World War II.

Lewis, J., comp. *Uncertain Judgment: A Bibliography of War Crimes Trials.* **Santa Barbara, CA: ABC-Clio, 1979. 251 pp.**

Comprehensive bibliography of war crimes trials, covering historical and philosophical issues, conferences and treaties, and war crimes trials dating from 1474 to the Mozambique mercenaries trial in Luanda in 1976.

Neumann, I., comp. *European War Crimes Trials: A Bibliography.* **Westport, CT: Greenwood Press, 1978, 1951. 113 pp.**

Lists materials published between 1941 and 1950. About two-thirds of the entries are annotated. Entries exclude newspaper articles and accounts in popular periodicals.

Tutorow, N., comp. and ed. *War Crimes, War Criminals and War Crimes Trials: An Annotated Bibliography and Source Book.* **New York: Greenwood Press, 1986. 548 pp.**

Contains 4,500 entries. Includes monographs, periodical articles, government documents, dissertations. Covers background and philosophical issues, pre-World War I historical aspects, World War I, World War II, allied and national trials, the Eichmann trial, and the Vietnam war. A final "miscellaneous" section includes information on the Korean War, the Algerian Civil War, the Pakistan Civil War, the Mozambique Mercenaries Trial, East Timor, the Dering-Uris case, the Beth-Din Trial, and the Afghanistan-Soviet Union War. Appendices include major documents. Contains a subject and name index.

CHAPTER FIVE.
HUMAN RIGHTS AND
UNITED STATES FOREIGN POLICY

I.   Access to U.S. Government Information Generally

Principal sources of information are generally documents produced by government agencies or departments; access to the most relevant of these is discussed below. In addition, however, contacting officials can often be useful if one has specific questions, or is attempting to locate a specific document. Ordinarily, NGO staffers or others involved in a particular issue will be able to identify the relevant government officials. For a general orientation, the following resources may be helpful.

Monthly Catalog of United States Government Publications. **Washington, DC: United States Government Printing Office, 1951-.**

> The main current bibliography of publications issued by all branches of the U.S. government. Because of its comprehensiveness, this source may be somewhat unwieldy. If possible, researchers should rely on the other reference tools described in this section which focus more narrowly.

> *Online:* The *Monthly Catalog* is available online in DIALOG (file 66), in WESTLAW (GPO-CTLG database) as a DIALOG database, in BRS (GPOM), in OCLC EPIC, and in OCLC FirstSearch from 1976 to date.

United States Government Manual. **Washington, DC: Office of the Federal Register, National Archives and Records Service, Governmental Services Administration, 1935-.**

> An annual official handbook on the federal government, providing basic information on the agencies in the legislative, executive and judicial branches. Also includes information on quasi-official agencies, international organizations in which the United States participates, and boards, committees, and commissions. A typical agency description includes a list of principal officials, an organization chart, a summary statement on the agency's purpose and role in the government, a brief history of the agency including its legislative or executive authority, a description of its programs and activities, and a "Source of Information" section.

> The *Manual* is a good first source to consult for a general description of the formal role of a particular agency. Detailed information about the organizational structures of agencies is available in the most recent agency statements of organization, published in the *Federal Register* or *Code of Federal Regulations.*

> *Online*: The *Federal Register* is available online in LEXIS (in the FEDREG file in the GENFED library) and in WESTLAW (FR database) from 1980 to present.

Online: *Code of Federal Regulations* is online in LEXIS (in the CFR file in the GENFED library) and in WESTLAW (in the CFR database).

A.   Congress

Congressional Information Service Index to Publications of the United States Congress. **(CIS/INDEX). Washington, DC: Congressional Information Service, 1970-.**

The primary tool for finding Congressional publications such as House and Senate hearings which are key to human rights research. Annual volumes, plus monthly updates. Contains a comprehensive, well-organized index (by subject, witness, committee, or subcommittee). Catalogs and abstracts all non-classified publications of the U.S. Congress, including hearings, committee prints, reports, documents, and special publications. The full texts are available in microfiche. A drawback to CIS/INDEX is its time lag: monthly updates are usually received by libraries some five weeks after the index is released. *Congressional Quarterly Weekly Report* should be used for more current, albeit less comprehensive, information.

Progress of legislation and treaties through the Congress can be tracked by using *CIS/ Index*, as well as the *CQ Almanac* (an annual detailed summary of legislative developments which includes all roll-call votes taken), presidential texts and lobby registrations.

Online: The CIS Index is available online in DIALOG (file 101) and in WESTLAW (CIS database) as a DIALOG database from 1970 to present. At present the CIS database on WESTLAW is not available to law schools through their WESTLAW educational contract.

Online: The *CQ Weekly Report* is available online in full text in Data Times (CQW) from 1986 to date.

Congressional Yellow Book. **Washington, DC: Washington Monitor, 1976-.**

Quarterly. A looseleaf service containing biographies and committee assignments of congressional representatives and senators, addresses and telephone numbers of members of Congress and their aides, as well as brief descriptions of committees, subcommittees, caucuses and other informal congressional groupings.

Goehlert, R. *Congress and Law-Making: Researching the Legislative Process.* **2d ed. Santa Barbara, CA: ABC-Clio; Oxford: CLIO Press, 1989. 306 pp.**

A good general introduction to information sources about the Congress and the legislative process. Designed to help users trace congressional legislation and to familiarize them with the major sources of information about Congress. Author, title and subject indices.

B.   Executive Branch

Federal Executive Directory. **Washington, DC: Carroll Pub. Co., 1980-.**

> Published six times a year. Contains the names, addresses and telephone numbers of executive branch personnel, including cabinet departments, independent agencies and commissions of the executive branch. Very useful for getting in touch with lower-level State Department people who can often be helpful in sending copies of hard-to-get documentation and reports, or by providing names of other people to get in touch with. This is especially true for "country desk" people—individuals who are assigned to a particular country to monitor developments there.

Federal Yellow Book. **Washington, DC: Washington Monitor, 1976-.**

> Quarterly. Contains much of the same information as in entry above.

II.   U.S. Non-Treaty Human Rights Legislation

A.   Generally

In the mid-1970's the United States Congress began passing legislation which conditioned U.S. trade with and aid to foreign countries based on observance of human rights. Legislation may be country-specific — imposing conditions on particular states — or it may be general in nature.

NGO publications provide the best succinct, general orientation to human rights-related U.S. legislation. Some of these resources are listed below, along with other helpful publications which can serve as starting points for the researcher.

Biel, E. *Linking Security Assistance and Human Rights.* 1988 Project Series, no. 3. New York: Lawyers Committee for Human Rights, 1989. 61 pp.

> A good review and critique of the development and functioning of U.S. human rights policy. Focuses on legislative and executive roles in the formulation and implementation of policy linking security assistance and human rights.

***Congressional Human Rights Bulletin.* Washington, DC: Congressional Human Rights Foundation, 1992.**

> Monthly from January 1992 until October 1992. Newsletter of the Congressional Human Rights Foundation, containing brief updates on congressional human rights activities, including legislative initiatives and hearings.

Congressional Quarterly Weekly Report. **Washington, DC: Congressional Quarterly, Inc., 1956-.**

> Contains information on current activities in the House and Senate, as well as key votes. Also contains information about important executive orders and presidential press conferences.

> *Online*: The *CQ Weekly Report* is available online in full text in Data Times (CQ WEEK) from 1980 to present. It is also available on NEXIS (NEXIS library, CQ file) from 1975 to present.

Human Rights Watch. *The Bush Administration's Record on Human Rights in 1989.* **New York: Human Rights Watch, January 1990.**

> Good critique of U.S. human rights policy in selected countries. This report has not been continued; its information has been incorporated in the *Human Rights Watch World Report*, described below. Contains section on U.S. human rights legislation.

Human Rights Watch. *Human Rights Watch World Report [year].* **New York: Human Rights Watch, 1991-.**

> An essential annual report analyzing the U.S. administration's human rights policy in a number of countries monitored by Human Rights Watch. See p. 72 for a full annotation.

Human Rights Watch and Lawyers Committee for Human Rights. *The Reagan Administration's Record on Human Rights.* **New York: Human Rights Watch and Lawyers Committee for Human Rights, 1980-1989.**

> Annual issues, spanning the eight years of the Reagan administration, were published, the final volume appearing in January 1989. Good critique of U.S. human rights policy in selected countries. Sections entitled "U.S. Human Rights Laws," "Treaties," and "Refugee, Asylum and Immigration Policy" provide succinct treatments of current U.S. legislation dealing with human rights and an assessment of U.S. performance.

Lawyers Committee for Human Rights. *Human Rights and U.S. Foreign Policy: Report and Recommendations: 1988 Project.* **New York: Lawyers Committee for Human Rights, 1988. 68 pp.**

> This report provides detailed discussions of the relevant U.S. legislation in force at the time of the report. Useful for a general orientation.

Maynard, F. *Bureaucracy and Diplomacy: Human Rights and Foreign Policy.* **1988 Project Series, no. 4. New York: Lawyers Committee for Human Rights, 1989. 96 pp.**

> A good review and critique of the development and functioning of the executive branch human rights offices and officers, and the way in which U.S. human rights policy is administered and implemented.

Turnball, B. *Worker Rights under the U.S. Trade Laws.* **1988 Project Series, no. 2. New York: Lawyers Committee for Human Rights, 1989. 77 pp.**

> Useful discussion of four U.S. laws linking foreign trade with workers' rights protection in exporting countries.

B.   *Texts of U.S. Legislation on Human Rights*

Human Rights Documents: Compilation of Documents Pertaining to Human Rights. **Washington, DC: U.S. Government Printing Office, 1983. 774 pp.**

> A comprehensive, although somewhat dated, compilation of U.S. laws having human rights provisions.

International Human Rights Law Group, comp. *U.S. Legislation Relating Human Rights to U.S. Foreign Policy.* **4th ed. Buffalo: W. S. Hein, 1991. 186 pp.**

> A very useful update to the above compilation. Although it does not contain an index, its detailed table of contents makes locating particular legislation or a specific subject fairly easy.

Legislation Aimed at Combating International Drug Trafficking and Money Laundering: A Staff Report. **Washington, DC: U.S. Government Printing Office, 1987. 213 pp.**

> Although not typically categorized as human rights legislation, these laws are relevant to human rights research because of human rights violations by officials trained or assisted in counter-narcotics work, and because security assistance prohibited under other legislation may be given under anti-drug-trafficking laws.

III.   Human Rights Treaties Ratified or Signed by the United States

To be ratified in the United States, a human rights treaty must go through the following steps. First, the President must sign and submit the treaty to the Senate which gives its advice and consent and may add qualifications (reservations, understandings, declarations, etc.) The Senate may also require implementing legislation. After the Senate's advice and consent, the treaty returns to the President for ratification.

The Senate Committee on Foreign Relations handles treaties submitted for advice and consent. Committee reports are published in the *Senate Executive Reports* series; these can be located using *CIS/Index* or the U.S. Government Printing Office's *Monthly Catalog*. *CCH Congressional Index* contains a section with a status table for all treaties submitted to the Committee on Foreign Relations and which are awaiting action by the Committee or by the full Senate. A full discussion of these matters can be found in Jacobstein and Mersky, *Fundamentals of Legal Research.* 5th ed., Westbury, NY: Foundation Press, 1990, pp. 397-412.

After signature by the President, but prior to ratification, treaty texts, with their accompanying presidential messages, are published in the *Senate Executive Documents* series. Before 1945, these were almost always confidential documents.

Before 1950, the final texts of ratified treaties were published in the *Statutes at Large*. Since then, they have appeared in *United States Treaties and Other International Agreements* (U.S.T.), Washington, DC: Department of State; U.S. Government Printing Office, 1931-. The first authoritative publication of treaties is in slip form as pamphlets in the *Treaties and Other International Acts Series* (T.I.A.S.), Washington, DC: Department of State; U.S. Government Printing Office, 1931-.

T.I.A.S. pamphlets are not always easily available, but texts of recently ratified treaties can be found in *International Legal Materials.* (See annotation on pp. 14-15.) I.L.M. citations and texts are usually accurate and are available before a treaty appears in T.I.A.S. I.L.M. also publishes the texts of important draft treaties.

If, after consulting the resources listed both above and below, researchers are unable to find the text of a treaty, or to determine its current status, contact the Assistant Legal Adviser for Treaty Affairs, United States Department of State, 2201 C Street N.W., Washington, DC 20520.

Lillich, R. *International Human Rights Instruments: A Compilation of Treaties, Agreements, and Declarations of Especial Interest to the United States.* **2d ed. Buffalo: W.S. Hein, 1990. 540 pp.**

> This periodically supplemented looseleaf gives the texts and citations of the principal human rights treaties (both those to which the United States is a party, as well as those which the United States has signed but not ratified). Also contains the texts and citations of non-treaty instruments, selected bibliographies, and references to U.S. executive and Congressional documents pertaining to human rights. Provides citations to U.S. cases in which international human rights instruments have been invoked.

U.S. Department of State. *Treaties in Force: A List of Treaties and Other International Agreements of the United States in Force on [date].* **Washington, DC: U.S. Government Printing Office, 1929-.**

> This source should be used to locate citations to the texts of all treaties to which the United States is a party. It is an official annual publication which lists all treaties and international agreements in force at the beginning of the year. The first section covers bilateral agreements, arranged by country and subject. Multilateral treaties, arranged by subject, and including lists of states parties, are covered in the second section.

IV.   Drafting History and Status of U.S. Treaties and Legislation

U.S. legislative history of treaties and human rights-related legislation—the reconstruction of the history of a bill or enactment and the identification of all the documents relevant to its interpretation—is facilitated by several research tools, some of which have been mentioned in the above sections of this chapter. Primary tools are listed below.

Buergenthal, T. *International Human Rights in a Nutshell.* **St. Paul, MN: West Publishing Co., 1988.**

> For a brief overview of the U.S. treaty ratification process, legislation, and human rights law in the courts, see Chapter 7, "The U.S. and International Human Rights."

A.   *Legislative Branch*

Congressional Index. **Chicago: Commerce Clearing House, 1937-.**

> A looseleaf service issued in two volumes for each session of Congress. Provides indices of all bills by subject and by sponsor; digests of each bill; a status table of actions taken on bills and resolutions; an index of enactments and vetoes; a table of companion bills; a list of reorganization plans, treaties, and nominations pending; tables of voting records of members of Congress by bill and resolution number; and a weekly report on major developments in Congress.

Kaufman, N. *Human Rights Treaties and the Senate: A History of Opposition.* **Chapel Hill, NC: The University of North Carolina Press, 1990. 256 pp.**

> Good discussion of U.S. Congressional and other materials relevant to the debates in the United States on the ratification of human right treaties.

B.   *Executive Branch*

The Department of State Bulletin. **Washington, DC: Office of Public Communication, Bureau of Public Affairs, 1939-1989.**

> Contains section on multilateral treaties, which includes current information on treaty status, recent developments and information on treaties to which the United States is not a party. These sections are reproduced in the monthly *International Legal Materials.* (See description on pp. 14-15.) The *Bulletin* ceased publication in December 1989. It is continued by the *U.S. Department of State Dispatch.* (See annotation below.)

> *Online:* The *Bulletin* is online in LEXIS from January 1984 to December 1989 in the DSTATE file in the GENFED, INTLAW, or ITRADE libraries.

Foreign Policy Bulletin. Washington, DC: Foreign Policy Bulletin, 1990-.

> A private bimonthly publication using the same format as the discontinued *Department of State Bulletin*. Stated goals are to maintain continuity with that publication while offering additional materials, and to provide a timely and systematic record of U.S. foreign policy and of complementary documents from international sources. Includes major addresses, diplomatic statements, and the texts of press conferences of the President and the Secretary of State; statements and Congressional testimony by the Secretary of State and other administration officials; treaties and other agreements to which the United States is or may become a party; special reports; and selected press releases issued by the White House, the Department of State, and other agencies.

U.S. Department of State Dispatch. Washington, DC: Office of Public Communication, Bureau of Public Affairs, 1990-.

> The Department of State's weekly paid subscription magazine, which serves as the basic source of official information on U.S. foreign policy. Includes major speeches and congressional testimony by senior U.S. officials, foreign policy summaries, fact sheets on global issues, updates on countries around the world, and current U.S. treaty actions. Indexed every six months. Seems to cover the same information as its predecessor, the *Department of State Bulletin*. The valuable "Treaty Actions" section has been continued. However, while the *Dispatch* is more timely, it is doubtful that it will be more complete.

> *Online*: The *Dispatch* is online in LEXIS from September 1990 in the DSTATE file in the GENFED, INTLAW, or ITRADE libraries.

V.   The Conduct of United States Foreign Policy and Human Rights

Many of the materials useful for research on the conduct of U.S. foreign policy and human rights have been discussed in the immediately preceding sections, and many sources noted in Chapter One will also be relevant to such research.

In addition to the *U.S. Department of State Dispatch* and the *Foreign Policy Bulletin* (both are described in the above section), documentation of U.S. foreign policy can be found in the following irregularly published series, which contain press releases, speeches, and statements made by the President, the Secretary of State and senior government officials about the foreign policy of the United States.

> U.S. Department of State. *Current Policy*. Washington, DC. U.S. Department of State.

> U.S. Department of State. *Press Conference*. Washington, DC: U.S. Department of State, Bureau of Public Affairs.

> U.S. Department of State. *Selected Documents*. Washington, DC: U.S. Department of State, Bureau of Public Affairs.

U.S. Department of State. *Special Report.* Washington, DC: U.S. Department of State, Bureau of Public Affairs.

U.S. Department of State. *Speech.* U.S. Department of State, Bureau of Public Affairs.

Restatement of the Law Third, the Foreign Relations Law of the United States. 2 vols. St. Paul, MN: American Law Institute Pub., 1987-.

For annotation, see p. 47.

Online: The full text of the *Restatement* is online in WESTLAW in the REST-FOREL database.

U.S. Department of State. *Foreign Relations of the United States.* Washington, DC: U.S. Government Printing Office, 1861-.

This series constitutes the official printed record of the foreign policy of the United States. The 25-year time lag in publication of documents, however, limits its use to historical studies. The Department of State also publishes other documentary compilations, discussed below, whose time lag is shorter.

The following three collections assemble foreign policy documents made public prior to the issuance of the volumes in the *Foreign Relations of the United States* series.

American Foreign Policy, 1950-1955: Basic Documents. 2 vols. Washington, DC: U.S. Government Printing Office, 1957.

American Foreign Policy: Current Documents. Washington, DC: U.S. Government Printing Office, 1981-.

U.S. Department of State. *A Decade of American Foreign Policy: Basic Documents, 1941-1949.* Rev. ed. Washington, DC: U.S. Department of State, 1985. 969 pp.

Authoritative sources of information about U.S. practice in international law include the following:

Whiteman, M. *Digest of International Law.* 15 vols. Washington, DC: U.S. Department of State, 1963-1973.

U.S. Department of State. *Digest of United States Practice in International Law.* Washington: Office of the Legal Adviser, Department of State, 1973-.

American Journal of International Law. **Washington, DC: American Society of International Law, 1907-.**

> Whiteman's *Digest* consists of 15 volumes published between 1963-1973. This was supplemented by the U.S. Department of State's *Digest of United States Practice in International Law.* Washington: Office of the Legal Adviser, Department of State, 1973-. Published annually since 1973, and supplemented in turn by the quarterly feature, "Contemporary Practice of the United States Relating to International Law," which appears in the *American Journal of International Law.*

> *Online:* The *American Journal of International Law* is available online in LEXIS from 1980 to present in the AJIL file in the INTLAW, ITRADE, or LAWREV libraries. Selected articles from the *American Journal of International Law* are online in WESTLAW (AMJIL database) from 1991 to present.

VI.   National Security and Military Affairs

The national security field is often of great relevance, given the extensive involvement of the U.S. government at home and abroad in areas such as intelligence, counter-insurgency, and military training and assistance. These activities are often closely connected to human rights conditions and policies in a particular country.

A.   Books and Articles

Franck, T., and M. Glennon. *Foreign Relations and National Security Law.* **2d ed. St. Paul, MN: West Publishing Co., 1993. 1142 pp.**

> Fairly standard presentation of U.S. doctrine and policy.

Graves, E. and S. Hildreth, eds. *U.S. Security Assistance: The Political Process.* **Lexington, MA: Lexington Books, 1985. 192 pp.**

> Details the evolution of U.S. security assistance policy since World War II, but with little critical analysis.

Koh, H. *The National Security Constitution: Sharing Power After the Iran-Contra Affair.* **New Haven: Yale University Press, 1990. 340 pp.**

> Analysis of the legal structure that regulates the relations among the President, Congress and courts in U.S. foreign affairs. Argues that the Iran-contra afffair exposed a serious constitutional imbalance in foreign affairs decision-making and proposes structural solutions. Footnotes provide many useful sources.

National Security Archive. *The Making of U.S. Policy.* **12 vols. Washington, DC: National Security Archive, [years vary].**

> Microfiche collection of more than 35,000 previously secret U.S. documents reproduced in 12 separate collections. Each contains extensive chronologies, glossaries, and indices.

For each document there is a catalog entry which describes the document's origin and provides complete bibliographic information. The collections are catalogued in most libraries under the titles listed below.

The 12 collections are entitled: *Military Uses of Space, 1945-1991; Nicaragua: The Making of U.S. Policy, 1978-1990; U.S. Nuclear Non-Proliferation Policy, 1945-1991; The Philippines: U.S. Policy During the Marcos Years, 1965-1986; South Africa, the Making of U.S. Policy, 1962-1989; The U.S. Intelligence Community: Organization, Operations and Management, 1947-1989; Afghanistan; The Making of U.S. Policy, 1973-1990; The Berlin Crisis, 1958-1962; The Cuban Missile Crisis, 1962; El Salvador: The Making of U.S. Policy, 1977-1984; Iran: The Making of U.S. Policy, 1977-1980; The Iran-Contra Affair: The Making of a Scandal, 1983-1988.*

Online: The Making of U.S. Policy is available on CD-ROM.

The National Security Archive is an independent nongovernmental research institute and library founded in 1985 to provide greater access to previously top secret and otherwise highly classified documents obtained through the U.S. law, the Freedom of Information Act. The organization can assist researchers searching for documents and can be contacted at: The National Security Archive, 1755 Massachusetts Avenue NW, Suite 500, Washington, DC 20036.

Richelson, J. *The U.S. Intelligence Community: Organization, Operations, and Management, 1947-1989.* (Microform). Alexandria, VA: Chadwyck-Healey: The National Security Archive, 1990.

870 items on 266 microfiches, plus guide and index. Sources on the history of U.S. national security and foreign relations. For more information on this resource and others in the same series, see above listing.

B.   *Newsletters and Periodicals*

Covert Action Information Bulletin. **Washington, DC: Covert Action Publications, 1978-.**

Quarterly. Focuses on intelligence operations, covert actions and related matters abroad and in the United States.

The Defense Monitor. **Washington, DC: Center for Defense Information, 1972-.**

Monthly. Focuses on U.S. defense issues.

First Principles. **Washington, DC: Project on National Security and Civil Liberties, 1975-.**

A civil-liberties oriented quarterly, focusing on U.S. national security issues.

NED Backgrounder. Albuquerque, NM: Inter-Hemispheric Education Resource Center, 1992-.

> Newsletter which follows developments of the National Endowment for Democracy as well as government agencies and private organizations that conduct U.S. government-funded foreign policy programs with the stated goal of building democracy.

Policy Focus. Washington, DC: Overseas Development Council. 1984-.

> A series of background papers on major U.S.-third world issues currently prominent on the U.S. decisionmaking agenda. Liberal orientation.

C.   Guides, Indices, and Bibliographies

Abstracts of Military Bibliography. Buenos Aires: Navy Publications Institute, 1968-.

Air Force University Library Index to Military Periodicals. Maxwell Air Force Base, AL: The Library, 1949-.

> These two quarterly indices provide subject and author access to publications dealing with national security problems, and military and strategic affairs.

Arkin, W. *Research Guide to Current Military and Strategic Affairs.* Washington, DC: Institute for Policy Studies, 1981. 232 pp.

> Contains information on military expenditures, the budget process in Congress, U.S. military bases overseas, and military issues in third world countries.

Blackstock, P. *Intelligence Espionage, Counterespionage, and Covert Operations: A Guide to Information Sources.* Detroit: Gale Research Co., 1978. 255 pp.

> Lists books and articles mainly in English, with detailed annotations. Arranged by subject.

Constantinides, G. *Intelligence and Espionage: An Analytical Bibliography.* Boulder, CO: Westview Press, 1983. 559 pp.

> Analytical bibliography of some 500 English-language books on the intelligence process and the history of intelligence, arranged alphabetically by author. Covers the 17th to the 20th centuries; emphasis is on later period. Includes works on U.S. and foreign intelligence services. Title and subject/author index.

Current Military & Political Literature. Oxford: Military Press, 1989-.

> Bimonthly. 200 journals abstracted. Continues *Current Military Literature.* Oxford: Military Press, 1983-1988.

Current World Affairs. Alexandria, VA: John C. Damon, 1990-.

> Quarterly bibliography which identifies and briefly abstracts the contents of periodical articles dealing with political, strategic or other subject matter affecting military forces. English, French, German, Italian and Spanish-language material abstracted. Access by personal name, country and topic. Continues *Quarterly Strategic Bibliography*, 1977-1989.

Naval Abstracts. Alexandria, VA: Center for Naval Analysis, 1978-.

> Quarterly bibliography which identifies and briefly abstracts the contents of periodical articles dealing with political, strategic or other subject matter affecting military forces. English, French, German, Italian and Spanish-language material abstracted. Access by personal name, country and topic.

Smith, M. *The Secret Wars: A Guide to Sources in English.* **3 vols. Santa Barbara, CA: ABC-Clio, 1980-1981.**

> 3 volumes: Vol. 1 (intelligence, propaganda and psychological operations, resistance movements, 1939-1945); Vol. 2 (intelligence, psychological warfare, covert operations, 1945-1980); and Vol. 3 (international terrorism, 1968-1980).

Watson, B., S. Watson, and G. Hopple, eds. *United States Intelligence: An Encyclopedia.* **New York: Garland, 1990. 792 pp.**

> Entries treat major terms, persons, and organizations in U.S. intelligence since World War II. Alphabetical list of entries with bibliographies. Concludes with appendices containing 25 relevant executive and congressional statements issued since 1941.

INDEX

This index is not exhaustive. It basically supplements the Table of Contents, using many of the same categories and adding others as useful. Geographic categories are broad: Africa, Asia, Eastern Europe and the Former U.S.S.R., Latin America and the Caribbean, Middle East, North America, and Western Europe. United Nations bodies are listed under the treaty which established them.